C000219742

Collectible Costume Jewelry

Identification & Values

Cherri Simonds

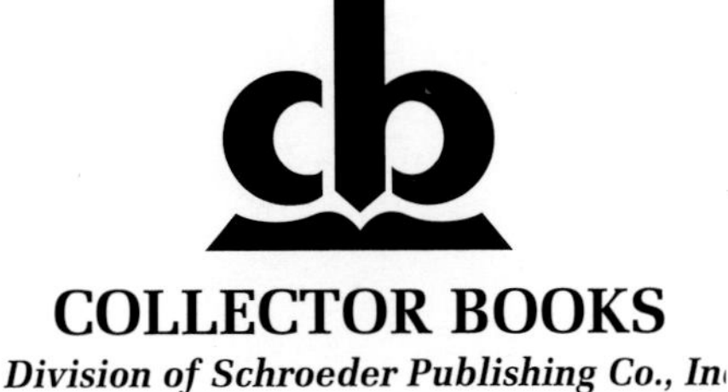

COLLECTOR BOOKS
A Division of Schroeder Publishing Co., Inc

The current values in this book should be used only as a guide. They are not intended to set prices, which vary from one section of the country to another. Auction prices as well as dealer prices vary greatly and are affected by condition as well as demand. Neither the Author nor the Publisher assumes responsibility for any losses that might be incurred as a result of consulting this guide.

Searching For A Publisher?

We are always looking for knowledgeable people considered to be experts within their fields. If you feel that there is a real need for a book on your collectible subject and have a large comprehensive collection, contact Collector Books.

Cover design by Beth Summers
Book design by Beth Ray
Photography by Charles R. Lynch

All items pictured are from the Author's collection unless otherwise noted.

Additional copies of this book may be ordered from:

COLLECTOR BOOKS
P.O. Box 3009
Paducah, Kentucky 42002-3009

@$24.95. Add $2.00 for postage and handling.

Contents

Silver-tone pendant necklace and ID style bracelet. The bracelet is silver-tone mesh with two interlocking G's. ¾" wide. Marked Givenchy Paris New York 1977. The 1¾" pendant is in a free-form spiral design and marked Givenchy Paris New York 1976. The clasp on the necklace is two interlocking G's. $75.00 – 115.00 each.

Dedication

Love to my family and friends who supported me and helped me through my bouts with "writer's block" and "deadline anxiety!" And to my grandmother who first introduced me to the glittering wonder of jewelry!

About the Author

Cherri Simonds has been collecting and wearing costume jewelry and fashion accessories for fifteen years. She earned a degree in fashion merchandising in 1989 and taught a junior college level course in fashion design at the same college. She managed several fashion/retail stores for a combined total of six years where she gained even more respect for the costume jewelry industry. Cherri is also a certified graphic artist and worked in this industry for two years. Cherri has choreographed and accessorized numerous fashion shows. Cherri was a amateur/semi-professional model for over fifteen years. Her hobbies include racquetball, roller blading, meteorology, arts and crafts, interior decorating, cooking, and collecting paperweights in addition to collecting fashion jewelry and accessories. Cherri resides in Huntsville, Alabama, with her husband, Darrell, and pet chinchilla, Poncho.

Acknowledgments

With special thanks to Koral Michael Whalton of Halcyon Studios in Montgomery, Alabama, and Beverly Gierow of The Glass Spoon in Huntsville, Alabama, for entrusting me with their personal collections.

To my friend Tracy Marshall of Moonlight Graphic Design for all her graphic artistry in this book — I am very grateful for all of your help and hard work.

Grateful appreciation to my publisher Collector Books, Paducah, Kentucky, for giving me the wonderful opportunity to make this "book dream" come true.

With many, many thanks to Lisa Stroup, editor, Collector Books, for believing in me and helping me along the way.

Thank you to Charley Lynch for his wonderful photography and patience with my pickiness.

With much appreciation to Lucille Tempesta of the Vintage Fashion and Costume Jewelry Collectors Club/Newsletter for giving me so much wonderful and helpful information!

Kudos to Robert Sorrell! Thank you so much for entrusting me with your rare jewelry photos! Your designs gave this book a dazzling and sparkling boost!

And much love to my family and friends who continue to put up with my costume jewelry obsession!

Introduction

Costume jewelry has come a long way. Since its inception, costume jewelry has brought on a wide variety of reactions. In the beginning, costume jewelry was created to mimic genuine jewelry worn by the upper class. Fake or imitation jewelry was looked down upon and considered in bad taste. In the 1920s and 30s designers Gabrielle "Coco" Chanel and Elsa Schiaparelli made costume jewelry widely accepted. However, it was still considered a disposable commodity — a fad item that was able to be thrown away when a certain style went out of fashion or at the end of a season. Chanel and Schiaparelli created their jewelry to go with each season's fashions and felt that the jewelry could affordably be renewed with each change of season. In the 1950s costume jewelry became a "hot commodity" and was considered a necessary adornment to the wardrobe. In the 1970s costume jewelry was once again frowned-upon as genuine gold jewelry became fashionable. In the 1980s costume jewelry of the past was rediscovered and became an appreciated art form only to become passé in the early 1990s as dainty "Y" chains and tiny single stone earrings replaced the funky, showy jewelry of the prior decade. However, as the late 1990s are approaching costume jewelry is once again becoming a much appreciated art form.

Often labeled disposable, junk, throw-away, and fake in the past, an appreciation for costume jewelry has been emerging and those former descriptions have been changed to works of art, brilliant, beautiful, *and* collectible. Everyone that collects costume jewelry can relate to this tale: "Once upon a time I was able to purchase costume jewelry at garage sales, junk sales, flea markets, and thrift stores jumbled up in cigar boxes for a mere $1.00 a box." Who would have dreamed that they were giving away "small works of art" at an unheard of price? I am sure whoever they were are now saying to themselves, "I *can't* believe I did that!" But who would have known that just a few short years later, "trash"

Silver-tone oriental-inspired earrings with tiny pagoda with dangling flowers. 1½". Marked Boucher 8274. $60.00 – 75.00. 1950s leaf earrings of unusual design. One leaf is attached to the back of the clip so it will show behind the ear. Chromium-plated stamped metal. Marked Coro. $30.00 – 45.00. Unusual 1950s wreath scarf pin. Silver-tone leaves with aurora borealis rhinestones glued in. Simulated gray Tahitian pearls. The largest central pearl is set with an aurora borealis rhinestone and attached to a thin piece of elastic cording — the elastic is then threaded through a small hollow tube on the underside of the pin. This elastic allows for the pearl to be moved to allow a scarf to be threaded through the pin. The pearl then snaps back into place holding the scarf securely. 2" x 2". Marked Hilco. $115.00 – 135.00.

costume jewelry would become so sought after? That the once-considered "junk" brooch that grandma has been wearing on her coat for decades is a rare Eisenberg figural worth quite a mint! This now-collectible fashion accessory is becoming more and more scarce to find at a good deal. However, on occasion a rare, collectible signed or unsigned piece might be purchased for a bargain. This is where this book comes into play. How do you know if the brooch is worth anything even though it is signed? How do you know if it is worth quite a bit if it isn't signed? How do you know if it is rare? What about fakes or phonies? Is it a reproduction? How do I take care of the jewelry once I start collecting it? What do I do if the item is broken? This book addresses all of these topics and more. Enjoy!

Why Costume Jewelry?

What prompts us to collect costume jewelry? Is it because for a very short space of time in our very ordinary day we can live out a fantasy or a fairy tale? That we could possibly be a glittering and glamorous femme fatale for just a little while? Or is it the compliments we receive when we wear the jewelry that prompts us? Whatever the reason, we seem to feel better about ourselves when we have that glittering brooch on our lapel. To those die hard costume jewelry fans — we often feel naked without it. What is it about that little lump of "worthless" metal when combined with glittering glass that makes us want more? Makes us want to turn it over and over in our hands and study it closer? Makes us want to know the why's and when's of that piece of jewelry? It is almost as if collecting costume jewelry has become a cult of its own. Hundreds of people are members of collectors' clubs, and those who collect love to discuss their favorite subject and digest any new infor-

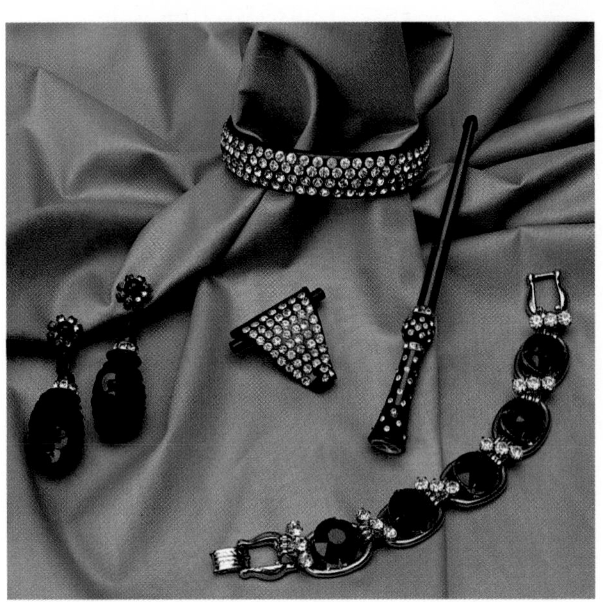

Beautiful finds in black and white! Clockwise from top: Black celluloid bangle bracelet set with four rows of clear rhinestones. $75.00 – 125.00. Courtesy of The Glass Spoon. Black celluloid cigarette holder studded with clear rhinestones. Very chic in its time! $60.00 – 100.00. Link bracelet in the Deco style but from the 1950s. Chromoim-plated chain lengths with prong-set black glass rhinestones and smaller prong-set clear rhinestone accents. ¾" wide. Unmarked. $50.00 – 95.00. Unusual dangling earrings by Miriam Haskell. The top of the earring is japanned with a cluster setting of black glass beads and rose monteé rhinestones. The bottom tear-drop dangle is covered in black sequins and is attached to the top of the earring with a black glass bead and rhinestone rhondelle. 2¼" long. Marked on the back of the clip Haskell and marked on the back of the earring Miriam Haskell. The inside of the screw-back clip is marked Pat. No. 3,176,475 (probably a patent for the components). $110.00 – 135.00. Center: Black celluloid dress clip. Scroll design set with clear rhinestone accents. Unmarked. $60.00 – 90.00.

mation like a starving person gobbling up scrumptious cheesecake. Ahhh, let them eat cake! We dream of finding that Eisenberg Original jumbled up in a shoe box at a garage sale, or bidding on that Chanel at the auction and getting it at a criminally low price, or finding that your grandmother has a box of old "junk" jewelry and you are welcome to it! It is a treasure hunt in its own right! We awake earlier than normal to get the front chair at the estate auction, are the first to squeeze through the door at the estate or garage sale, and we hunt for our jewelry via the Internet. Costume jewelry collectors also network and get the word out who they are and what they want. When we network it is often the jewelry that finds us. I remember getting many a phone call that started out, "Cherri, I remember you collect costume jewelry, and...." Which was usually followed up by someone arriving at my front door with their unwanted accessories. Going through these boxes is like Christmas every time. This passion and pursuit of knowledge about our favorite collectible is what this book is all about.

The Evolution of a Collector

It seems that the costume jewelry collector goes through many stages of growth, or a metamorphosis, and evolves each time with more knowledge about their favorite subject. The new collector begins in much the following way: They are attracted to a certain jewelry item for some strange reason. They start out by purchasing one or a very few items. They begin to want more. They then begin to buy up anything and everything with a rhinestone in it, regardless of signature, mark, or subject matter. Then after a period of time they begin to notice that for some reason, the jewelry with the names on it is more expensive. Why? The "baby collector" begins to ask questions and wants to learn more. The evolution begins and the "newby" collector moves up to the next stage: "the inquisitive intermediate." The collector, during this stage, stops indiscriminately buying up *all* the rhinestone jewelry they can find. They begin to be a little pickier. Often by this time they have a favorite maker or designer they recognize on sight. Who was this designer or manufacturer? When did they make the jewelry? How was this item made? Sometimes, a few questions are answered by the person the item was purchased from. Sometimes, though, only a few questions can be answered, and the collector finds her/himself wanting to know more. The collector begins to ask anyone and everyone about the jewelry. The collector, after a space of time, is sometimes put in contact with the authority on this favored collectible. This brings the collector to stage three: the "guru." They have had all their questions answered, and now the collector knows everything they could possibly know about the subject. This often leads them to wanting to know more about other designers and manufacturers. A thirst of knowledge is what makes the expert collector.

I would call myself an intermediate collector. I, by no means, know everything about costume jewelry. Each day I learn something new about my

favorite subject. I reflect upon my new-found knowledge and store it in my mind and write it down in a notebook for later reference. One reason I am writing this book is to help others along the way. To keep new collectors from making the same mistakes I did as a newby collector. When beginning on your journey for knowledge, it is easy to make errors and the following addresses them.

A new collector often makes the mistake that just because a jewelry item is signed by the designer or marked by the manufacturer, it is worth more than an unsigned item.

From the collection of Koral Michael Whalton

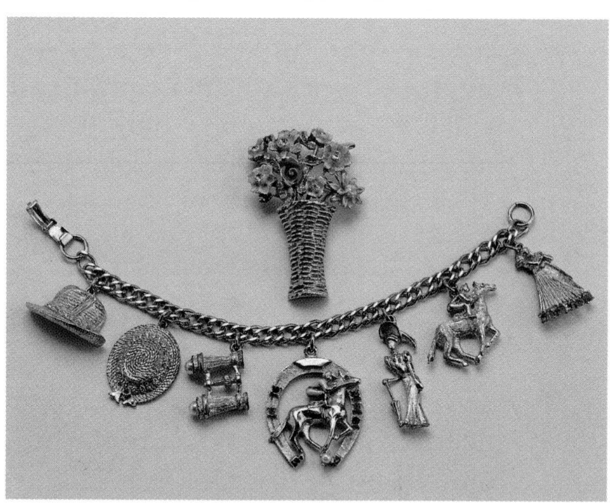

My Fair Lady collectibles from BSK. Features a charm bracelet, Eliza Doolittle's flower basket, Eliza's opened and closed parasols, and Professor Higgins' slippers. The parasols and slippers are scatter pins. The charm bracelet is gold plated with glued in rhinestones. The pins are gold plated with enameling and glued in rhinestone accents. All are marked BSK and My Fair Lady. 1950s. Bracelet: $65.00 – 80.00. Pins: $40.00 – 55.00 each.

A new collector will often purchase an attractive item without first studying it, often finding out later that it was not in like new condition. I had made the mistake in the past of scarfing up a Trifari parure without first closely examining it. I was afraid the seller would realize her mistake in selling it so ridiculously low. I got home and found out the hard way why it was so cheap. Both the necklace and the bracelet had been broken two or three times and had been soldered back together. However, the base metal did not take well to the solder and had fallen to pieces during the bumpy ride home. That "good deal" is now gathering dust in my parts box.

Often a new collector will buy anything without regard to price or subject matter. Many unscrupulous people are eager and willing to sell the new collector an item and tell them it is worth far more than it really is. The new collector unwittingly pays the high dollar.

Often the seller claims to be an expert and attempts to sell you an item as something it is not. Sometimes this is done intentionally, and sometimes it is due to lack of knowledge. For example, I had spied two beautiful pins sitting side-by-side in a glass case in an antiques shop. One of the pins I felt sure was an Eisenberg, the other I was unsure of. The owner told me they were

both Eisenbergs but upon examination the other Eisenberg turned out to be a 1950s Weiss. I showed her the mark and she went on to explain to me that Eisenberg and Weiss were the same company. Couldn't I tell, the pins looked identical? *Not!*

I picked up a pair of earrings at a flea market and wanted to purchase them, not for their collectibility, but for their wearability. Having sold 1928 jewelry in a department store in the 1980s, I knew the earrings to be made by that company. The dealer told me the earrings were a valuable antique that her mother had worn. When I explained to her that it was new 1928 she said, "1928! That sounds old to me!" And went on to tell me she wanted $100.00 for the pair of earrings which were valued at $25.00. Needless to say, she didn't make a sale. Who unknowingly came along some time later and bought those false antiques for that high price?

Many people sell knock-off's or bootlegs of big name, high priced collectible jewelry. Sometimes the seller knows the jewelry is a new antique and will price it accordingly. However, many times they will not tell you if they think they can pass it off to you at an extremely high price.

Collection of silver-tone beauties. Top to bottom and left to right: Rhodium-plated earrings with prong-set clusters of pear and chaton cut clear Austrian crystal rhinestones. Rhinestones are of excellent quality. ¾". Marked Weiss. $40.00 – 55.00. Clear rhinestone pin from the 1950s. Silver-tone stamped metal with prong-set clear rhinestones in a star design. Chaton, baguette, and square cut rhinestones. 2" in diameter. $65.00 – 80.00. Small rhodium-plated star pin with prong-set clear Austrian crystal rhinestones of excellent quality. Chaton and pear cut rhinestones. 1¼". Unmarked. $25.00 – 40.00. On each side of the dangling cluster earrings: Large cluster earrings from the 1950s. Chromium-plated with clear prong-set baguette and chaton cut rhinestones. 1¾" in diameter. $45.00 – 60.00. Screw-back dangling earrings of chaton and pear cut clear rhinestones. All rhinestones are prong-set. Chromium-plated. 1¾" long. 1950s. $35.00 – 50.00. Sarah Coventry tiny snowflake jewelry. Clip-on earrings with tiny pin in the same size. Silver-tone with clear rhinestones and central simulated pearl. 1¼" in diameter. Marked S. Coventry. $55.00 – 85.00 set.

Pricing Costume Jewelry

Oh boy...I feel like I am going to be getting into a hornet's nest over this one. Giving value to an item always seems to open Pandora's box. Values always bring on a mixture of emotions. The collector is always astonished and pleased to find the brooch they bought at a garage sale for $5.00 is valued in *the book* for $100.00! However, the collector is dismayed when he tries to re-sell it and can't get more than $25.00. They become angry and want to know *why*! *The book* said it was worth $100.00 *why* could I only get $25.00? *You said...*! Giving a value to an item is a *very* touchy subject and I often have wished I didn't have to do it. If you get several dealers and collectors together this will always be a very misunderstood topic. Some dealers go very high on their jewelry whereas others often may go ridiculously low. Pricing depends on many different influences:

Tassel necklace of white simulated pearls, aurora borealis crystal beads, gold-tone filigree caps and piercework beads with matching 1" earrings. $75.00 – 115.00 set. Miniature rag doll pin made of gold-tone beads and chains, white simulated pearls, gold-tone filigree caps, and aurora borealis crystal beads. The pin is 1¾" long. $35.00 – 55.00. All are unmarked.

How desperate is the seller for income?
How long has the seller been trying to sell a particular item?
Is it an item that is rare?
Does the item have eye-catching appeal, unusual subject matter, or a different combination of stones?
Is it a large item?
Is it an item that is a current "in" collectible?
Economic influences of the area.

Sometimes the answers may settle the price, but often there are other influences. Sometimes if you purchase items in bulk quantity from a seller they will give you a discount. Are you willing to pay in cash or do you want to charge or lay-away the items? As the saying goes "money talks" and cash will usually get you a discount before lay-away or a costly credit card transaction. Are you familiar with the dealer? Often if the dealer knows you and feels you are a good customer, he will give you a special discount. Also by knowing your dealer, he will often purchase items he knows you will like and save them especially for you!

I have found out in the past that when I am going on a jewelry hunt if I wear jewelry the dealer is less likely to give me a discount because they see I already adore jewelry. They feel I will like the item thus I will buy it at any price. If I act too knowledgeable about an item they seem to always tell me, "Well, you know it is *more* than worth the price I am asking!" Which translates to, "I am not coming down on the price at all. Take it or leave it!" I have often worn blue jeans and T-shirts on my junkets and come home with more

treasures because I acted like I thought they were merely pretty but I didn't *have* to have them. If the dealer thinks you are just lukewarm to the sale, they may make it more lucrative for you to take those babies home. *Never* act too attracted to an item. If the seller knows you want the item badly enough they know you will eventually pay the price.

How *did* I arrive at the values in this book? It depends on a great many factors. The prices the dealer was asking for the items, the age, condition, rarity, and the "eye-catching quality" of a particular item all come into play. Some may think my values are much too high, some may think they are way too low, and other's may say they are just right. I tried to stay in the middle of the road when giving values to the jewelry. However, I *do* know that some dealers as well as collectors are invariably going to be disappointed. Please remember that the values given in this book are not carved in stone! There is always a flexibility in pricing! I gave a range to the pricing and this range covers jewelry that is only in good to excellent

Schreiner New York earrings and unmarked 1950s cushion pin. The 1¼" earrings are in a beautiful cluster design set with inverted chocolate brown rhinestones and flower clusters of glass turquoise and faux peridot rhinestones. The 2¼" pin is gold plated with prong-set rhinestones in varying shades of brown topaz. Earrings $90.00 – 110.00. Pin $70.00 – 85.00.

Classic bracelet by Miriam Haskell of gilded antique brass and simulated freshwater pearls. $250.00 – 325.00. Rope length necklace of gold-tone chains and simulated freshwater pearls. Marked Freirich. $40.00 – 65.00.

condition. Keep in mind that if an item is not in good condition the value decreases substantially. Regional factors also come into play when giving values to jewelry. Location, economic conditions of the area, and regional popularity of a certain item all influence values. For instance, for a while Bakelite was a hot commodity in New Orleans and was bringing high prices, whereas in Huntsville, Alabama, it was rhinestone brooches. Also, is it the holiday season or time for the prom? Sales of rhinestone sets often soar during this time of the year when consumers want something glittery and glitzy to wear with their formal attire. Unfortunately, the sales of these items often plummet during the off season. Is the area where the item is being sold in a recession? If so, it is unlikely that anyone who is worried about paying their bills is going to purchase an item not considered a necessity.

Remember all these factors when buying and selling costume jewelry as well as other collectibles.

French jet jewelry. Top to bottom and left to right: Shoulder brooch and matching earrings in a looped floral design. Black prystal beads made to resemble black cut glass. The pin must be worn on the shoulder or the flower petals will flop over. The pin is 3¾" in diameter and the earrings are 2" in diameter. Marked West Germany. $75.00 – 95.00. Three strand necklace of faceted black glass beads. Marked deluxe. $50.00 – 75.00. Earrings are a cluster of faceted black glass beads. 1" in diameter. Marked W. Germany (West Germany). $20.00 – 30.00. Genuine jet bug. Black japanned metal. Unmarked. Has a crack in one wing. 2½" long. $35.00 – 65.00. Earrings in a cluster of faceted black glass beads and clear rhinestone rondelles. 1¼" in diameter. Unmarked. $25.00 – 35.00.

Designer/Manufacturer Identification Chart

Designer/Manufacturer	Dates in Business	Most Known For
Accessocraft	1930s to present	Unusual gothic designs highly popular in the 1960s. Many items have a Renaissance, Victorian, Art Nouveau, or Rococco style. Use of antique gold-tone or bronzed metals with unusual stones. Many of the 1930s pieces had a decidedly Deco look.
Art (ModeArt)	1940s to 1970s	Unusual designs usually with a Victorian or Deco style done in antique gold-tone metals. Commonly used unusual color combinations of rhinestones and cabochons.
Barclay, McClelland (Not to be confused with Barclay – another jewelry line.)	1930s to 1940s	Highly stylized Art Deco designs. Use of geometric shapes and rhinestones in the colors of genuine stones. Usually plated in gold, silver, or rhodium. Very hard to find.
Boucher, Marcel	1930s to early 1970s	Highly imaginative designs that sometimes mimic "the real thing" or boldly flaunt its "fakeness." Boucher's whimsical birds, insects, flowers, leaves, and many other three-dimensional designs are highly prized by collectors.
Cadoro	1940s to 1970s	Three-dimensional fish, animals, and Russian-inspired jewelry often in brushed gold-tone metal. Frequent use of glass cabochons. Many of Cadoro's items are mistaken on sight for Kenneth J. Lane.
Carnegie, Hattie	1920s to 1980s	Whimsical designs that often made the best use of unusual combinations of rhinestones, enameling, simulated pearls, beads, and other materials. Her line of Oriental influenced jewelry and figurals are highly collectible.
Carolee	1973 to present	Known for very classic designs of high quality. Carolee's "Duchess of Windsor" inspired jewelry from the 1980s is much sought-after today.
Castlecliff	1940s to 1960s	Designs that range from almost an Art Deco to a heavy gothic or Renaissance stylization.
Caviness, Alice	1945 to present	Unusual combinations of colors and stones. All Caviness items have eye-catching appeal (even the simple strands of beads!). Rare or hard to find due to Caviness' items being sold only in exclusive specialty shops and boutiques.

Designer/Manufacturer	Dates in Business	Most Known For
Chanel, Gabrielle "Coco"	1920s to present	Astounding items often with a Byzantine or Renaissance flair. Many items have the look of India. Best known for her "poured glass" jewelry by Gripoux, Maltese cross cuffs designed by Verdura, and an abundance of ropes of simulated pearls and gold-tone chains.
Ciner	1892 to present	Jewelry that often has Art Deco appeal and often appears to be the "real thing." High quality jewelry that is still in production today — and still keeps with the high standards that have always made them popular.
Coro (Cohn & Rosenberger)	1901 to present (Presently still in operation in Canada)	One of the most highly mass-produced line of costume jewelry in history. A collector can easily find Coro items still in excellent condition. Most popular Coro items are its unusual duettes, enameled tremblers, and whimsical designs by Adolph Katz.
DeMario, Robert	1940s to late 1950s or early 1960s	Use of lacy gilded brass filigree and clusters of simulated pearls and glass beads. Not to be confused with Originals by Robert (Robert Levy). Hard to find.
De Nicola	Late 1950s or early 1960s to 1970s	A name not widely seen due to the short time span of the company's existence. The few pieces found always have exquisite craftsmanship and are quite imaginative.
DeRosa (Ralph DeRosa)	1935 to 1955	Highly imaginative and very collectible jewelry. Fantastic use of enameling and unusual stones with unusual cuts. Very detailed craftsmanship.
di N, Mimi (di Niscemi, Mimi)	1962 to present	Eye catching jewelry often large in scale — often considered fantasy jewelry. High usage of glass cabochons and Byzantine-influenced settings. Very dramatic and highly collectible.
Eisenberg	Late 1920s to present	Eisenberg began as a dress manufacturer. These dresses were given brooches and clips as an accessory but these glittering accents proved to be so popular that they were being stolen, leaving the dresses bare. This left Eisenberg no choice but to leave off the accessories and create a separate fashion jewelry line. Eisenberg jewelry is almost always recognizable on sight. Swarovski's Austrian crystal rhinestones are used exclusively in Eisenberg's larger-than-life jewelry. Known for large, high quality rhinestones in very eye-catching settings.

Designer/Manufacturer	Dates in business	Most Known For
Florenza	Late 1940s to late 1970s or early 1980s	Intricately detailed jewelry, often Victorian in appearance. Lots of use of antique gold-tone metal.
Givenchy	Early 1950s to present	Classic design work in large scale. Lots of use of gold plating, Lucite, and other plastics.
Hagler, Stanley	1950s to 1996	Large and imaginative jewelry often created of filigree and clusters of simulated seed, freshwater, and baroque pearls.
Haskell, Miriam (Haskell Jewels Ltd.)	1920s to present	Intricate and detailed craftsmanship using gilded brass filigree, clusters of baroque and seed pearls, Bohemian glass beads, and rose montee foil-backed rhinestones in stunning arrangements. Haskell jewelry is yet another that is almost always recognizable on sight. Not to be confused with Robert DeMario, Eugene, or Robert Levy's jewelry which often had a similar design style.
Hobé	1887 to present	Highly imaginative designs with a Byzantine or Victorian look. Stones are usually bezel set. Highly intricate designs with a stunning variety of stone colors.
Hollycraft	1940s to 1970s	Designs with a decidedly Victorian look usually in antique gold plate with a riot of pastel colored rhinestones — a Hollycraft trademark. Much of Hollycraft jewelry is marked with a date, much to the delight of today's collectors.
Joseff	Used mainly for Hollywood films, however, during the 1940s and 1950s a Joseff retail line was for sale in limited quantities at very select department stores and boutiques.	Use of antique gold-tone metals which did not have a high reflective quality for use in the film industry. The use of this type of metals carried over to the retail line as well. All highly imaginative designs with fantastic detail.
Korda, Alexander (Thief of Bagdad, Korda)	1940s	Oriental-style jewelry produced in conjunction with the movie *The Thief of Bagdad.* Jeweled scimitars, Aladdin, stars, leopards, and many more items inspired by the movie.
Kramer	1940s to 1970s	Beautiful jewelry produced with an abundance of sparkling Austrian crystals in either clear or a variety of colors. All rhinestones are of the highest quality.
Lane, Kenneth J.	1960s to present	Bold, monumental jewelry of exquisite design. High quality that often takes its ideas from mythology, the zodiac, figurals, animals, and other bold designs with often striking and startling color combinations.

Designer/Manufacturer	Dates in Business	Most Known For
Ledo-Polcini	1911 to present	Hand-set rhinestone jewelry often in deco designs. Resembles genuine jewelry in style, design, and quality.
Les Bernard	Originally founded in 1936 as Vogue and changed to Les Bernardin 1963. Still in operation.	Unusual combination of marcasite with gold-tone or gold-plated jewelry. Les Bernard jewelry ranges from Art Deco influences to whimsical figurals.
Mazer/Jomaz	Produced costume jewelry from 1939 to 1951	Beautiful craftsmanship with spectacular use of rhinestones — often mimicking genuine jewelry. The Royal Orb pin is a favorite Mazer collectible.
Moini, Iradj	1980s to present	Large, exotic runway jewelry often produced for Oscar de la Renta.
*Monet	1937 to present	Widely known for their classic designs in silver and gold tones and their comfort-clip earrings. Monet also produced jewelry for a short period of time in the 1980s for Yves St. Laurent.
Napier	1875 to present	Earlier designs by Napier are quite unique and are the most sought after. The early sterlingdesigns and the unusual Oriental-inspired coin and charm bracelets of the 1950s are becoming very popular with collectors.
Panetta	1945 to the early 1980s	Fantastic jewelry with exquisite detail. Designs ranged from rhinestone encrusted Art Deco styles to enameled figurals. All very collectible.
Pennino	Unknown, however Pennino jewelry was very popular in the 1940s.	Beautiful jewelry with heavy plating and intricate design work. Most of Pennino's jewelry used rhinestones of the best quality that mimicked fine gemstones. Since Pennino was popular in the 1940s most of its jewelry is created in sterling silver or in gold or rose gold vermeil over sterling silver. Panetta was also known for using flat unfoiled rhinestones with metal "frames."
Rader, Pauline	1962 to unknown	Highly imaginative designs usually massive in size. Rader jewelry often shows mystical Greek or Italian influences.
Robert (Robert Levy)	1949 to 1960 was under the name of Fashioncraft. Changed to Robert Originals then to Ellen Designs, Inc. from the 1980s to present	Usually known for his work in filigree, which is often mistaken for Miriam Haskell jewelry. However, in the 1950s and 60s he created a line of enameled jewelry in whimsical fruits and flowers which has become the epitome of that era.
Rosenstein, Nettie	Early 1930s to 1960s	Nettie Rosenstein jewelry often takes its cue from heraldry, the Victorian era, and surrealistic figurals. A popular Rosenstein line is the Victorian-inspired portrait jewelry.
Saint Laurent, Yves	Early 1960s to present Monet produced jewelry for St. Laurent in early to mid 1980s.	Saint Laurent's runway accessories are highly collectible. Couture jewelry.

Designer/Manufacturer	Dates in Business	Most Known For
Sandor (Sandor Goldberger)	1930s to 1970s	Sandor's jewelry came in a wide variety of styles from figurals to dainty flowers. All of Sandor's jewelry is highly collectible, but the enameled flowers seem especially so.
Schiaparelli, Elsa	Late 1920s to mid 1950s or early 1960s.	Best known for her whimsical designs taking inspiration from nature, the circus, and the zodiac. Often received her surrealistic inspiration from Salvador Dali. Schiaparelli jewelry is often found with a wide variety of colored stone combinations. Highly sought after and very collectible.
Schreiner	1950s to 1970s	Unusual and distinctive jewelry which often utilized gun-metal plating, unusual stone cuts, inverted-set rhinestones, and unusual color combinations. Stunning!
Swarovski (jewelry)	1985 to present	Swarovski has been creating high quality Austrian crystal rhinestones since the late 1800s. In 1985, Swarovski launched their first line of fashion jewelry utilizing these rhinestones. The jewelry in the collectors series is destined to go up in value due to its being manufactured in limited quantities and only being offered to members of its collectors club.
*Trifari (TKF) (Trifari, Krussman & Fishel)	1918 to present	Trifari jewelry traverses all the genre that fashion jewelry possibly can. From the imaginative sterling vermeil figurals of the 1940s to its classic gold and silver-tone jewelry of today. The Trifari figurals, retro florals, and jelly-bellies from the 1930s and 40s are in high demand by today's collector.
Volupté	1926 to the late 1950s or early 1960s.	Mostly known for the production of lovely ladies' compacts, Volupté jewelry was produced for a short period of time and thus is scarce.
Weiss	1940s to early 1970s	Jewelry which was always produced with high quality Austrian crystal rhinestones. Known for its jewelry that was similar to Eisenberg, as well as its lovely rhinestone encrusted butterflies, fruit, and flowers from the 1950s.
Whiting & Davis	1876 to present	The name Whiting and Davis usually brings to mind their lovely and highly collectible mesh evening bags. However, the company also has crafted some very lovely jewelry often with a Victorian or Art Nouveau look. Their mesh spiral snake bracelets are highly collectible.

* Please note: Trifari, Monet, as well as Marvella are now all owned and operated by the Crystal Brands Jewelry Group.

The "Lost Wax" Casting Method

The jewelry you have been collecting began in a skilled artisan's imagination. The design idea was first put to paper as a rough sketch or a thumbnail sketch. If the idea was approved a fully detailed rendering was then created. This fully detailed drawing was done three dimensionally on paper as the jewelry item was to be seen from all angles. The colors were then drawn in, the placement of rhinestones, beads, and pearls noted, and all other relevant details are shown. Next, a full scale model of the paper rendering is made. Often the model is made in two or more parts which are put together when the piece is completed. The model is shaped using engraving tools, files, and other equipment necessary to meet structural requirements. A rubber mold is then made of the acceptable model. Wax models are then made using this mold. Molten metals are poured into this mold and allowed to cool. Once the metals have cooled a precision cutting tool is used to trim away any rough edges. The surface is then polished. The product now has earring clips, fastenings, or added components or parts soldered on. The almost complete jewelry product is now passed on to the department that takes care of the final stages of production. It is given a galvanizing bath then plated in gold, rhodium, or silver. The semi-finished piece is now ready for enameling, adding of stones, or any other finishing touches. The finished jewelry is then packaged for distribution and sale.

Jewelry making in stages. Top row, right to left: Flower cluster to be added to the almost finished main body of the brooch (this brooch was made in two parts). The sterling silver main body of the brooch before gilding and adding the flower cluster. The sterling silver polished brooch with the flower cluster attached. Bottom row, right to left: The brooch after its gold vermeil bath. The finished brooch with the prong-set rhinestones. Packaging for distribution.

Jewelry, models, and archival information courtesy of Koral Michael Whalton's "Adrian's Archives."

Adrian M. Scannavino and Robert Adrian Scannavino

Adrian M. Scannavino was born on April 26, 1901, in Genoa, Italy. He trained as an apprentice machinist making tools for jewelers, engravers, and precision craftsmen. The threat of World War I forced his immigration to New York in the fall of 1917. Adrian worked temporarily at his father's bakery, and later began working as a floor sweep at the costume jewelry factories. Bulova watch company taught Adrian his first trade in America. Watch repair was not enough for Adrian's talents so he started to work in costume jewelry production.

Adrian was trained to produce each piece of jewelry entirely by hand. This process involved selecting a design, milling the white metal, stacking the sheets of white metal, transferring the design to the sheets, frilling, sawing, and then dapping the design if required. Hand working with tools to create a refined look and layout for the stones were the next steps. Pin shaft hinges and catches were now soldered into place and stones were bead set by hand to finish the piece. The basic training for Adrian would become the format of his future as one of the industries most sought-after artisans.

Adrian worked for various companies, including Trifari, during the 1920s and 1930s. In 1939 the doors to "Adrian Classic," his own business, were opened. During the 10 year business span of Adrian Classic, the line consisted of animated, floral, figural, moderne, and heraldic motifs. A variety of Italian and other ethnic motifs were produced along with compacts and accessories.

Adrian Classic jewelry was cast from hand-carved tin models. Some styles called for plaster of Paris models to be used in sand casting, however, the majority of the jewelry was machine cast.

Koral Michael Whalton of Adrian's Archives explains that the "By Adrian" hallmark was rarely used due to the fact that Adrian Classic jobbed-out their styles to New York City companies and distributors. The majority of styles were simply stamped sterling from 1941 to 1945. Hallmarks that are known to exist are usually found on raised blocks in pieces finished in 18K pink, yellow, and rose vermeil. After the war white metal was used with the same plating until the business closed in 1949.

With Adrian Classic closed, business was conducted from their 83rd street home studio. Mr. Adrian and Robert produced models, jobbed piecework, specialty work, and layouts for all top level costume jewelry companies. The Scannavino's skills were in high demand.

Robert's training started at Adrian Classic when he was 11 years of age. His work for setting certain types of stones was often commended by the Mazer Co. He set stones, engraved, and produced custom trim for frames.

Mr. Adrian's highly skilled layout talents were now being employed by Panetta, Pennino, Hollycraft, Pell, Marvella, Mazer, Boucher, Jomaz, Ora, Ciner, and Symphony. Watch repair was always a mainstay, and watch case layouts were produced for Natacha Brooks Ltd. and Milton Manufacturing Co.

The mid 1960s brought retirement for Mr. Adrian and his home studio was moved to Florida. After 60 years of mainstream industrial experience, Mr. Adrian closed his bench at the age of 83. Adrian M. Scannavino died on August 4, 1993. He was 92. Robert Adrian Scannavino continues to produce very limited editions of high quality costume jewelry through Halcyon Studios, Inc.

Gold vermeil over sterling silver lobster pins shown in its model stage, finished stage, and packaging for distribution stage.

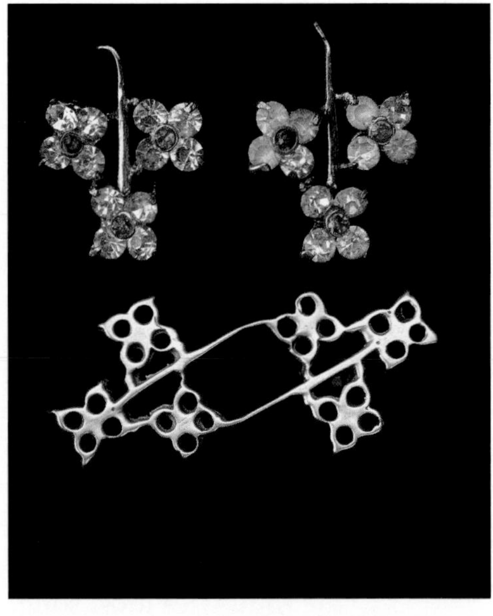

Earrings still in the unfinished stage. Sterling silver outline done in one piece, then cut apart, plated in gold, and set with rhinestones. At top are the earrings when finished and ready for packaging for distribution.

Gold vermeil over sterling silver turtle pin and earring set shown with original model.

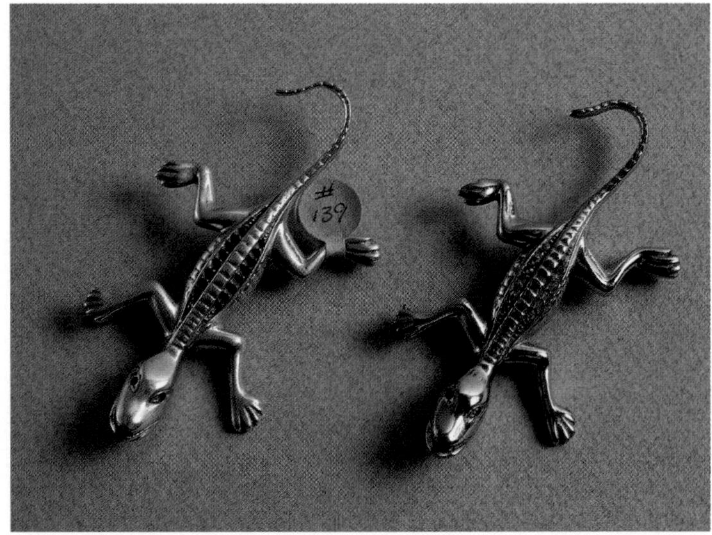

Smiling alligator brooch shown in its sterling silver unfinished stage with the notches for rhinestones in its back and its finished stage — ready to be packaged for distribution.

Jewelry, models, and archival information courtesy of Koral Michael Whalton's "Adrian's Archives."

 *Tips for Care of Your Costume Jewelry* 

Many collectors make the mistake of rationalizing that since costume jewelry is just a relatively inexpensive combination of glass and base metals that it doesn't require much care. The opposite is true, however. Genuine jewelry can be immersed in cleaners, where your fashionable baubles must be handled with tender loving care. It is very easy to accidentally peel the foil backing off rhinestones, or catch and pull the prongs loose on a pin and lose a stone, or chip the enamel, so be extremely cautious when cleaning, storing, and wearing your faux jewels. The following is a few helpful tips that can be useful when caring for your collectibles.

Be extremely cautious when cleaning your simulated pearl jewelry with the nacre on the outside of the bead. After a period of time the pearlized shell will eventually flake off. Especially vulnerable are necklaces with rhinestone and simulated pearl combinations. It is very easy for the rhinestones to scratch the pearlized casings when the necklace is unintentionally wadded up in storage or after being haphazardly thrown into a bag after purchasing. Store this type of jewelry flat and protect the pearls to keep them from flaking or peeling.

Sometimes items are stored wrapped in loose cotton, but this is not recommended for jewelry with prong-set rhinestones. The cotton gets caught in the prongs and you end up with "fuzzy" jewelry. This is not harmful, it is just time consuming to remove all the bits of cotton from the item. Flat-sided cotton used in jewelry boxes works better for storage!

If you are going to wear your costume jewelry — let it be the last item you put on before leaving the house. *Never* have your jewelry on while applying cosmetics, perfume, and hairspray. *Never* wear your jewelry against skin with perfume or perfumed lotions. The metal will react to the chemicals causing it to tarnish.

Make sure that metals don't react to your skin! Some people's skin reacts easier to the metals in jewelry causing the jewelry to tarnish quickly and their skin to temporarily turn green where the jewelry has touched. If you have an item that you want to wear but do not want to keep for its collectibility and you have trouble with your skin reacting to the metals causing it to tarnish or if you have allergic reactions to jewelry made with nickel, paint a thin coating of clear nail polish in the areas where the item touches your skin. For instance, on the inside of the clip and the back of the earring. Do not cover the whole item in clear nail polish! Remember — Do *not* use nail polish on an item you are adding to your collection for its value and collectibility. Also, it is not recommended you paint enameled jewelry with clear nail polish as it might cause the enamel to later flake off with the nail polish. I have heard that some collectors do, however, use clear nail polish on enameled jewelry where the enamel is starting to flake off. They paint the areas that are peeling to keep this from continuing.

 *Tips for Cleaning Your Costume Jewelry*

With an extremely soft toothbrush, very mild dishwashing soap, and distilled water, lightly brush dirt, grime, dust, or old hairspray from rhinestone jewelry. Be cautious with very old foil backed stones. It is very easy to brush the flaking foil off the rhinestones and you do not want to do that!

Immediately after cleaning, pat dry with a clean, soft cotton or muslin cloth. Use a blow dryer on the lowest/coolest setting to remove any remaining dampness. Lay flat to continue drying. Do not use the toothbrush around glued-in stones. The water may cause the glue to break down causing the stones to become loose and eventually fall out.

For sterling jewelry, use a silver polishing cloth only. These are usually made up of two cloths sewn together. One cloth has a cleaning agent additive and the other is for polishing after cleaning. Do not use this cloth on jewelry that is sterling with a gold plating — the chemicals will gradually clean the plating off. Only use the cloth on plated jewelry if the plating is almost completely worn away and you just want the sterling showing.

Never clean your jewelry with harsh abrasives. Never immerse your jewelry in cleaners meant for fine jewelry. Never immerse your costume jewelry in cleaners that *say* they are safe for costume jewelry. Do not use silver polishing compound meant for cleaning large items and silverware on sterling or sterling plated jewelry. The polishing compound gets stuck under the stones and around small parts and components and is about impossible to remove without taking the piece apart.

Do not use acetone on plastic jewelry.

To clean simulated pearl jewelry, do not use a toothbrush unless the pearlization is on the inside of the glass bead. Otherwise, use a cotton swab and distilled water to lightly remove dust and grime, then blot dry. If the pearl casings are already starting to flake — by all means, do not clean. It takes very little to cause the rest of the casings to flake off.

Be cautious when cleaning your jewelry; less is best. Be as gentle as possible, use no abrasives and store your jewelry in the following ways so that you won't have to clean your jewelry....

Tips for Storing Your Costume Jewelry

Never jumble your jewelry up in a box — the metal will get scratched up, pearl casings will flake off, pin backs may scratch stones, and rhinestones will pop out.

If possible store your jewelry in the box originally purchased in. These boxes are usually lined with flat-sided soft cotton inserts which are great for the jewelry. If you are storing a pin or earrings in one of these boxes, fasten the pin or clip the earrings to the removable cotton lining. Remember, don't press loose cotton against rhinestone jewelry unless you desire "fuzzy" jewelry. If you preserve your jewelry in the original boxes if the brand name, manufacturers name, jewelry logo, or department store name is on the outside of the box — in the future the jewelry stored in this box will be worth more. This information on the box lends to dating, value, and credibility. If you are storing in plain white cardboard jewelry boxes, mark on the outside what the contents are so you won't have to open every box you own to find a particular item. Do not write on the outside of collectible boxing — this will decrease the value.

Never store Bakelite or Catalin jewelry with metal jewelry. The two react to one another and you could end up with flaking Bakelite and corroding metal!

Store jewelry in plastic baggies. This makes your jewelry easy to see and admire as well as keeping the items safe. Air tight plastic baggies also keep your sterling silver jewelry from turning so you won't have to polish it as often.

Never subject your jewelry to harsh temperature changes. The metal in the jewelry expands and contracts in the extreme temperatures causing stones to fall out, pearl casings to peel off, and enamel to flake.

Do not store your plastic jewelry in areas with extremely bright light.This will cause your jewelry to fade and discolor over a period of time. This is very harsh on jewelry constructed of paper, leather, and plastic (especially celluloid).

Be careful when storing your jewelry in wooden jewelry boxes and drawers. Oak, for instance, has certain chemicals that react adversely with the metals in costume jewelry.

This is a fantastic bracelet with only one flaw — it was purchased with the original clasp missing. The rose gold-plated clasp from the 1940s was impossible to match, so a newer one was used. The newer clasp is from the 1950s and the gold plating is not the same. If the bracelet had originally been marked, then it was probably marked on the missing clasp. This obvious repair brings the value down drastically although it is still very stylish and certainly wearable. This bracelet, if perfect, might have been valued anywhere from $200.00 to 800.00. With it being so obviously repaired and thus, not in perfect condition, the value is only about $40.00.

Tips for Repairing Your Costume Jewelry

Remember the saying, "an ounce of prevention is worth a pound of cure?" If you take proper care of your costume jewelry it is not likely you will have much repairing to do. However, if you do purchase an item that needs repair work, this section is for you. Remember that obvious repairs bring down the value of the jewelry. Following are some tips for home jewelry repair:

Purchase old broken jewelry for its components and stones. Replace broken components and missing stones with these old ones for authenticity.

Remember, when replacing missing rhinestones with new rhinestones, it will be obvious. With time some older glass rhinestones turn yellow or take on a grayish cast (often called "dead" or "dulled" rhinestones). The new stones will be much brighter and will stick out like a sore thumb in your repaired jewelry.

When in doubt, have an expert repair your jewelry.

When gluing in rhinestones don't use fast drying-type glues, or cheap household glues. Often these glues will eat away the foil backing of the rhinestones. Slow drying expoxy comes highly recommended from craft supply stores and hobby shops. This type of glue is stronger and does not react to the foil backing.

If your jewelry has an oxidized patina, remember it is rust and thus, is an actual part of your jewelry. It is best not to purchase jewelry in this state unless it is on the back of the item and not in great abundance.

Purchase a jewelry loupe or strong magnifying glass. When making purchasing decisions look the piece over thoroughly to make sure there are no defects. Often, if a piece is not thoroughly examined you will get the item home only to realize that the pin back no longer works or a major part of the brooch has been soldered back together. Then it is often too late!

When purchasing jewelry that needs major repairs, the value of the item is drastically reduced. Remember this when purchasing as well as selling!

REPAIR LISTING

Costume Jewelry Repair House
10 North Michigan at Madison
Street Level
Chicago, IL 60602
(312) 782-7810

Halcyon Studios
Koral Michael Whalton
P.O. Box 11525
Montgomery, AL 36111
(334) 834-9560

Tanner's Jewelry
Raymond Tanner
2510 Memorial Parkway
Huntsville, AL 35801
(205) 536-5558

Bootlegs, Phonies, Fakes, Knock-offs, and Remakes

With the values of some items of costume jewelry skyrocketing, it is only common that some very shady characters are cranking out some phonies. Some of these fakes are done poorly and one can tell on sight that they are new. However, many of these bootleg manufacturers are getting smart. They are using the old techniques, stockpiling old stones and findings, and even adding "wear" to the new jewelry in order to make them appear old. These manufacturers are boldly putting the original company mark or signature on the back of the item or soldering on a tag with the mark or signature on it. Some even go as far as adding a patent number. But how can you tell if it is not an original when it says "Eisenberg Original"? Sometimes it is almost impossible to tell, but here are some tips that I have found that work for me:

Know your dealer. If this is someone you have a good buyer-seller relationship with, you bring this person a steady flow of revenue. The seller may not want to lose your business by selling you a bootleg — only for you to angrily find out later that it was a fake.

Another good reason for knowing the dealer is you become familiar with the inventory flow. If you visit their shop once a week and each week they have two or three different rare "Eisenberg Originals" — it is a very good chance they are phonies.

Look at the inventory of the seller. Do they sell a majority of new jewelry with a few rare "Bouchers" thrown in for good measure?

2¾ x 4¼" Eisenberg script "E" bootleg brooch. The original brooch was produced in two separate pieces then put together with rivets. This brooch was made in one piece then the rivets were added to look like it was made the old fashioned way. The plating is newer but already starting to flake off in places. The gold plating was not done as neatly as the real thing and will not last as long. The large, pink stones are old, but the smaller clear stones are new and sparkling. The small rhinestones are not glued in very well in some places.

Does the seller have several Eisenberg's together, with the larger flashier items being lower priced than the smaller items with some stones missing? Chances are the seller knows the item is a fake, is not going to tell you, but out of guilt is not willing to sell the item too high. However, this is a rare occurrence and many unscrupulous dealers will mark the fakes just as high as the originals — some even higher!

Scrutinize the item. Is the pin skewer longer than the brooch? Does it stick out beyond the edge? Does the item look new? Does the item show signs of wear or any patina? Are all of the stones present and accounted for? Do the stones look new (no cloudiness, all foil perfectly intact)? Is the item extraordinarily large — larger than the original one you saw like it that another collector had? Does the gold plating or enameling show any signs of flaking? Does the metal have unfinished lumps or swirls? Is the item done in base metal when you know it was originally done in sterling or vice-versa? All of these questions are good to ask yourself and the seller before purchasing. However, not even these techniques always work. I have seen some bootlegs that were almost impossible to recognize as fakes. These pieces had been rubbed to appear to be aged due to repeated wear (I noted later that all of the wear marks were going in the same direction, as if it had been scrubbed with fine sandpaper — another tell-tale clue). Even some of the stones had been intentionally chipped! If I had not been informed that the item was a bootleg, I might have not guessed until much later. That is just how convincing some of these items are.

Know your bootlegs! Get to know through the collector grapevine which items have been reproduced and avoid them like the plague. That is, unless you are buying the item cheaply to be worn, not to resell as an "original." These bootlegs are often created with as fine of craftsmanship as the original, and they do wear nicely when you don't want to risk wearing the "real" thing!

Items seen commonly reproduced: Bakelite figurals, Eisenberg Originals, Eisenberg script "E," Boucher, Trifari, and jelly bellies (marked as well as unmarked ones), Hobé, and any other item that brings extremely high prices.

Why do they make bootlegs? Often the scenario goes something like this: An item brings $1,000.00 – 2,000.00 at an auction. The bootleg manufacturer purchases the item at the high price, takes the item back to the workshop and takes it apart. A mold is then made of the original. Hundreds, if not thousands, of copies are made of the item in many different stone color combinations. Each is sold for, let's say, $50.00. Sold in quantity, the bootleg manufacturer has just made a profit. Most of the time this is a gray area when inquiring rather or not this practice is against the law. Most of the items either had no patent, the patent has expired, or the original manufacturing company is no longer in existence. Thus, there is no breach of the law. The only thing that is hurt, besides the unknowing buyer, is honesty.

Many manufacturers occasionally introduce a retro line. The company

manufactures items that had been in their popular line in the past. Many times these items are given a new or different mark, marked as retro or sometimes dated. Eisenberg has a new retro line that is signed in script "Eisenberg Ice," but is signed differently than the way it was originally signed in the 1960s.

How to tell if your Bakelite figural is a fake? Does the plastic look new? Is the piece extremely lightweight? Bakelite was actually a heavier, thicker plastic. Is the item made of Lucite, Bakelite, and Catalin buttons? Are the buttons held together by obviously shiny new findings? Is the pin back new and glued on to the back of the pin? The pin backs used with the early plastics were either sunk into the back of the item or riveted on. Does the face look like it has been painted on by marker? Below is a photograph of three phony Bakelite figurals. These items are actually constructed of Lucite and Bakelite remnants and buttons. This type of figural is often called remnant figurals due to the fact that they are new items constructed of old materials. The Halloween figural has a face stamped "Made in Hong Kong" on the back. Definitely a give-away!

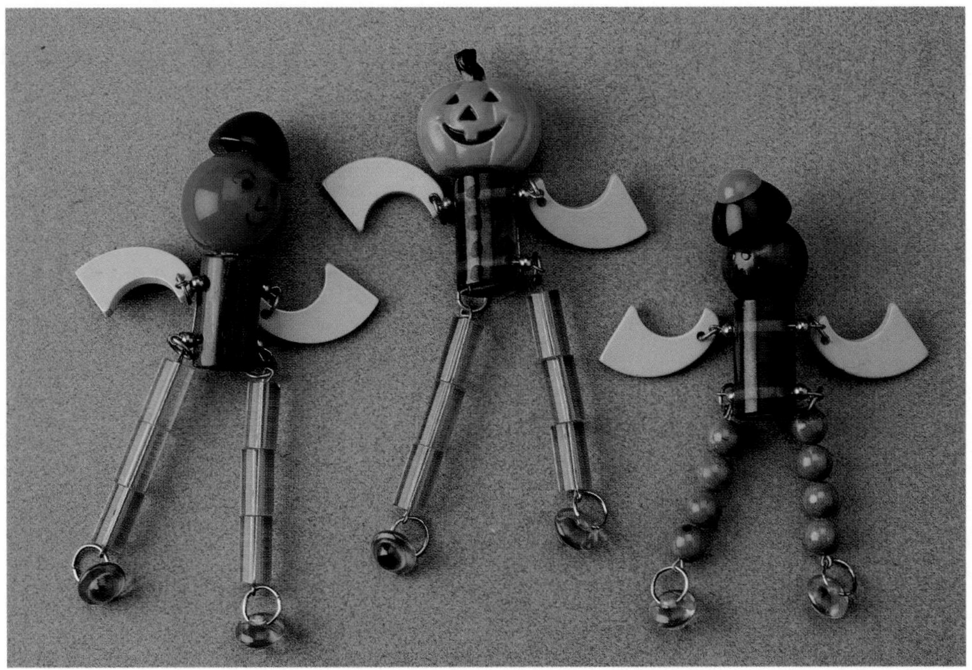

Three remnant pins. These pins are created from bits and pieces of old Bakelite, Catalin, and Lucite jewelry and buttons. Often these are passed off as Bakelite figurals and sold at high prices. All three of these pins have new glued-on pin backs and new gold-plated findings.

 Design Influences through the Years 

Costume jewelry was directly and indirectly influenced by both historical and social events. This section is dedicated to both contributing factors. Since this book contains jewelry designed mainly from the mid 1920s through today, earlier period influences will not be addressed.

Art Deco Influences

The 1925 Paris Exhibition Internationale des Arts Decoratifs et Industriels Modernes had a great impact on the styles of the period. The term "Art Deco" was directly derived from the name of this Parisian World's Fair. However, the term "Art Deco" was not widely used until the mid-1960s when the Paris Museé des Arts Decoratifs did a comprehensive study of the design styles of the 1920s. At the time only the term "modern" was given to this particular design form. During this period the modernistic designs were directly influenced by cubist artists, geometric design, and new technology. This bold new design form was attributed to scientific thinking and was applied to architecture, interior design, decorative objects as well as fashion and jewelry. An obsession with sleek and geometric objects was directly reflected in fashion as feminine curves, found attractive just a few years before, became outdated. The garçon style (thin women with boyish figures) became the fad. It is believed that this unisex fashion was a direct result of the male to female ratio imbalance after WWI. Women began dieting to meet the masculine proportions and the older generation became shocked when the women began bobbing their hair, sporting short skirts, tanning, wearing cosmetics, and smoking cigarettes. Boxy dresses with hemlines above the knees were worn with long flowing ropes of pearls, chains, or crystal beads. The hair, being geometrically bobbed, called for long dangling, swinging earrings often grazing the shoulders. The new evening dresses left the shoulders and arms bared which called for armloads of bracelets which were worn around the wrists, up the forearms, above the elbow, and around the upper arm. Often these bracelets were in the form of coiled serpents in imitation of Egyptian jewelry in response to the discovery of King Tutankhamun's tomb in 1922. Streamlining became popular as fussy styles of the past were cast aside for the sleek new modern designs. Chromium, Bakelite, and Catalin were being used in many household items as well as jewelry. The Deco influence was felt all the way up until 1941 when the threat of war overshadowed the optimism of the previous decade.

Popular Influences on Jewelry and Related Accessories in the Deco Era

The modernistic styles of the Deco era were influenced by cubist artists, geometric design, the workings of industrial machinery, air travel, and fascination with speed and grace. Air travel was reflected in jewelry in the form of airplanes and zeppelins. Fascination with speed was seen in the form of streamlined trains, automobiles, steamliners, leaping gazelles, antelopes, whippets, horses, and Afghan hounds. Dogs were popular as themes, and a favorite was the Scottie — a direct influence by President Roosevelt's Scottie companion, Fala. The Scottie theme began showing up on playing cards, dish towels, and serving trays as well as costume jewelry. After Admiral Byrd's expedition to the South Pole, polar bears, penguins, and seals began appearing as themes. Also popular during this era was Mexicana. Mexican images popped up in brightly colored Catalin and Bakelite costume jewelry. One of the most recognized symbols of the Deco era was the Florida Deco theme (sometimes simply called Miami Deco after the popular Miami Art Deco district). Catalin and Bakelite jewelry in brightly colored palm trees, flamingos, tropical fish, and parrots became favored. Even though the Depression was making a huge impact upon people's lives as well as their budgets, this brightly colored and affordable early plastic jewelry seemed to give just a little lift to the spirits.

In 1922 King Tutankhamun's tomb was discovered and the breathtaking opulence of the find prompted the Egyptian craze. Egyptian hieroglyphic motifs, Tut faces, ankhs, streamlined felines, and serpents began appearing in jewelry.

Early Plastics in Jewelry

A widely used medium in the Deco era was plastic. The best known of these early plastics was invented in 1909 by Leo Hendrick Baekeland. This plastic innovation was named Bakelite after its inventor and was later produced in mass quantity by Union Carbide. However, the American Catalin Corporation out of New York also had a new plastic discovery they named Catalin. Catalin appeared in a wide variety of colors such as pumpkin orange, vibrant red, deep blue, butterscotch yellow, white, deep green, marbleized green, maroon, chocolate brown, and amber. Both Catalin and Bakelite are phenolics. However, Bakelite is often mistakenly used as a catch-all term for all phenolics and other early plastics as well. Another early plastic used for jewelry and hair accessories was Celluloid, a pyroxylin. Casein was a plastic most often used for buttons. Catalin is believed to be the most often used plastic for costume jewelry due to its high shine, durability, and wide range of colors. In 1936 it was referred to as the "gaudy brother of Bakelite" by *Fortune* magazine. Jewelry can still be found on its original cards which are marked "Catalin." The crash of 1929 marked the beginning of the Depression era and the value of genuine jewelry hit rock-bottom. Precious metals and genuine gemstones could not be afforded, thus could not also be sold at their original value. At this time, the market was ripe for mass-produced inexpensive novelty plastic jewelry. The 1930s is often referred to as the Age of Plastic as a result.

The Great Depression

During the Depression when frivolities were not affordable for the majority of the women, costume jewelry could be handmade at the kitchen table. Items that were on hand were often used in the construction of this jewelry. Cloth, sequins, wood, marbles, and clothes pins were some of the many house-

Depression era fringe-style necklace constructed of small (2½") wooden clothespins strung on braided cording in primary colors. Same primary colors are painted in stripes on the clothespin fringe. Oxidized brass clasp. Unmarked. $40.00 – 75.00.

hold items that were used. Cheap metals and make-at-home Catalin and Bakelite jewelry kits could also be purchased for very little.

Depression era double fringe-style necklace. Brass with turquoise glass marbles. Unmarked. $45.00 – 90.00.

World War II

During WWII base metals which formerly had been used for costume jewelry was utilized instead for the war effort. Costume jewelers were forced to use sterling silver as a substitute metal since it was not scarce nor rationed. Prior to the war rhinestones had been imported from Austria. However, during the war these stones could no longer be imported. Jewelry during this war era made the best use of one large central glass stone or a few strategically set rhinestones. Some sterling pins were often made larger, plated in gold and had no stones at all—the boldness of the piece made it attractive even without the rhinestones. Costume jewelry of this time period was also crafted from either plastics or wood as well as in sterling silver and sterling silver with gold plating. Patriotic jewelry became a favored theme — red, white, and blue rhinestones or enameling on a brooch, "V" for victory, soaring eagles, order brooches, military insignia, flags, soldier pins, sweetheart jewelry, and "Remember Pearl Harbor" brooches.

Sometimes it is difficult to date jewelry during this era because many women just went on wearing what jewelry they had before the war (due to shortages). However, after the war America had a resurgence of prosperity. Once again, femininity became the fashion. The straight-skirt and wide-shouldered look of the previous decade was traded-in for the "new look" as inspired by Christian Dior. This new look placed accentuation on the bust and tiny waist — and with the feminine clothing went feminine jewelry. With this newly found prosperity and the new feminine fashions, jewelry was in great demand — especially costume jewelry.

The 1950s

In the 1950s new technology and the obsession for space exploration spread over into the business of fashion. Comet and atomic pins became prevalent. Since costume jewelry was in such a great demand — the jewelry making techniques of the 30s and 40s became costly and time-consuming. Supply could not meet the demand. Thus, technology was relied upon to find an alternative to jewelry production. In the 1950s the lost-wax casting method as well as old handcrafting techniques for creating fashion jewelry were almost all replaced by machine stamping. The jewelry could now be mass produced at a much reduced price to the manufacturer and the demands of the consumer could be met. Gradually, the prong-setting of stones by hand was replaced by the much faster and cheaper gluing-in of rhinestones using airplane glue.

Into the 1960s

By the late 1950s, rhinestone jewelry was becoming less popular. The industry had literally been flooded with rhinestone costume jewelry. As the 1960s progressed, the nation's youth were rebelling against the structured guidelines their parents had grown up with. Along with the removal of these principles went a rebellion against the stricture of fashion. Jewelry became constructed of plastics during the Op-Art fad of the late 1950s – early 1960s. Still a great influence in the 1960s was space exploration inspired by the Apollo campaign. Rhinestones were used less and less and were gradually replaced with plastics and metals as an accessory to the imagined couture of the future. By the time miniskirts became the fad, jewelry was no longer considered a wardrobe necessity. By the late 1960s to early 1970s costume jewelry took a definite downturn.

The 1970s and the Downfall of Costume Jewelry

By the late 1960s to early 1970s, costume jewelry, as well as fine jewelry, was no longer a "had to have" wardrobe addition. In the 1970s costume jewelers took a great blow. Gold had become increasingly expensive and the fashion conscience of the time invested their hard-earned money in gold chains and simple hoop earrings. It became a sign of wealth to own gold. Those costume jewelers in the mainstream of fashion managed to hang-on to their business by a thread by creating imitation gold jewelry targeted to those individuals who wanted to have the look of real gold but who could not afford the exorbitant price of the real thing. Sadly, the late 1960s and early 1970s saw many costume jewelry houses close shop forever.

The Return to Glamour — 1980s Style

In the mid-1980s there was a revival of glamour. The clunky, funky, and unflattering styles of the 1970s gave way to more appealing, feminine, and flashy styles of the 1980s. As in the past, fashion was greatly influenced by the stars of

Hollywood. Meryl Streep's character in the movie *Out of Africa* represented strength as well as feminity in the 1980s. The *Out of Africa*-influenced fashions (lacy, feminine blouses worn with cameos, longer sweeping skirts, and leather riding boots) were reflected in the most exclusive shops all the way down to the bargain basements. However, even with the popularity of *Out of Africa,* during this time period television made more of an impact than the silver screen. Programs such as *Dynasty* portrayed women as strong, intellectual, independent, stylish, and bedecked in jewels 24 hours a day. Joan Collins and Linda Evans, among others in television, were bedecked in dazzling faux gems by Joseff. Joseff had earlier made its mark on the film industry in the 1940s and had bedecked all the great stars of Hollywood. Joseff jewelry was seen in *Gone with the Wind, That Hamilton Woman,* and *Camille,* as well as hundreds of other films. In the 1980s there was an appreciation for costume jewelry of the past and many people began wearing costume jewelry that had belonged to their mother and grandmother. Old fashion jewelry that had been considered junk during the prior decade started showing up clustered on denim jackets, at the neck of a severe blouse, on the lapel of a wool business suit, or at the waist on a sash. Glittering rhinestones were no longer worn for night time only and began showing up during the day. With this appreciation for costume jewelry of the past, the prices of old pieces and parures began to soar. People began asking "When, where, and how was this made?" Costume jewelers of the 1980s saw increasing popularity of old designs and began copying them in great quantities. Companies such as 1928 began making reproduction Victorian, Edwardian, and Art Deco jewelry in mass quantities to meet the demands of the 1980s consumer.

The 1990s and the "1970s Revival"

Once again in the early to mid-1990s costume jewelry took a down turn as a renaissance of the 1970s style took place. Once more, "plain Jane" jewelry became commonplace and simple chains, Y-necklaces, tiny peace-signs, and love beads became popular. Large, rhinestone-encrusted jewelry became a scarce occurrence on store racks and displays. However, now it looks like a return to glamour is once again reappearing, with the majority of consumers again wearying of unflattering modes. The reappearance of glamour goes hand-in-hand with the necessity of costume jewelry of the past as well as the present. However, this time, even fewer pieces are to be found and the values are once again soaring.

The Influence of Hollywood

From the 1930s through the 1950s glamorous Hollywood film stars made a huge impression on fashion. Styles worn by the stars on and off the silver screen were readily copied and adapted to fit any budget. The genuine gems and baubles worn by the most elegant of Hollywood were mimicked in costume jewelry — from the pricier designer costume jewelry on down to the cheaper dime store imitations. Anyone who was fashionable did not leave the house in the 30s, 40s, and early 50s without being perfectly coifed, without a hat, gloves, and glittering jewelry. During the Second World War, a majority of the French couture houses were forced to close. America could no longer look to Paris for fashion influence. At this time, Hollywood became the new fashion focal point for the fashionable American consumer.

***Life**, November 1959*

***Life**, November 1959*

The Influence of Royalty

Besides the great effect of Hollywood on fashion, the royal style was also imitated. Jewelry given to The Duchess of Windsor by The Duke of Windsor was purchased at the most elegant and imaginative of jewelers. Staggering, ingenious jewelry was custom made for the royals by the great jewelers Van Cleef in New York, Van Cleef & Arpels in Paris, Cartier, Harry Winston, David Webb, and Suzanne Belperron. When these fanciful and expensive jewels were first worn at social functions by the Duchess, society columnists raved about it in articles — everyone wanted *those* jewels! Costume jewelers produced copies out of sterling silver, base metal, and glass stones. Many of these replicas were done with different colors of materials and rhinestones. The same bracelet, for instance, might have been done in emerald green rhinestones, as well as in ruby red or sapphire blue rhinestones. Joan Rivers has created a plastic and rhinestone flower pin influenced by the Duchess's blue chalcedony, sapphire, and diamond flower necklace and matching leaf earrings. However, Joan's beautiful replica is done in faux ivory and tortoise cabochons. Wallis Simpson's famous Cartier jeweled panthers and tigers were sources of inspiration for Trifari, Jomaz, Kenneth J. Lane as well as numerous other companies. Her rubies and diamonds inspired replicas by Mazer, Jomaz, and Trifari. The Cartier aquamarine Deco-style clips presented to Queen Elizabeth in celebration of her eighteenth birthday were swiftly copied into costume jewelry in rhinestones. The influence of the Queen's pear drop earrings, modern baguettes and brilliants bracelet, Queen Victoria's collet necklace with matching earrings and her bow brooches, and Queen Mary's Dorcet's bow brooch was seen in similar Eisenberg and Weiss designs. Trifari also made designs similar to the Queen's jardiniere and flower bas-

ket brooches (these brooches were done in the Indian design with carved stones often called "fruit salad" jewelry). Copies of Queen Mary's ever-fashionable Kensington bow brooch are still being done today. In the 1940s a focus was made on India and Indian-inspired jewelry became all the rage. The May 1948 issue of *Harper's Bazaar* featured an article on the Maharaja of Baroda's thirty-ninth birthday with an excerpt on the regal jewelry worn to the royal gala. Amazingly, the gala event was a benefit to feed the poor.

In preparation for a traditional event of feeding the poor. The Maharani of Baroda adorning her massive collar of diamonds, which once belonged to Napoleon.

Jewelry Time Table

Victorian Era............	1837 – 1901	Transitional................................	1910 – 1920
Art Nouveau.............	1895 – 1915	Art Deco.....................................	1910 – 1941
Edwardian................	1901 – 1910	Heyday of Hollywood................	1930 – 1955

Victorian era jewelry is so called due to the styles influenced by England's Queen Victoria during her reign from 1837 – 1901.

The label "Art Nouveau" was attributed to the free-flowing style that was influential mainly from approximately 1895 through 1915. Late Art Nouveau jewelry began to show Art Deco influences during the first decade of the 1900s. The free-flowing lines of the "new art" (Art Nouveau) became combined with the sleek and geometric influence of the "modern" Art Deco and the "line" between the two styles became obscure.

The term "Edwardian" refers to the jewelry that was created during the reign of England's King Edward VII from 1901 to 1910.

In the years from approximately 1910 through the late 1930s many styles were reflected in the jewelry industry. It is often difficult to place a date to the particular jewelry items that have a combination of Art Nouveau and Art Deco stylizations. These jewelry items are referred to as transitional. The beginning date of World War II is often considered to be the termination date of the Art Deco era.

Remember when trying to put a date to costume jewelry that the old adage "what goes around, comes around" holds very true in this genre. Many styles that proved to be bestsellers of the time, are often remade every few years. Often these new items are made in the same way as they were years before with just a change in metal plating or rhinestone color combinations. There was a Victorian revival in the 1940s, a Black Mourning Jewelry revival in the 1950s and 1960s, an Art Deco revival in the 1960s, a Glamorous 1930s revival in the 1980s, and a Disco and 1970s revival in the 1990s.

During the heyday of Hollywood screen stars made a huge impact on the fashion industry. Jewelry in the 1930s became more detailed and larger in size with more rhinestones than ever before. However, during the years of World War II the use of white metals was outlawed as these metals were strictly utilized for the war effort. Sterling silver (with and without gold plating) replaced the usage of cheaper base metals. The importing of Austrian crystal rhinestones was halted and most of the jewelry items created during this period used one or two large stones or had no stones at all and relied on their dramatic design. Many of these dramatic pieces without rhinestones are referred to as "retro."

Vogue, September 15, 1942

A DRESS THAT WILL BE YOUR STAND-BY the Winter thru has a beautifully detailed blouse and a skirt with rhythm. Available in sizes 14½ to 24½ at the following stores: Abraham & Straus, Brooklyn; Bloomingdale's, New York City; Boston Store, Milwaukee; Bullock's, Los Angeles; H. C. Capwell's, Oakland; The Dayton Company, Minneapolis; The Emporium, San Francisco; Wm. Filene's Sons Company, Boston; B. Forman Co., Rochester; Joseph Horne Co., Pittsburgh; The J. L. Hudson Company, Detroit; Hutzler Brothers Co., Baltimore; The F.&R. Lazarus & Co., Columbus; The Rike-Kumler Company, Dayton; The John Shillito Company, Cincinnati; Strawbridge & Clothier, Philadelphia; Taylor's, Cleveland; Thalhimers, Richmond

DAYTIME CHARM IN MIRACLE
A FABRIC DISTINCTIVELY
Evergrand

TUBIZE *certified quality* RAYON

***Vogue**, September 1942*

In the fashion magazines of the 40s, bold jewelry dotted and accented most of the feminine-targeted advertisements. Glamour was the selling point of many items from toiletries, shoes, foundations, wigs, as well as the latest fashions.

"Fashion Plate"

Cream Wafer Face Make-Up by REVLON

IT'S GOING PLACES . . . in the smartest handbags! It's *designed* to keep the poreless-as-porcelain perfection of the "Fashion Plate" complexion . . . at your fingertips . . . always.

REVLON
Fashion Plate
THE CREAM WAFER MAKE-UP

JUST FINGER-STROKE IT ON . . . Not a cake, "Fashion Plate" needs n water or sponge. It *ends* the old-fashioned, dry, mask-y look! Choose from exclusive fashion-genius colors.

The great new fashion in make-up! New vanity-case size 1.00 plus tax

***Harper's Bazaar**, September1948*

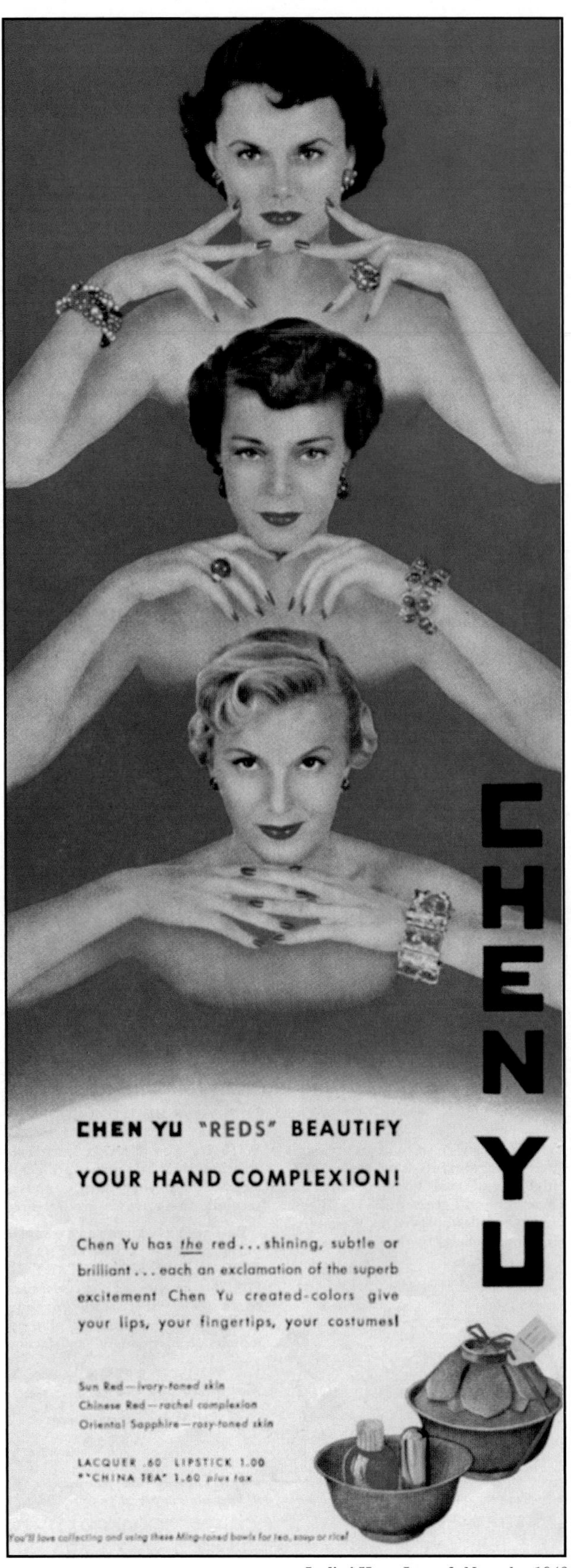

Ladies' Home Journal, *November 1948*

HORST

Indian Summer Look

A look that distills the golds and reds of autumn. The gold that lights her skin, her hair, and her dress. The red that brightens her lips, her nails, and matches (she planned it!) the tip of her Marlboro cigarette. Revlon's "Scarlet Slipper" lipstick, polish. Richelieu's Satinore earrings, bracelet. Bonwit Teller; Neiman-Marcus; Marshall Field; I. Magnin

***Vogue**, September 1942*

Sirocco-Blue

69

Vogue, September 1942

Jewelry in the 1930s and 40s was used as an adornment in imaginative ways — on glove cuffs, on jaunty hats, at the waist, on shoes, at the edge of a sleeve, on a poufed scarf, in the hair, as well as countless other ways.

Mazer

JEWELS OF ELEGANCE

In jewelry departments of fine stores everywhere.

MAZER BROS., 20 WEST 33rd STREET, NEW YORK 1, N. Y.

Harper's Bazaar, *April 1947*

Vogue, May 1948

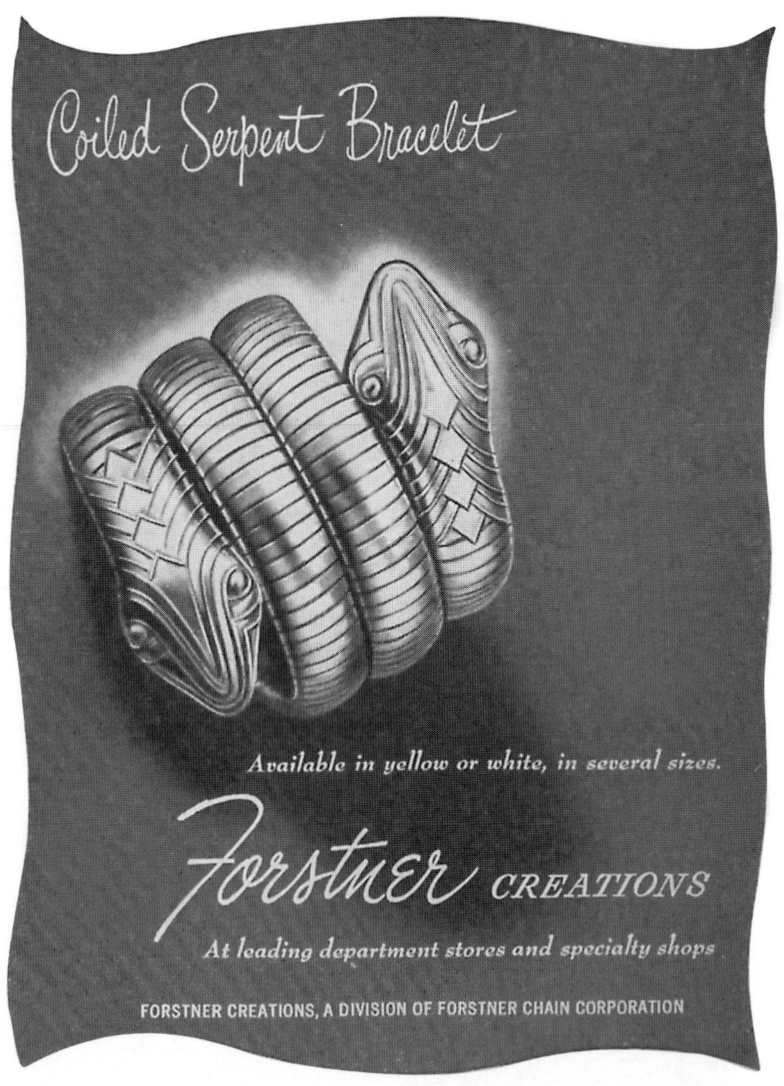

Harper's Bazaar, April 1947

Vogue, May 1948

Coro plays Cupid
with "SWEET TALK" *jewelry*

in harmony with REVLON'S new "SWEET TALK" color.

"SWEET TALK" wins the lady fair.
Coro's original conversation pieces that speak the language of love...in golden, jeweled accents.

Pin pair about $11., matching bracelet about $4., earrings about $3., plus tax.

At all leading stores, or write Coro, Inc., N. Y. 1

Coro JEWELRY ®
design patents appl'd for

***Vogue**, May 1948*

"HEAVENLY TWINS"—
out of never-never land
dances this merry pair of
winged creatures. Brightened
by rhinestones and make-
believe emeralds and rubies,
cast in gold-plated Trifanium.
Special magic for your
favorite Summer costume.
$7.50 a pair. Tax extra.

Jewels by TRIFARI

Design patents pending.

Harper's Bazaar, May 1948

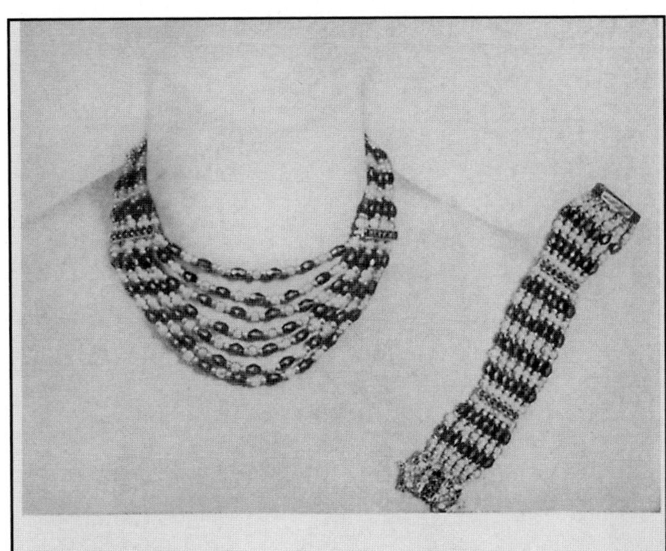

THE EMPRESS. Seven luxurious strands of jewel toned cut beads interspersed with small golden beads and simulated pearls. Unusual side ornament and back clasp interest. Matching bracelet boasts the same exquisite clasp . . . golden latticework studded with pearls and stones; a distinguished replica of an antique design. In garnet, topaz, amethyst, crystal, crystal and jet, and aquamarine tones. Necklace, $25.00. Bracelet, $19.00. Price plus 20% tax.

Harper's Bazaar, September1948

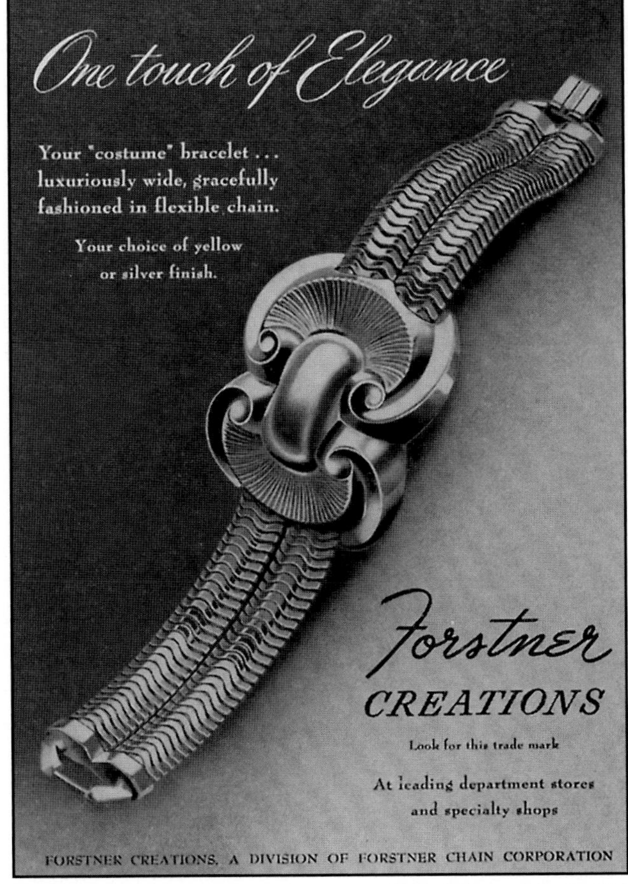

Harper's Bazaar, September1948

Life, *November 1959*

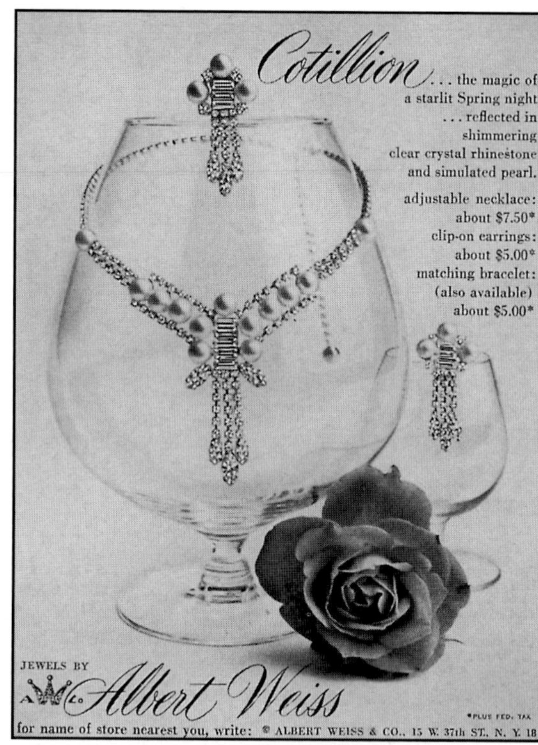

Harper's Bazaar, *May 1954*

"SIROCCO"... COOL SPLENDOR CAUGHT IN...

Jewels by BOGOFF

dress by JERRY PARNIS

Harper's Bazaar*, May 1954*

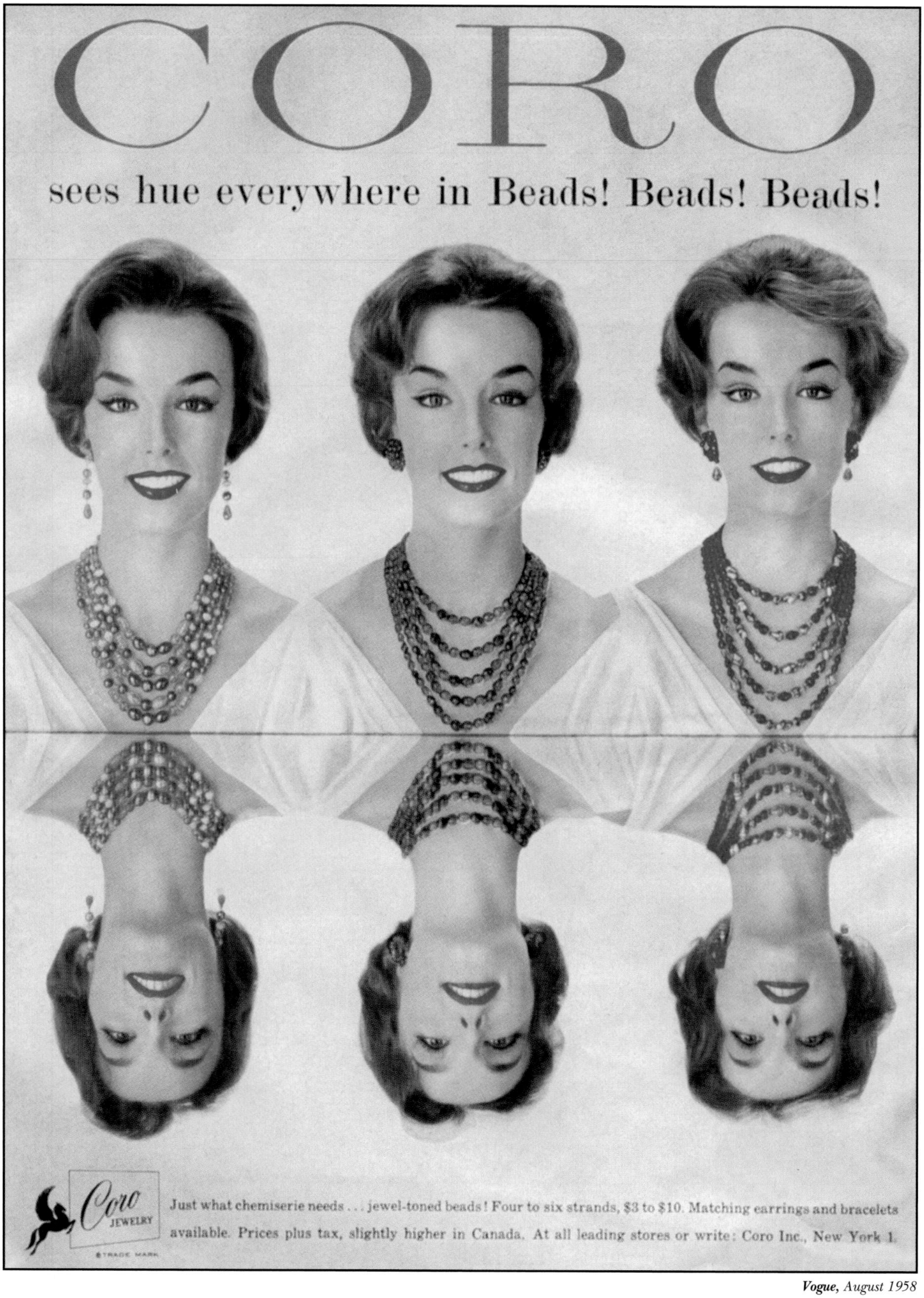

CORO

sees hue everywhere in Beads! Beads! Beads!

Coro JEWELRY
®TRADE MARK

Just what chemiserie needs . . . jewel-toned beads! Four to six strands, $3 to $10. Matching earrings and bracelets available. Prices plus tax, slightly higher in Canada. At all leading stores or write: Coro Inc., New York 1.

Vogue, *August 1958*

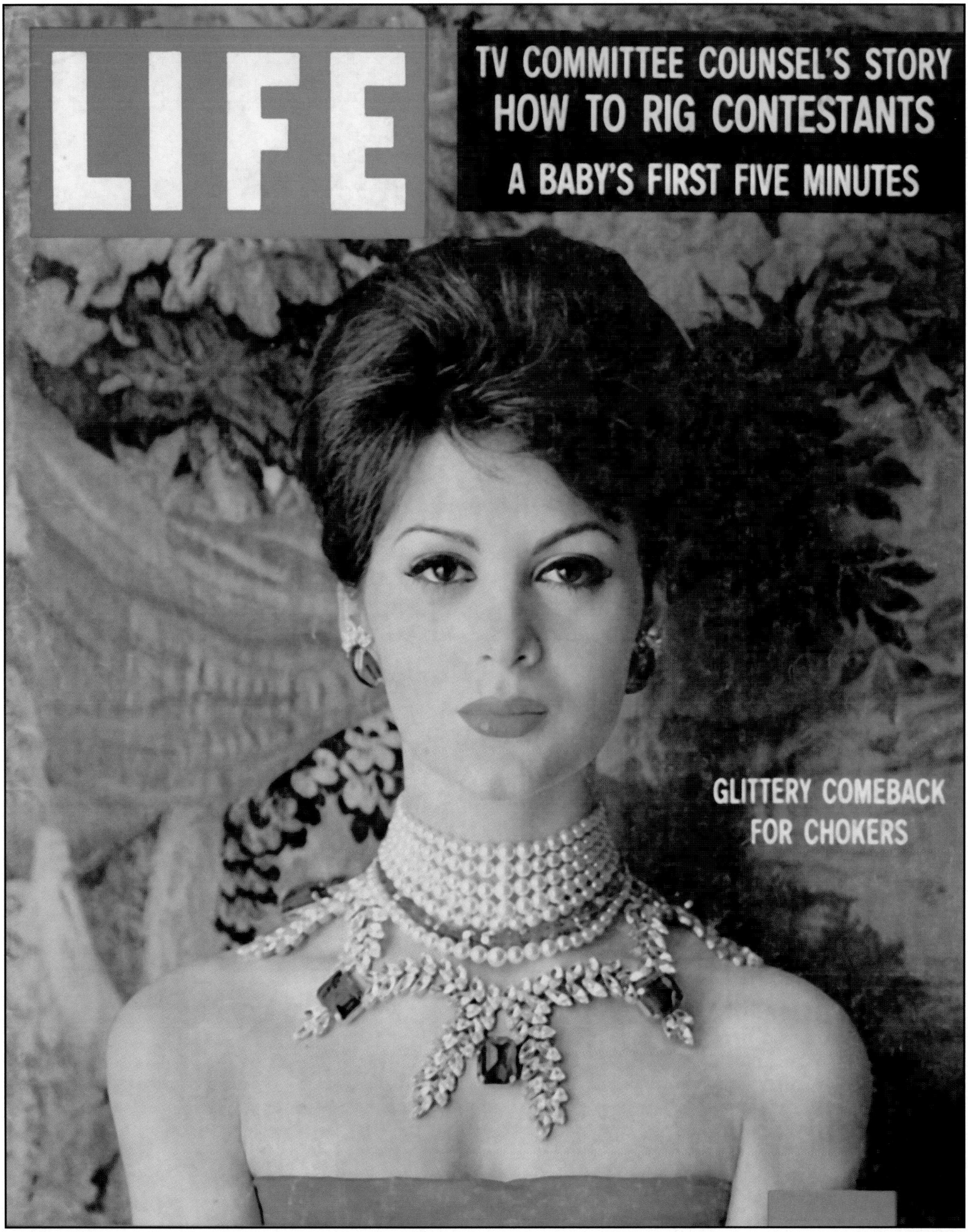

LIFE

TV COMMITTEE COUNSEL'S STORY
HOW TO RIG CONTESTANTS
A BABY'S FIRST FIVE MINUTES

GLITTERY COMEBACK
FOR CHOKERS

***Life**, November 1959*

Do us a favor. Before you buy Majoricas, look at them beside a strand of real pearls.

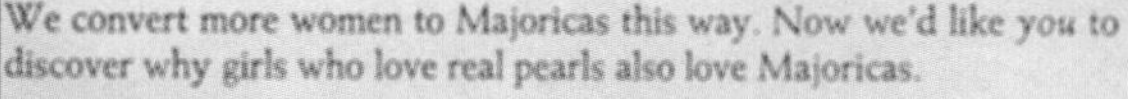

We convert more women to Majoricas this way. Now we'd like *you* to discover why girls who love real pearls also love Majoricas.

They love the same things in both. The warm lustre. The iridescence that shares its glow with your complexion. The creaminess of color that seems to go all the way to the heart of the pearl.

No other simulated pearl captures the extraordinary beauty of the real pearl as Majoricas do. (Women who are fortunate enough to own both sometimes can't tell which is which!)

Majoricas are not the only simulated pearls which are made on the island of Majorca, but they are the only ones that can rightfully claim to be the world's most precious simulated pearls.

So please, look at Majoricas side by side with real pearls. Do us—and yourself—a favor.

Majorica necklaces, $25 to $150, only at the most discriminating stores.

MAJORICA®
INTERNACIONAL
the world's most precious simulated pearls

Harper's Bazaar, *May 1967*

Harper's Bazaar, *May 1967*

1967 model wearing Kenneth J. Lane earrings.

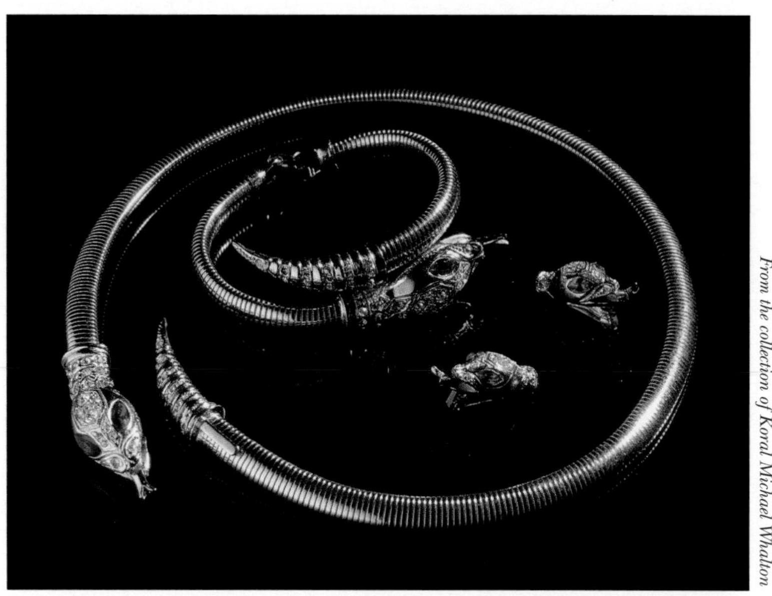

From the collection of Koral Michael Whalton

Coro parure. Gold-plated serpentine necklace and bracelet. The serpent's head and tail is clear rhinestone pavé with emerald green rhinestone eyes. The earrings are 1", the serpent's head on the necklace is 1¾" long, and the serpent on the bracelet is 1¾" long. Late 1940s to early 1950s. $600.00 – 750.00 set.

From the collection of Koral Michael Whalton

Miriam Haskell brass Egyptian-motif choker with 3¾" x 3¾" repoussé work square disk. Mesh bracelet with the same Egyptian motif on the clasp. $500.00 – 650.00 set.

From the collection of Koral Michael Whalton

Trifari parure consisting of cuff bracelet, necklace, pin with drop, and dangle-style earrings. Glass milkstones in kidney-bean, round, and pear-shaped cabochons. Sapphire blue inverted square-cut and clear chaton-cut rhinestones. Antiqued gold plate. All marked Trifari and the pin is marked with patent number 2066969. The pin is 2" long, the hinged cuff is 1" at the widest point, and the earrings are 1¼" long. $400.00 – 600.00 set.

From the collection of Koral Michael Whalton

Early 1950s Hollycraft beauties. Each in antiqued Russian gold-plated base metal set with the foil-backed pastel rhinestones Hollycraft is famous for marking almost every piece with the date. The top right brooch is 1½" x 1¾" and is marked 1950. $75.00 – 95.00. The 1" jeweled hoop earrings at top left are undated (probably 1951). $55.00 – 75.00. The 1" wide bracelet is marked 1950. $155.00 – 200.00. On the right, the 2" long, dangle-style earrings are set with simulated seed pearls marked 1951. $75.00 – 95.00. The necklace is marked 1950. $145.00 – 190.00. The large brooch in the center is 2" x 2½", marked 1951. $100.00 – 150.00. The smaller oval cluster-style earrings on the left are 1" long, marked 1950. $55.00 – 75.00. The brooch at bottom left is 1¾" long, marked 1951. $75.00 – 95.00.

Korda "Thief of Bagdad" necklace and brooch. Alexander Korda had this jewelry made in conjunction with the movie The Thief of Bagdad. Gilded brass filigree with pale blue enameling set with simulated pearls and ruby, sapphire, emerald, and amethyst rhinestones. The brooch is 2¼" in diameter and the center of the necklace is 1¾" in diameter. Marked 113 Thief of Bagdad Korda 6. $600.00 – 700.00 set.

From the collection of Koral Michael Whalton

An elaborate demi-parure consisting of floral pendant necklace and earrings. Gold plated. The flowers are in lavender enamel and the leaves are apple green enamel. Pink and aqua prong-set flower clusters and accents. Mesh chain. The pendant is 1½" in diameter and the earrings are ¾" in diameter. Unmarked. Possibly from Austria or Czechoslovakia. $200.00 – 300.00.

Hobé necklace and earrings set. Three strands of marbleized apple-green thermoset plastic beads and Venetian glass beads strung on fine chains. The push-slot clasp is gold plated with prong-set marbleized "bubbled" glass. The earrings are made of the same glass as the clasp. The earrings and the clasp are all 1¼" in diameter. All marked Hobé. 1950s – 1960s. $250.00 – 275.00.

1950s rope of peach and apricot simulated pearls and yellow carnival glass beads. The matching 1" earrings are marked Japan. $40.00 – 65.00.

Miriam Haskell necklace and earrings demi-parure. Antiqued gold-plated set with large flat simulated pearls. $375.00 – 425.00.

Courtesy of The Glass Spoon

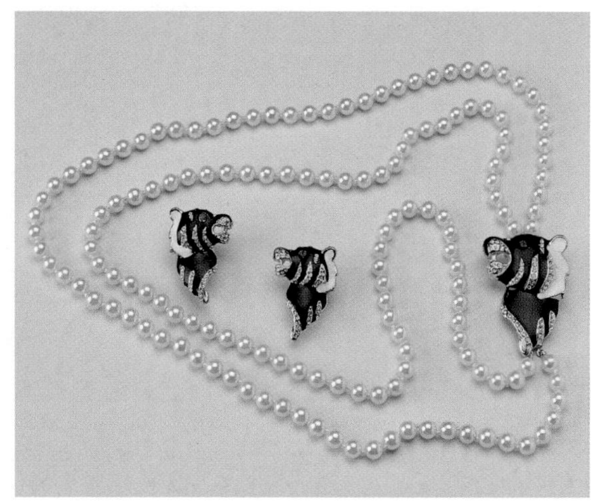

Unmarked demi-parure in a style resembling the work of Kenneth J. Lane. The black enameled tiger clasp converts to a brooch and the pearls can be worn without it. The faux pearls are heavy and of good quality. The tiger clasp/brooch and matching earrings are gold plated with black and cream enamel. The tiger's stripes and muzzle are set with clear rhinestones. The eyes are ruby red rhinestones. The clasp/brooch is 2¾"l x 1¾"w, the clip-on earrings are 1¾" x 1¼", the double strand of 7mm uniform simulated pearls is matinee length. $175.00 – 225.00.

Trifari necklace, earrings, and bracelet set. Faux coral and white opalescent cabochons in gold trifanium. 1960s. The necklace and bracelet are ¾" wide and the earrings are 1¼" long. $200.00 – 300.00.

From the collection of Koral Michael Whalon

Collection of Miracle Victorian Scottish agate style jewelry. Scottish agate jewelry was popular in England and Scotland during the rein of Queen Victoria. 1" wide silver-tone Art Nouveau-style bracelet. Simulated turquoise with aqua and green enameling. Marked Miracle. Silver-tone Scottish Agate brooch with a Maltese cross design. Glass stones are used to imitate agate and turquoise. 2" in diameter. Marked Miracle A.S. The Scottish agate brooch is 1¾" in diameter. Silver-tone metal. Glass stones are used to imitate agate and turquoise. Central round rose-cut glass amethyst. Marked Miracle. Silver-tone base metal pendant necklace is set with simulated turquoise. 2½" long. Marked Miracle Britain. $400.00 – 500.00 set.

Sarah Coventry's Celebrity pendant/brooch and earring set. Rhodium plated with large emerald-cut smoked glass stone and clear rhinestone accents. 1960s. $110.00 – 145.00.

Copper necklace and matching bracelet of openwork rectangular links by Renoir. 1950s. ¾" wide. $110.00 – 165.00.

Emerald-cut garnet glass rhinestones set in heavy antiqued brass in Victorian style. Pendant is on an antique gold-tone "S" chain. The bracelet is 1¼" wide and the pendant is 1¾". Both are marked Judy Lee. Excellent quality. $125.00 – 175.00.

Necklace and earrings of prong-set marbleized glass. The silver-tone necklace is marked Christian Dior Germany (A Grosse design for Christian Dior). The chromium-plated earrings are unmarked but have the same marbleized glass stones. The necklace is ¾" wide at the center and the earrings are 1¼" in diameter. Both necklace and earrings are from the 1950s. Necklace $200.00 – 275.00. Earrings $40.00 – 55.00.

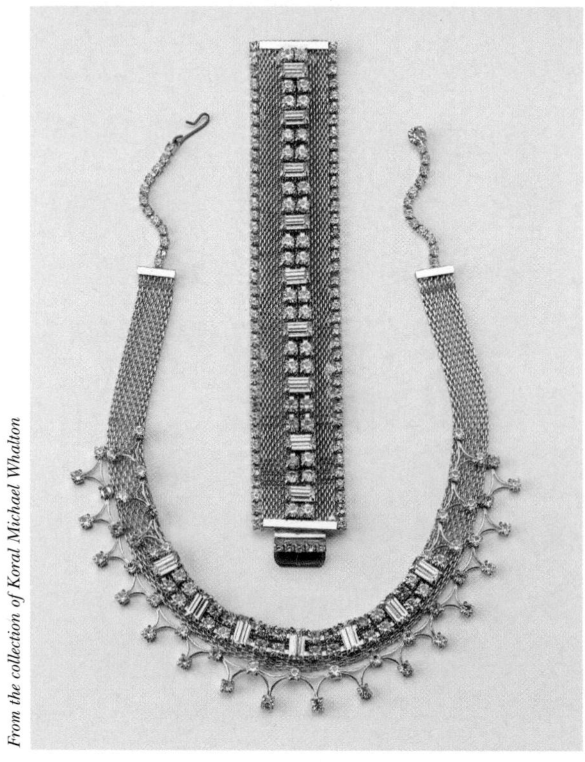

From the collection of Koral Michael Whalton

Hobé gold-plated mesh bracelet and necklace set. Clear chaton-cut and icy blue emerald-cut, prong-set rhinestones. The bracelet is 1¼" wide. 1950s. $400.00 – 500.00.

From the collection of Koral Michael Whalton

1950s parure with unusual glass stones. Iridescent flesh-tone domed glass in a diamond-shaped cut with blue aurora borealis rhinestone accents. All stones are prong-set and foil-backed. Chromium plated. Excellent quality and highly collectible although unmarked. The bracelet is 1¼" wide, the earrings are 1½", and the necklace is ½" wide. $250.00 – 375.00.

Large and showy rhinestone festoon-style necklace and matching earrings. Prong-set aqua and aqua frosted glass rhinestones. Gold plated. The earrings are 1¼" in diameter. Unmarked. 1950s. $200.00 – 300.00.

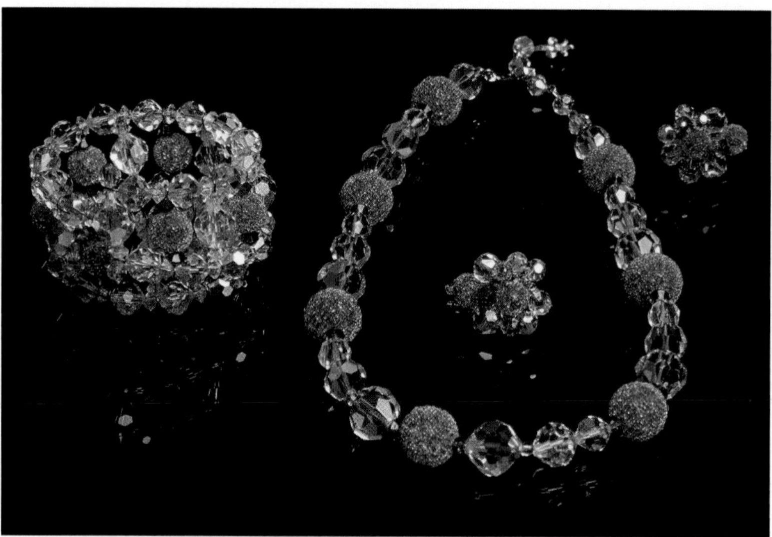

1950s Vendome set. Excellent quality clear and green aurora borealis crystal beads and glass raspberry beads comprise this 1" wide spiral bracelet, single strand necklace, and 1" cluster-style screw/clip earrings. The findings are rhodium plated. Marked Vendome on the necklace's hook clasp with the fleur-de-lis emblem at the open end of the necklace. $150.00 – 225.00.

Spectacular bib and 1½" long matching dangling earrings. Cascading aurora borealis Austrian crystal beads and rhinestones. Gold plated. Marked Hattie Carnegie. Still has original paper tags (not shown). $500.00 – 600.00.

1950s Eisenberg necklace and matching earrings. Emerald-cut clear Austrian crystal rhinestones and smaller chaton-cut accents. All rhinestones are prong-set. The necklace and earrings are marked Eisenberg. The 1¼" wide bracelet is unmarked but original owner purchased it with an Eisenberg brooch. The bracelet has a push-slot clasp and a safety catch chain. The earrings, bracelet, and necklace are rhodium plated. Bracelet $100.00 – 150.00, the necklace and earring set $450.00 – 575.00. Necklace and earrings set courtesy of The Glass Spoon.

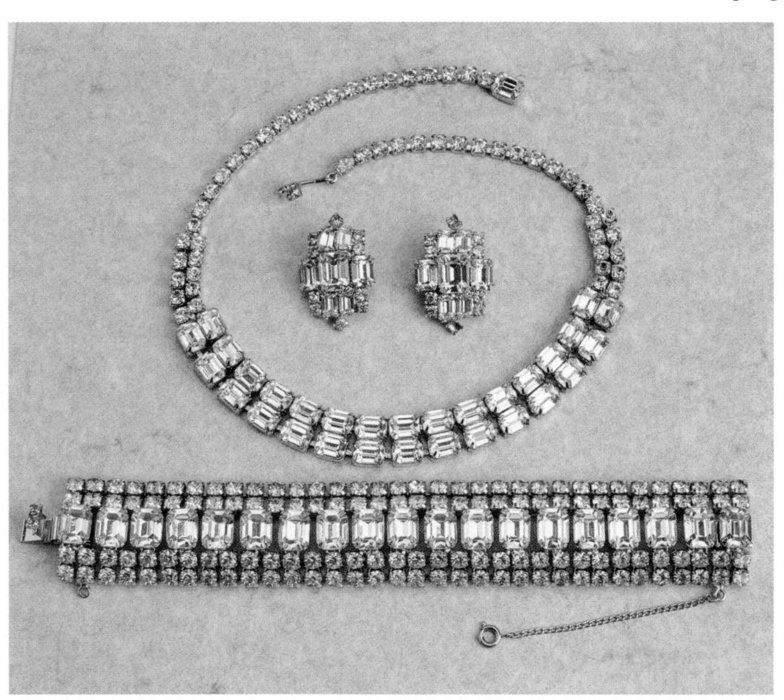

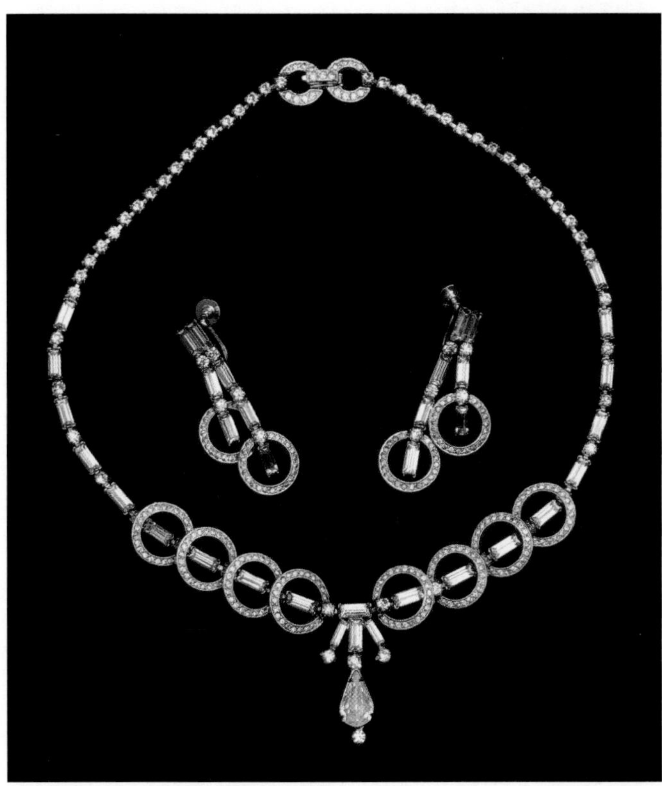

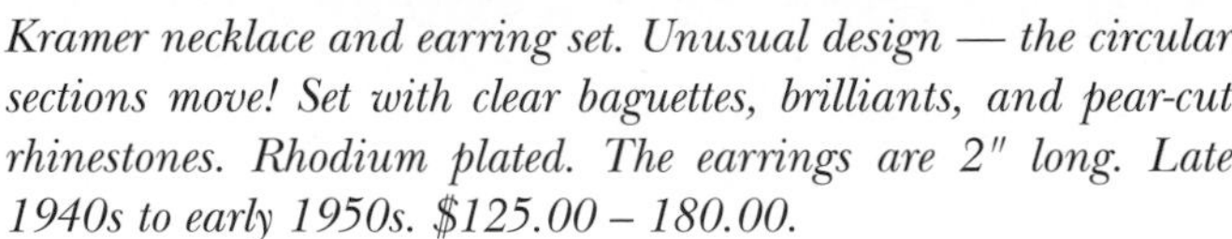

Kramer necklace and earring set. Unusual design — the circular sections move! Set with clear baguettes, brilliants, and pear-cut rhinestones. Rhodium plated. The earrings are 2" long. Late 1940s to early 1950s. $125.00 – 180.00.

1950s Weiss demi-parure. Prong-set lavender rhinestones in chaton and pear cuts. Prong set pink aurora borealis rhinestones in chaton and marquise cuts. Lavender Austrian crystal beads are added to the necklace and earrings to give the set a moving three-dimensional effect. $275.00 – 350.00.

Grouping of 1950s rhinestone jewelry. The fringe-style earrings are 1¼" long and have emerald-cut marbleized Venetian glass and chaton-cut lavender rhinestones. The choker-length necklace has purple round-cut cabochons and chaton-cut lavender rhinestones. The outer necklace has chaton-cut lavender and aurora borealis rhinestones. Both the necklaces and the earrings are chromium plated with prong-set rhinestones. The use of rhinestones in shades of purple was a popular practice in the 1950s. None of the jewelry is marked. Earrings $35.00 – 45.00, necklace $85.00 – 110.00 each.

Hobé parure from the 1950s – 1960s. Spiral bracelet, cluster earrings, and fringe necklace. The earrings are designed to fit along the shape of the ear (a popular style in the 1950s). The parure is constructed of silver-tone metal, faux white pearls, and blue, clear, and aqua glass bugle beads. $400.00 – 500.00.

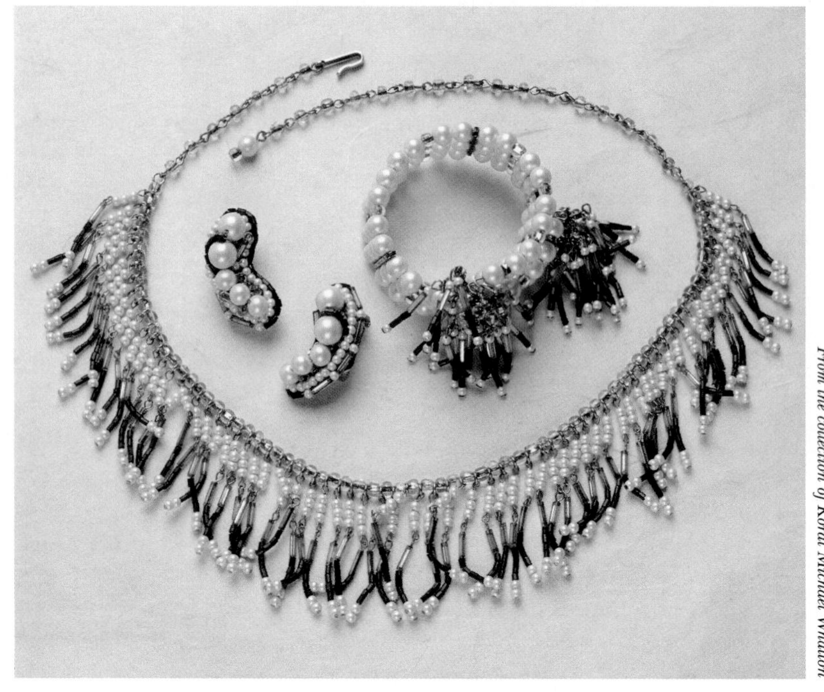

From the collection of Koral Michael Whalton

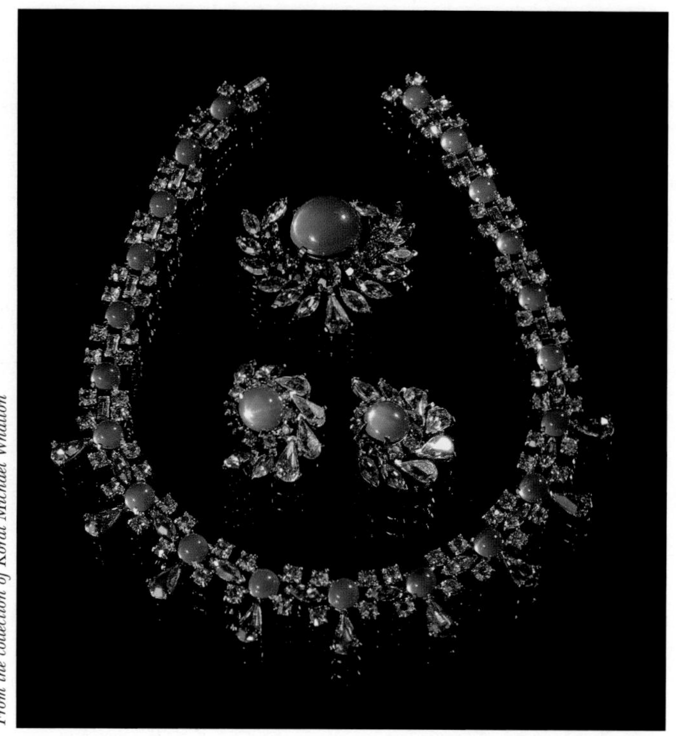

From the collection of Koral Michael Whalton

Breathtaking parure of simulated blue star sapphire cabochons and blue and peach aurora borealis rhinestones in chaton and pear cuts. All the rhinestones are prong set and the cabochons are claw set. Rhodium plated. Marked Jomaz. The pin is 1¾" x 1¼" and the earrings are 1¼". 1950s. $1,200.00 – 1,500.00.

From the collection of Koral Michael Whalton

Spectacular unmarked parure of excellent quality. Purple Venetian-style glass cabochons, amethyst and lavender rhinestones prong set in brush-tone gold plate. Twisted-rope chains. Possibly made in Austria or Czechoslovakia. The brooch is 2" wide x 4" long, earrings 1¼", the clasp on the bracelet is 1½" x 2¼", the clasp on the necklace is 1¾" x 2½". 1950s. $900.00 – 1000.00.

Gold-plated set by Emmons. Molded plastic flowers to imitate jade with tiny rhinestone accents. Leaves are ivory enamel. The necklace and bracelet is ½" wide and the earrings are 1¼" long. $250.00 – 325.00.

Gilded brass floral disk choker-length necklace and earring set. Prong-set aquamarine, emerald, amethyst, and clear rhinestones. Marked BK. $75.00 – 100.00 set.

Unmarked parure. Aqua marbleized plastic cabochons in gold-plated base metal. The bracelet is ¾" wide, the earrings are ¾" in diameter, and the necklace is ½" wide with a ¾" drop. Late 1950s. $125.00 – 150.00.

Pinchbeck necklace and dangling earrings. Faux seed pearls and genuine turquoise. Gold cording with turquoise glass seed bead, simulated pearl, and red glass bugle bead tassel. The necklace is 1¼" wide and the earrings are 2¼" long. Probably made in India. $125.00 – 225.00.

Courtesy of The Glass Spoon

Trifari parure. Aurora borealis, emerald, and peridot green rhinestones gives this parure a leafy quality. Gold plated. $200.00 – 300.00. The pin is 2¼", the earrings are 1¼" long, the bracelet is ½" wide, and the drop on the necklace is 2" long.

Silver-tone metal chains, aqua and navy blue glass beads with antiqued brass spacers. Marked W. Germany (West Germany). The earrings are 1¼" in diameter and are marked Made in West Germany. 1950s. $55.00 – 85.00.

1950s silver-tone metal chains with ball and tassel center accent. Aqua blue and smoky gray glass beads. Marked W. Germany (West Germany). 1970s silver-tone tassel earrings marked Monet. The central necklace tassel is 4¾" long and the earrings are 2¼" long. $40.00 – 60.00 necklace and $25.00 – 40.00 earrings.

Necklace and earrings set in an openwork floral design. The simulated pearls and sapphire-blue rhinestones are glued in. Rhodium plated. Unmarked. 1950s. The necklace is 1½" wide at the center and the earrings are 1½" long. $75.00 – 105.00.

Etruscan-style bib necklace and earring set. Silver-tone metal with bezel-set smoky-gray rhinestones. The central section of the bib is 5¼" long and the earrings are 2¼" long. Unmarked, similar to work done by Kenneth J. Lane. 1960s. $175.00 – 275.00.

Bedouin silver-tone filigree rigid collar with glass simulated turquoise from Pakistan. Wire earrings are also set with glass simulated turquoise and are from 1994. Neither marked. The collar is 2" wide at the center and the earrings are 1½" long (including the wire). $100.00 – 200.00 collar and $15.00 – 25.00 for earrings.

Retro-style necklace and earring set. Pear-shaped faux topazes set in 2¼" long gilded brass pendant on a rattail chain with 1½" long matching dangle clip-on earrings. Unmarked. $115.00 – 175.00.

Unmarked necklace and earrings of oxidized copper set with blue moonstone cabochons, simulated pearls, and sapphire rhinestones. The earrings are ¾" in diameter and the pendant is 2" long. Original box from Bullock's not shown. $100.00 – 125.00.

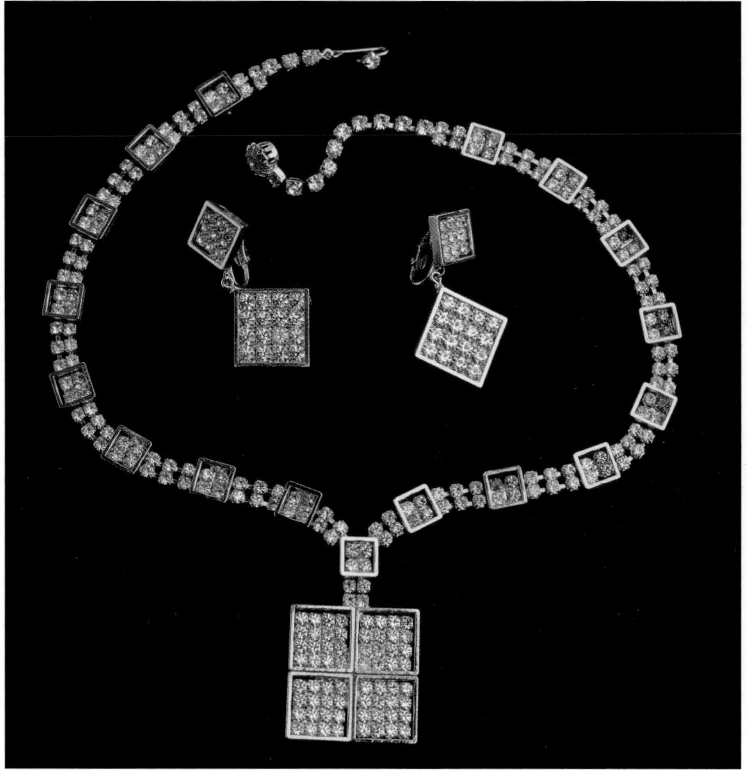

Unusual necklace and dangle-style earrings. Gold-plated squares with prong-set clear chaton-cut rhinestones. Unmarked. Late 1960s to 1970s. The necklace is ¼" wide with a 2" long central pendant. The clip-on earrings are 2" long. $135.00 – 180.00.

Buddha and pagoda pendant necklace and dangle-style earring set. Faux carnelian plastic beads, gold plated. Marked ART. This type of Oriental jewelry is quickly becoming very collectible. The pendant is 5" long and the earrings are 2½" long. $125.00 – 200.00.

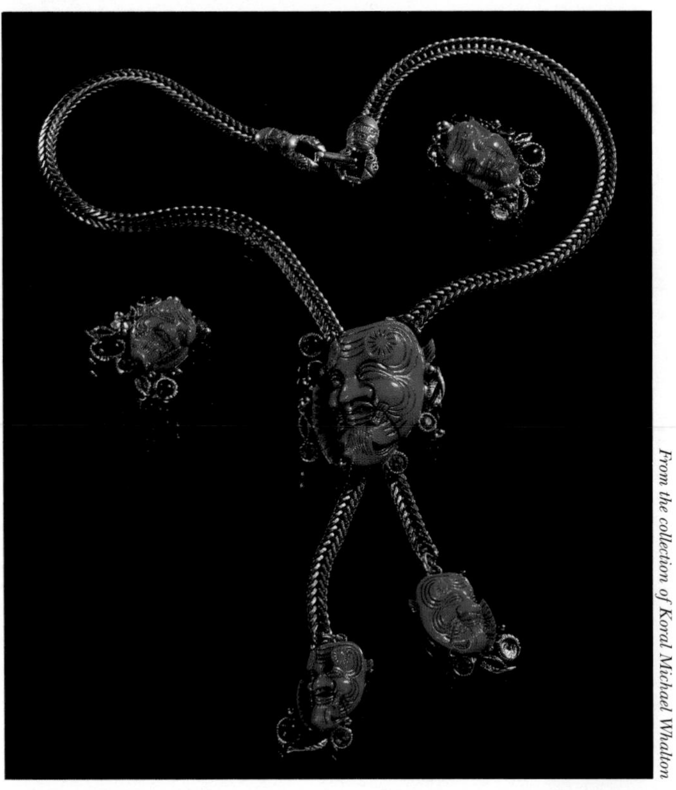

From the collection of Koral Michael Whalton

Selro Corp. bolo-style necklace and earring set. Silver-tone base metal. Red plastic molded devil faces, black plastic cabochons and red rhinestones (all glued in). The earrings are 1¾". 1950s. $350.00 – 450.00.

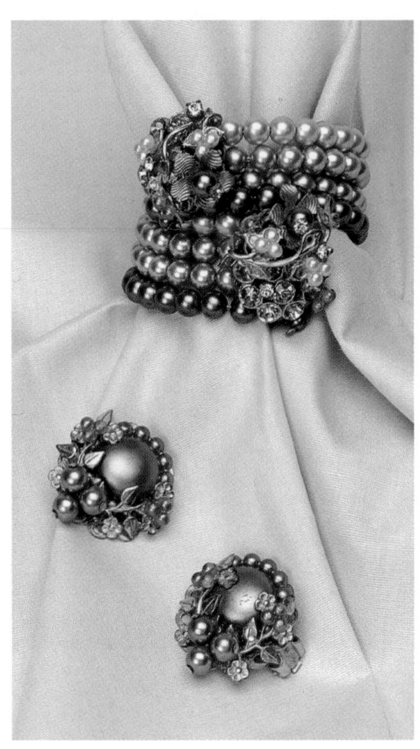

Beige and tobacco colored simulated pearls make up this spiral bracelet. The ends of the bracelet are done in a cluster (a style made popular by Miriam Haskell) and are brass filigree with brass flowers and leaves set with clear and aurora borealis rhinestones. The 1¼" clip-on earrings are of a similar style except without the rhinestone accents. Earrings and bracelet are unmarked. 1950s. $40.00 – 60.00 bracelet and $20.00 – 35.00 earrings.

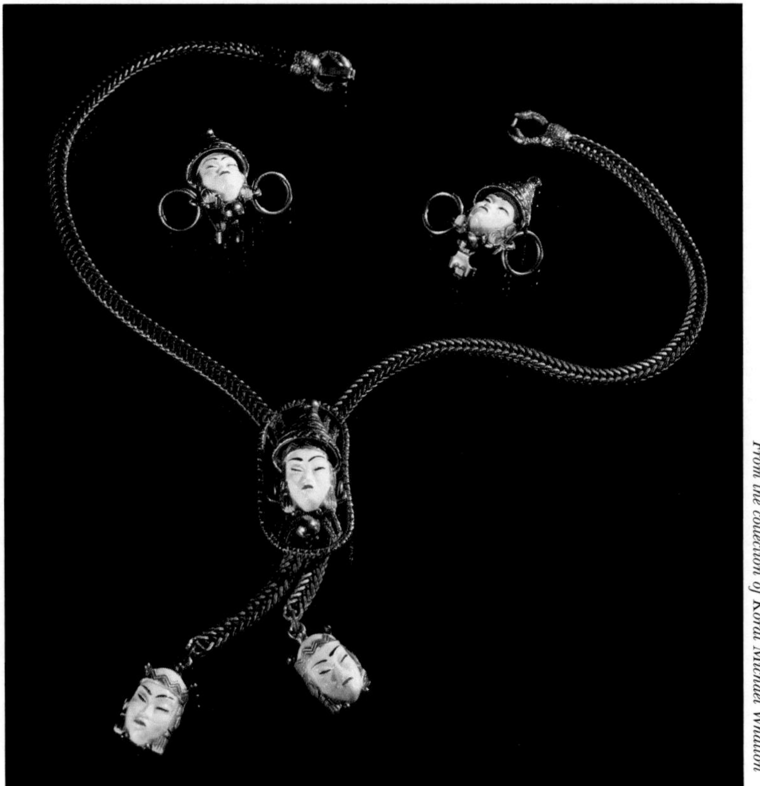

From the collection of Koral Michael Whalton

Bolo-style necklace and earrings with Oriental inspiration. Gold-tone base metal with plastic molded faces. Unmarked. 1950s. $250.00 – 325.00.

1950s Napier jewelry. Antiqued silver-tone Oriental coin charm bracelet with unusual coiled antiqued silver-tone hoops. The largest coin on the bracelet is 1¼" and the earrings are 1". Bracelet $125.00 – 185.00. Earrings $25.00 – 50.00.

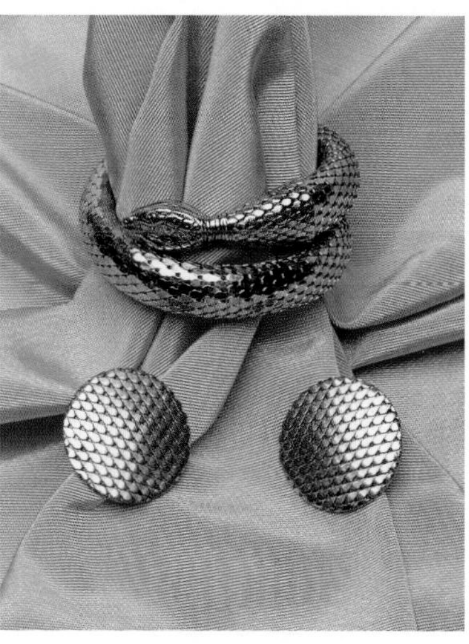

Serpent spiral bracelet and matching scaly earrings. Gold plated. 1950s. Marked Whiting and Davis on the earrings and the bracelet. The snake bracelet is ½" wide and the earrings are 1¼" in diameter. $200.00 – 275.00 set.

Trifari serpent scarf brooch and cobra-style spiral bracelet. Set with ruby red and emerald green rhinestones which are glued in. Gold-tone trifanium plate. The brooch is 3" x 2¾". $325.00 – 450.00 set.

From the collection of Koral Michael Whalton

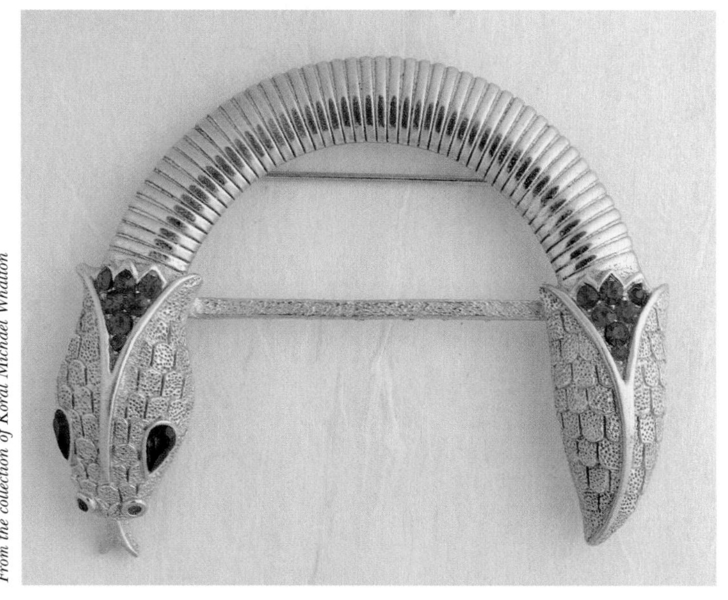

Courtesy of Leon & Lurleen Tetreault.

Left: Panetta gold-plated 1" wide cuff. Pavé clear rhinestones. Art Deco style. $350.00 – 450.00. Right: Christian Dior 1" gold-plated cuff. Pavé clear rhinestones. $175.00 – 250.00. Lanvin-Paris earrings. Gold plated with pavé clear rhinestones. 1¼" long. Purchased in Paris in the early 1950s. $200.00 – 250.00.

Egyptian-motif link bracelet and earrings. Pale green enameled disks depicting Egyptian scenes set in gold-plated nugget-style links. Unmarked. The bracelet is 1¼" wide and the earrings are 1¼" square. 1960s Egyptian revival. $125.00 – 200.00.

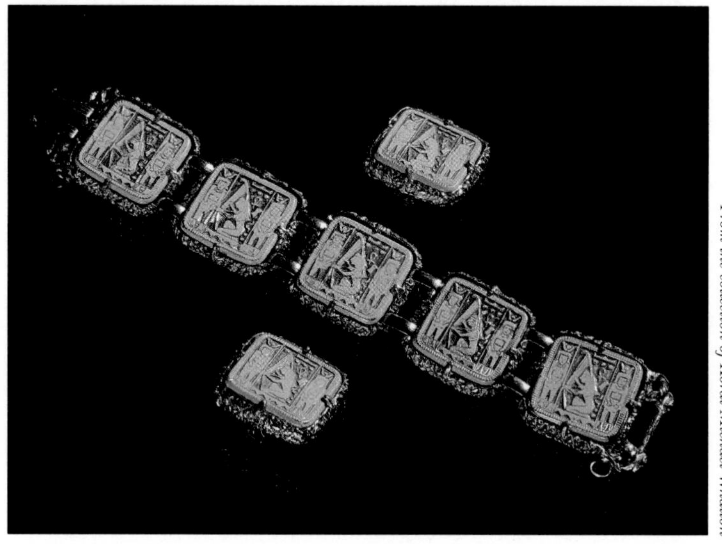

From the collection of Koral Michael Whalton

From the collection of Koral Michael Whalton

Gold-plated scroll-leaf design bracelet and earrings. Marked Schiaparelli. The earrings are 2½" long and the bracelet is 1" wide. $250.00 – 325.00.

Antiqued gold-tone bracelet and earrings. Red confetti glass pear-cut cabochons and ruby red rhinestones. Earrings are 1¾" and the bracelet is 1¾" wide. 1950s. Unmarked. $100.00 – 150.00 set.

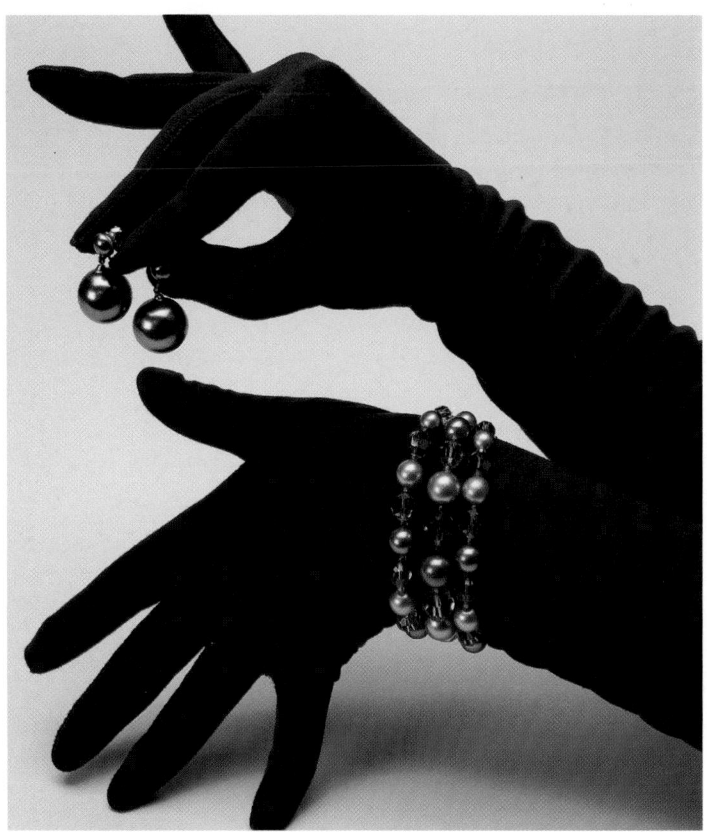

1950s Marvella brown crystal bead and tobacco faux pearl, three-strand bracelet. Unmarked earrings of tobacco faux pearls. $50.00 – 75.00 bracelet and $15.00 – 25.00 earrings.

Clusters of prystal beads and simulated pearls with pastel pink, aqua, and blue rhinestones on silver-tone filigree. The earrings are 1¼" and the bracelet is 1¼" wide. 1950s. Unmarked. $75.00 – 115.00.

Antiqued gold-tone bracelet and earring set. Triangular-shaped opalescent glass cabochons, simulated pearls, pale yellow and deep green rhinestones. Marked Florenza. $150.00 – 250.00.

From the collection of Koral Michael Whalton

Glittering rhinestone bracelet and earring set. Excellent craftsmanship. Gold tone with prong-set rhinestone mesh in each disk. Clear chaton-cut rhinestones with smaller brown chaton-cut rhinestone accents. Bracelet is marked Ann Vien on a soldered-on tag. A rare name. $375.00 – 475.00.

From the collection of Koral Michael Whalton

Unusual parure from approximately 1910. Gilded brass disks with apple green and lavender enamel cloisonné. Each disk has a claw-set emerald green glass rhinestone. The brooch is topped with a gold-filled feminine bow and the bottom disk is finished on both sides. The earrings are screw-back. The bracelet has an unusual clasp — it is the type usually used with watch fobs. The brooch is 3¼" long, the bracelet is 1" wide, and the earrings are 1" in diameter. The bow is marked FM Co. and hallmarked 120 10KGF, however the rest of the jewelry is gilded brass. May possibly be suffragette jewelry. *$200.00 – 250.00.

*The colors chosen to represent the women's suffragette movement were purple, white, and green. Jewelry during this time period could be found in combinations of those colors, often in genuine amethysts, pearls, peridots, and emeralds for those that could afford the real thing and done in simulated pearls, rhinestones, and enamel for those who could not.

From the collection of Koral Michael Whalton

Unmarked Sarah Coventry parure. Silver-tone base metal bracelet, brooch, earrings, and ring set with smoky glass and pink rhinestones (foil-backed). Earrings are 1¼", brooch is 2½" l x 1¾" w, and the bracelet is 1¼" wide. $175.00 – 250.00.

Gun-metal plated bracelet with green tourmaline, sapphire, and aurora borealis rhinestones. Brooch and earring set is silver-tone metal with pewter leaves and emerald, sapphire, and aurora borealis rhinestones. The brooch and earrings are marked Patent Pending. $125.00 – 150.00 for the bracelet and $100.00 – 145.00 for the set. Bracelet is courtesy of The Glass Spoon.

From the collection of Koral Michael Whalton

Beautiful parure of prong-set faux watermelon tourmalines, emerald-green, and olive-green rhinestones. Blue-green and pink aurora borealis rhinestones. Gold plated. Unmarked. 1950s. The earrings are kept on original card (not shown). The brooch is 2½" x 2½", the earrings are 1¼" long, and the bracelet is ¾" wide. All hand-set rhinestones. $300.00 – 400.00.

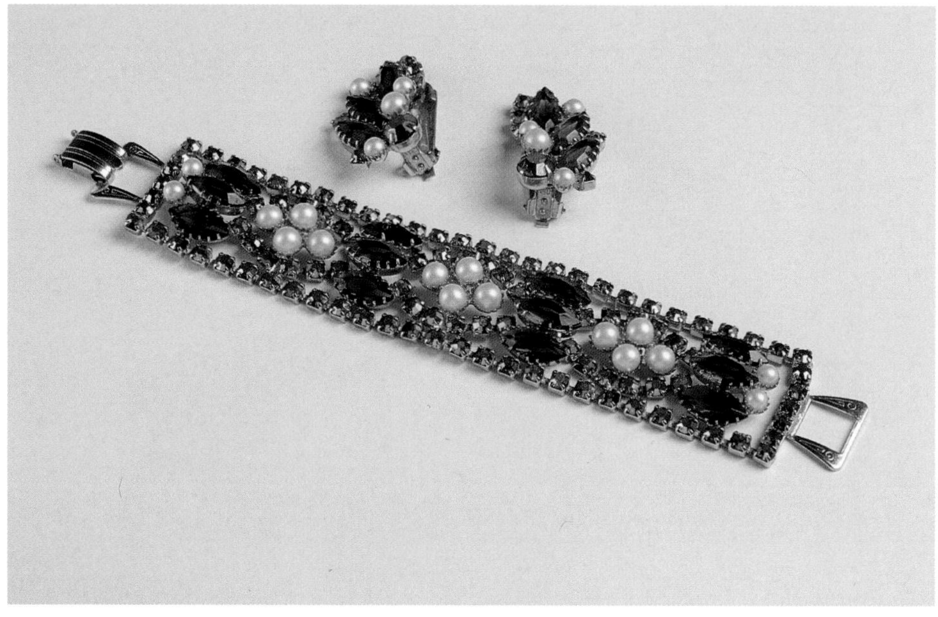

Beautiful 1950s bracelet and earring set. Gold plated with prong-set simulated pearls, chaton-cut aurora borealis rhinestones, and marquise-cut amethyst rhinestones. The bracelet is 1¼" wide and the earrings are 1½" long. Unmarked. $145.00 – 175.00.

From the collection of Koral Michael Whalton

1950s bracelet and earring set. Peacock glass cabochons, simulated gray Tahitian pearls, amethyst and sapphire rhinestones. Gun-metal plated. Marked Kramer N.Y. The bracelet is 1¼" wide and the earrings are 1¾" long. $200.00 – 300.00.

Unmarked bracelet and earring set of fine quality. Chromium plated with prong-set chaton and emerald-cut frosty blue rhinestones. Bracelet has a three-dimensional quality with the "S" shape overlapping the main body of the bracelet. Bracelet has a safety clasp with catch-chain. The earrings are 1½" long and the bracelet is ¾" wide and the "S" design 1¾" wide. 1950s. $175.00 – 250.00.

Jewelry that copies the look of the real thing: Marcel Boucher Deco-style earrings with channel-set baguette-cut ruby red rhinestones. Clear rhinestone pavé. Rhodium plated. 1¼". Marked Boucher 6245. $75.00 – 125.00. Jomaz ¼" wide Deco-style bracelet with channel-set square-cut ruby red rhinestones. Rhodium plated. Safety clasp with catch-chain. Marked Jomaz 2. $175.00 – 225.00. Rhodium finished link bracelet with clear channel-set baguettes. Deco-style bracelet. Safety clasp with catch-chain. ¼" wide. For the size, this bracelet is heavy. Marked E.B. $500.00 – 600.00.

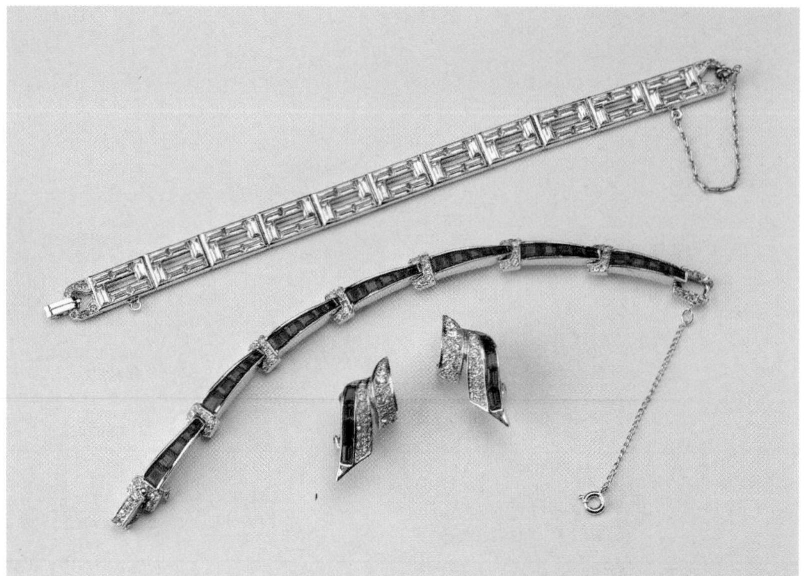

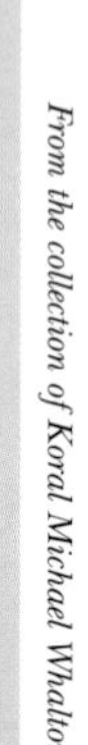

From the collection of Koral Michael Whalon

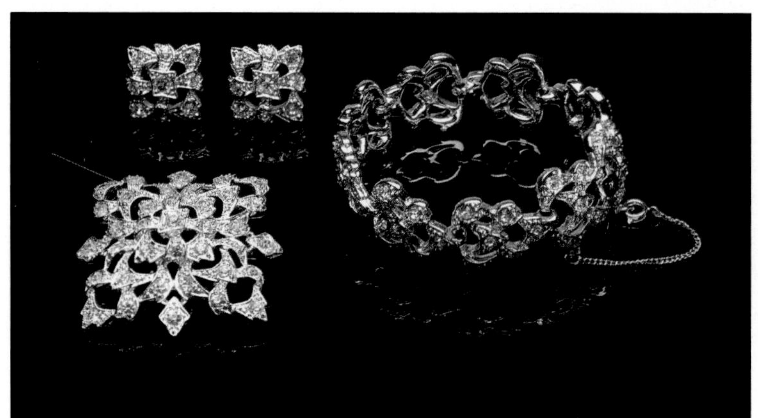

Sarah Coventry parure. Bracelet, brooch, and earrings in a snowflake design. Rhodium plated with pale beige glued-in rhinestones. Safety clasp and catch-chain on bracelet. The brooch is 2¼" x 2¼", the bracelet is ¾" wide, and the earrings are 1". Marked Sarah Cov. $75.00 – 110.00 set.

1950s bracelet and knot earrings. Round and baguette-cut clear Austrian crystal rhinestones. The earrings are 1½" in diameter and the bracelet is 1¾" wide. Marked Eisenberg. $450.00 – 550.00 set.

Courtesy of The Glass Spoon

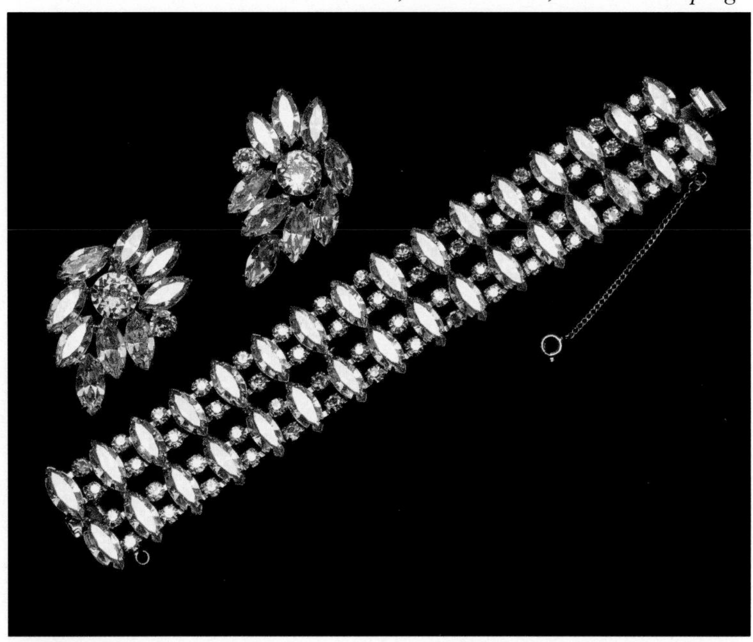

Spectacular 1¼" wide bracelet and 2" long matching earrings. High quality aurora borealis prong-set rhinestones in marquise and chaton cuts. Gold plated. Push-slot clasp with safety catch chain. 1950s. Marked WEISS. $250.00 – 350.00.

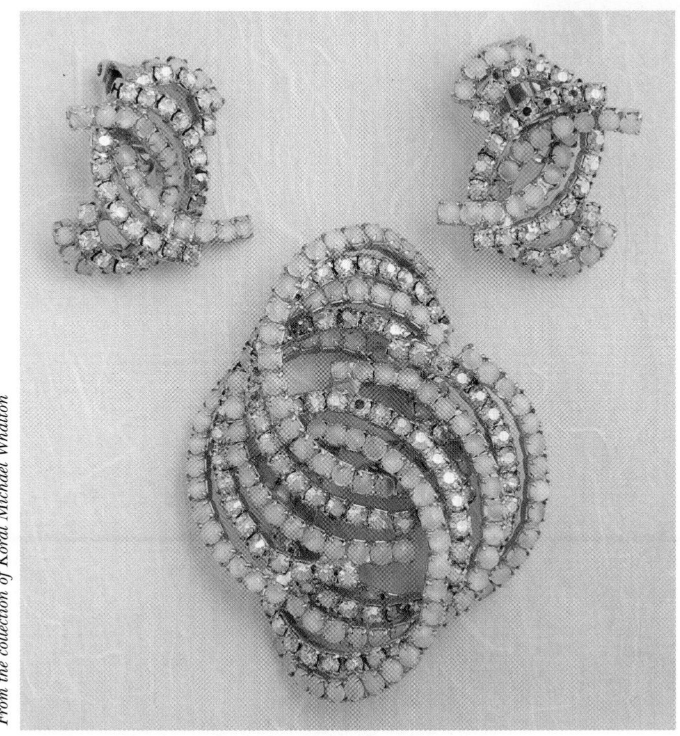

From the collection of Koral Michael Whalton

Brooch and earring set in a knot design. Prong-set aurora borealis rhinestones and tiny cabochon milkstones. Gold plated. The brooch is 2¾" long x 2¼" wide and the earrings are 1¼" long. Signed Alice Caviness. 1950s. $325.00 – 400.00.

Courtesy of The Glass Spoon

Rhinestone bracelet and earring set in original box. Olivine and clear prong-set rhinestones. Rhodium plated. Both the box and the jewelry are marked B. David. The bracelet is ¾" wide and the earrings are 1" in diameter. $150.00 – 200.00.

Unusual three-dimensional brooch and earring set in a geometric design. High quality aurora borealis prong-set rhinestones. Gold plated. Unmarked. The brooch is 2¾" in diameter and the earrings are 1¼" in diameter. 1950s. $155.00 – 200.00.

Robert filigree pin and earring set. Much of Robert's jewelry was custom made to coordinate with a customer's clothing ensemble (which may be the case with this set). The filigreed metal backing was enameled with an ivory color. The 3¾" pin has orange domed glass marquise-cut stones and beads, apple green rhinestones and crystal beads, and aurora borealis rhinestones. The stones are all prong set and the beads are strung on metal wire. One large emerald-cut lemon yellow rhinestone on the brooch. Marked Original by Robert. 1950s. $165.00 – 215.00.

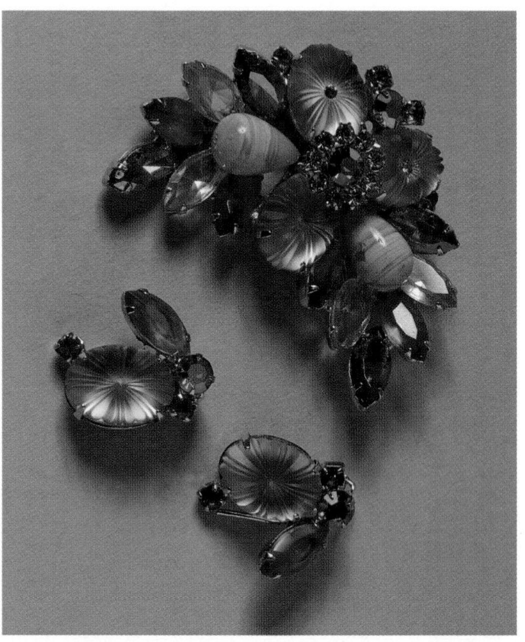

A conversation piece. The brooch is a cluster of molded plastic (in imitation of frosted topaz glass), Venetian glass beads, aurora borealis rhinestones, and citrine and topaz marquise-cut rhinestones. All stones are prong set. Gold plated. Unmarked. The brooch is 1½" x 2½" and the earrings are 1¼". 1950s. $80.00 – 115.00.

Unusual BSK pin and earring set with glued-in marquise-cut rhinestones representing topaz, peridot, and emeralds of varying shades. Simulated pearls and Venetian-style plastic beads. Gold plated. 1960s. The pin is 2¾" long and the earrings are 1" in diameter. $80.00 – 125.00.

From the collection of Koral Michael Whalton

Brooch and earring set. Antiqued gold plate. Molded tobacco-colored frosted glass pear-shaped center. Smoky gray, smoky topaz, and onyx glued-in rhinestones (with faux prong settings). White enameled leaves. The brooch is 2¾" long x 1¾" wide and the earrings are 1¼". Late 1950s – early 1960s. Marked Florenza. $150.00 – 250.00.

1950s brooch and earring set with prong-set Venetian glass cabochons, ruby and topaz rhinestones. Gold plated. The brooch is 3" x 3" and the earrings are 1¾" long. Unmarked. $125.00 – 160.00.

Red and pink prong-set rhinestones comprise these two floral pin and earring sets. Both sets are in stamped silver-tone base metal. Top set: the brooch is 1¾" x 2¾" and the earrings are 1½" long. Unmarked. Bottom set: the pin is 2" in diameter and the earrings are 1¼" x 1¼". Marked Beau Jewels. $85.00 – 100.00 top set and $95.00 – 115.00 for bottom set.

Grape cluster-style pin and earrings. Ruby red rhinestones in marquise and baguette cuts. Clear rhinestones in baguette cut and pavéd on the grape leaves. The pin is 2" l x 2½" w and the earrings are 1½" l x ¾" w. Rhodium plated. Marked Wiesner. $125.00 – 200.00.

1950s wreath pin and earring set. Prong set with excellent quality light pink, dark pink, ruby red, and clear Austrian crystal rhinestones. Rhodium plated. Marked Eisenberg. The pin is 2¼" in diameter and the earrings are 1½" long. $425.00 – 525.00.

From the collection of Koral Michael Whalton

Grouping of emerald green and clear rhinestone jewelry. Top left: 3¼" long dangling pierced earrings with emerald green marquise-cut rhinestones and clear chaton-cut rhinestones. Early 1980s. Chromium plated. Unmarked. $75.00 – 95.00. 2½" shield pin and earring set. Marquise-cut emerald green rhinestones and chaton-cut clear rhinestones. Earrings are 1¼". Chromium plated. Unmarked. 1950s. $135.00 – 200.00 set. Bottom pin: 2¼" Jomaz pin set with emerald green baguettes, clear marquise-cut and chaton-cut rhinestones. Rhodium plated. $150.00 – 200.00.

From the collection of Koral Michael Whalton

One double and one single Weiss strawberry pin. Pair of matching earrings. Japanned with ruby red and emerald green chaton-cut rhinestones. The double pin is 1¾" x 1¾", the single pin is 1¼" and the earrings are 1". $300.00 – 400.00 set.

Egyptian-inspired scarab pin and earring set. Gold-plated scarab beetles with red texturized plastic insets. The pin is 1¼" x 2¼" and the earrings are ½" x 1". Marked Mosell. $200.00 – 215.00.

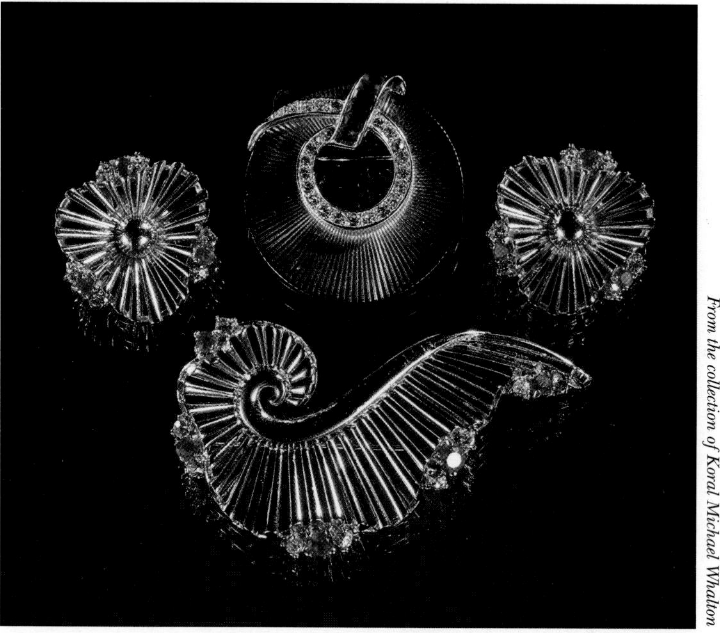

From the collection of Koral Michael Whalton

Boucher spoked leaf design pin and earring set and unmarked circle pin. Pin and earrings are gold plated with prong-set Burmese ruby rhinestones and clear rhinestones. The pin is 2½" long and the earrings are 1". The earrings are marked Boucher and the pin is marked Boucher 3817. $200.00 – 300.00 set. Unmarked Art Deco-style 1¼" circle pin. Gold plated with channel-set Burmese ruby square-cut rhinestones. Rhodium accent set with clear pavé rhinestones. Unmarked, probably Boucher. $110.00 – 175.00.

Clip and dangle-style earring set. Gold plated with prong-set oval-cut emerald green rhinestones, teal pear-cut rhinestones, and ruby red glass cabochons. The clip is 1½" x 3½" and the earrings are 2" long. Marked Schiaparelli. $400.00 – 500.00.

Courtesy of The Glass Spoon

Star brooch and earring set. Ruby red and aurora borealis prong-set rhinestones. Rhodium plated. $130.00 – 175.00.

From the collection of Koral Michael Whalton

Large floral brooch and earring set. Four layers of marquise-cut rhinestones in varying shades of pink and bottle green. Aqua aurora borealis accents. Fuchsia chaton-cut rhinestone in the center. Gold plated. Marked Hobé on both brooch and earrings. Original paper tag reads "Hobé Jewels by Hobé." The brooch is 3¼" l x 2¾" wide and the clip-on earrings are 1¼". 1950s. $225.00 – 300.00.

Three-dimensional floral cluster pin and earring set. Prong-set pink, red, and aurora borealis rhinestones. The beads are plastic but painted to imitate Venetian glass. Pink enameled flowers. Set in gold-plated stamped metal. 1950s. The pin is 2½" in diameter and the earrings are 1¼" long. Unmarked. $85.00 – 110.00.

Weiss flower brooch and red rhinestone earrings. The brooch is gold plated with pear, marquise, and chaton-cut rhinestones. The lever-back earrings have prong-set marquise-cut red rhinestones and are marked Winecraft Pat. 2414382 (which is the mark of the company that patented the lever-back component not the earrings). Gold plated. 1¼" long. Pin $70.00 – 90.00. Earrings $40.00 – 55.00. The brooch is courtesy of The Glass Spoon.

Courtesy of The Glass Spoon

Brooch and earring set. Red glass cabochons with red and pink rhinestones. Gold plated. The brooch is 2¼" and the earrings are 1¼" long. Unmarked. $85.00 – 100.00.

Pendant/brooch and dangle-style earrings with prong-set pastel shades of lavender, pink, aqua, and yellow-gold rhinestones. All rhinestones are foil backed. Chromium plated. The brooch is 2¼" in diameter and the earrings are 1¼" long. Marked Kramer of New York. $125.00 – 175.00.

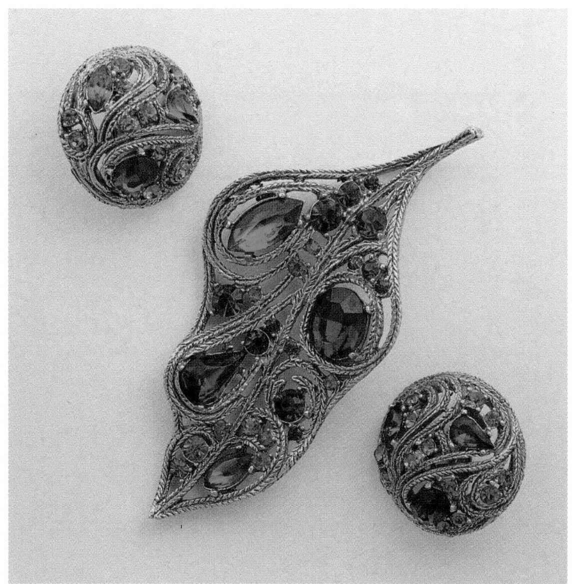

1960s leaf pin and earring set. Antiqued gold-tone etched design. Glued-in sapphire and emerald rhinestones in chaton, marquise, and pear cuts. All stones are foil-backed. The pin is 1½" x 3¼" and the earrings are 1" in diameter. Unsigned, possibly made by Florenza or Art. $125.00 – 145.00 set.

Courtesy of The Glass Spoon

Vogue cushion brooch and earrings. Iridescent peacock rhinestones in shades of purple, green, and blue. The brooch is 2" in diameter and the earrings are 2" long. $125.00 – 160.00.

From the collection of Koral Michael Whalton

Schiaparelli icy blue pin and earring set. Prong-set molded iridescent prystal and glass aurora borealis rhinestones, chaton-cut ice-blue rhinestones, and simulated pearls. Gun-metal plated. The pin is 2¼" and the earrings are 1½". $300.00 – 375.00.

From the collection of Koral Michael Whalton

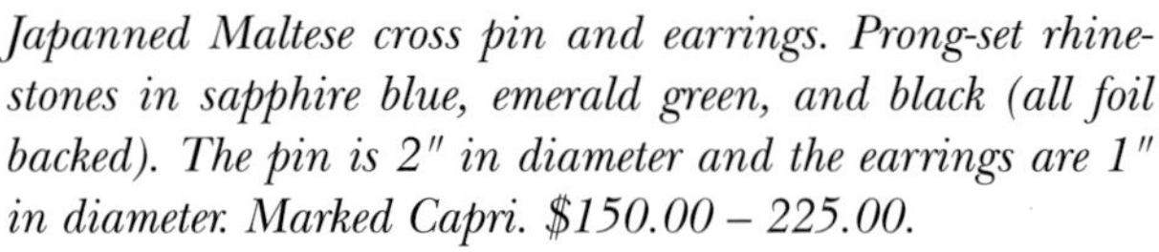

Japanned Maltese cross pin and earrings. Prong-set rhinestones in sapphire blue, emerald green, and black (all foil backed). The pin is 2" in diameter and the earrings are 1" in diameter. Marked Capri. $150.00 – 225.00.

From the collection of Koral Michael Whalton

Cluster brooch and earrings. Prong-set rhinestones in green tourmaline, blue aurora borealis, and emerald green. Marquise-cut domed glass cabochons are marbleized green and orange. Gun-metal plated. The brooch is 2½" x 1¾" and the earrings are 1¼" in diameter. Marked Art. $175.00 – 225.00.

Comet-style cluster brooch and earrings. Harvest color rhinestones in topaz brown, ruby red, and blue aurora borealis. Marquise-cut domed glass cabochons in marbleized green and orange, solid green, solid red, solid orange, solid golden yellow, brown, and marbleized brown and golden yellow. Antiqued gold plated. The brooch is 2¾" long x 2" wide and the earrings are 1¼" in diameter. Marked Art. $175.00 – 225.00.

From the collection of Koral Michael Whalton

Large 2¾" Sarah Coventry brooch and 1¼" matching earrings. Gold plated with glued-in pink plastic oval cabochons, green marquise-cut and chaton-cut rhinestones, and simulated pearls. An unusual Sarah Coventry set. Marked Sarah Cov. $80.00 – 120.00.

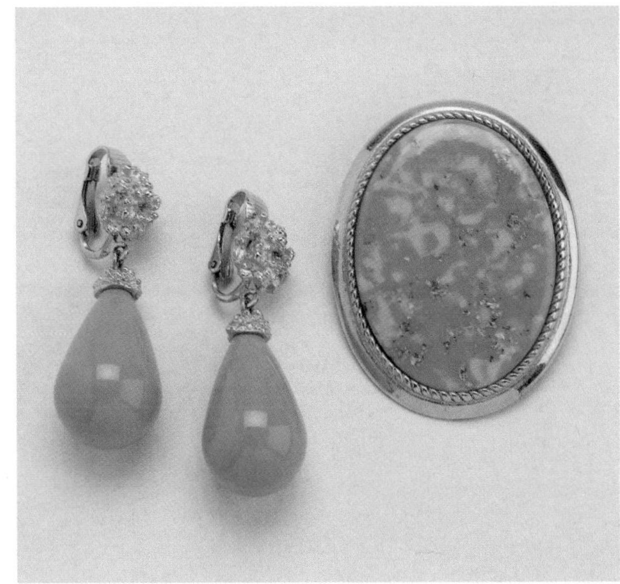

Gold-plated oval pin/pendant with coral ceramic center. Marked Sarah Cov. The 1960s unmarked earrings are gold-plated nuggets with a plastic coral drop. The pin is 1¾" long x 1½" wide and the earrings are 1¾" long. $45.00 – 60.00 pin, $40.00 – 50.00 earrings.

From the collection of Koral Michael Whalton

Massive Maltese cross and matching earrings. Simulated plastic cabochon bloodstones and carnelian. Twisted rope design. Gold plated. The brooch is 3" in diameter and the earrings are 1". 1960s. Marked Sarah Coventry. $200.00 – 300.00.

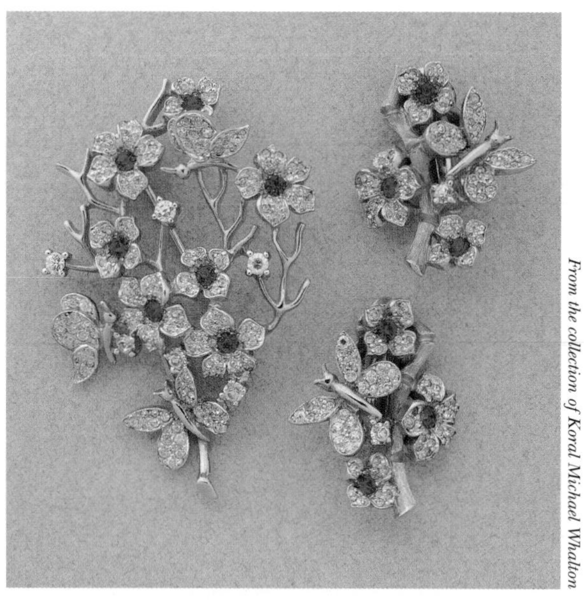

From the collection of Koral Michael Whalton

Delicate pin and earring set by Jomaz. Tiny pavé flowers and butterflies. Gold plated. The flower centers are ruby red rhinestones. The pin is 2½" long and the earrings are 1¼". $225.00 – 325.00.

From the collection of Koral Michael Whalton

Brooch in the shape of a tropical plant with matching earrings. The leaves are rhodium plated with pavé clear rhinestones. The swirled fruit is gold plated. A heavy set that mimics fine jewelry. The pin is 1½" long x 2" wide and the earrings are 1". Unmarked, but of excellent quality. $600.00 – 750.00.

From the collection of Koral Michael Whalton

Conch shell pin and earrings. Green enameled leaves and simulated pearls. Gilded brass. The pin is 2¼" long and the earrings are 1". Marked Mimi di N. $225.00 – 275.00.

From the collection of Koral Michael Whalton

Bridge jewelry — Alice Caviness carved and dyed red genuine ivory roses. Green enameled leaves, brown enameled stems. Set with tiny marcasite accents. Sterling silver, Germany. The pin is 2¼" and the earrings are 1¼". $375.00 – 450.00.

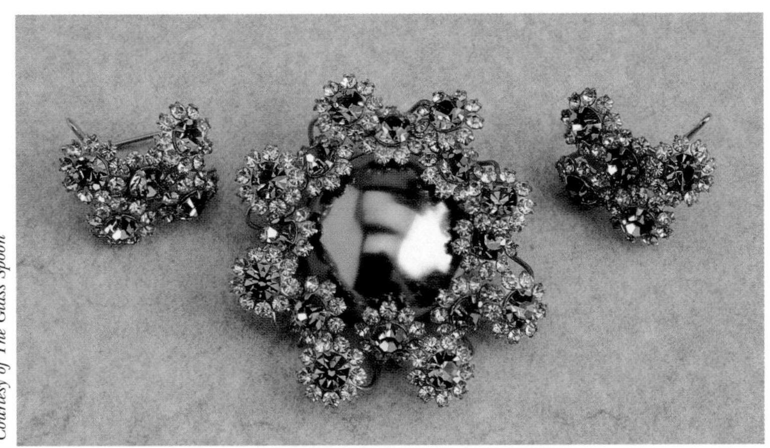

Courtesy of The Glass Spoon

Brooch and earring set. Large Tahitian mabé pearl surrounded by clusters of smoky gray and clear chaton-cut rhinestones. Gold plated. Unmarked. $115.00 – 140.00.

Lily of the Valley brooch. Rhodium plated. The leaves have invisible settings with clear baguette rhinestones. The flowers are pavé clear rhinestones. 3". Marked Trifari. $175.00 – 275.00. Unmarked earrings with rhinestones similar to the ones used in the brooch. Rhodium plated. 1½". $35.00 – 45.00.

From the collection of Koral Michael Whalton

Miriam Haskell floral leaf brooch and earrings. Prong-set aurora borealis rhinestones. Antiqued gold-plated flowers, stems, and leaves. The brooch is 3" and the earrings are 1½". $250.00 – 350.00.

Sarah Coventry large hurricane swirl brooch and earring set. Rhodium plated with simulated pearls. The brooch is 2¾" in diameter and the earrings are 1¼" in diameter. Marked Sarah Cov. $85.00 – 110.00.

Emmons free-form leaf pin and earrings. Rhodium plated with icy-blue prong-set rhinestones. The brooch is 2½" x 3" and the earrings are 1½" x 2". $95.00 – 125.00.

From the collection of Koral Michael Whalton

Eisenberg bar pin and drop-style earrings. Rhodium plated with large Austrian crystal rhinestones of excellent quality. The bar pin is 3¼" long and the earrings are 1¾" long. Late 1930s to early 1940s. $400.00 – 475.00 for the pin and $200.00 – 275.00 for the earrings.

Lacy leaf brooch and matching earrings. Smoky-gray glued-in rhinestones. Silver-tone base metal. The brooch is 2¾" long and the earrings are 1¼" long. 1960s. Unmarked. $65.00 – 105.00.

Flower pin and earrings. Flower petals of clear marquise-cut rhinestones, leaves of apple green marquise-cut rhinestones, flower centers of fuchsia and royal blue chaton-cut rhinestones. Sterling plated. The pin is 2" x 2½" and the earrings are 1¼" long. Unmarked, probably from Austria. $75.00 – 95.00.

From the collection of Koral Michael Whalton

Vendome flower brooch and earring set with the original card and tag. White iridescent enameled petals, simulated pearls, and prong-set clear chaton-cut rhinestones. Brushed gold-plated leaves and shiny gold-plated stems. The brooch is 3½" long x 2¼" wide and the screw/clip earrings are 1½". Late 1950s to early 1960s. $275.00 – 350.00.

From the collection of Koral Michael Whalton

HAR Chinaman brooch and earrings. Plastic molded simulated ivory faces. Ivory enameled base metal. Imitation jade cabochons. Tiny aurora borealis accents. The brooch is 2¼" x 1½" and the earrings are 1¼". Late 1950s to early 1960s. $400.00 – 475.00.

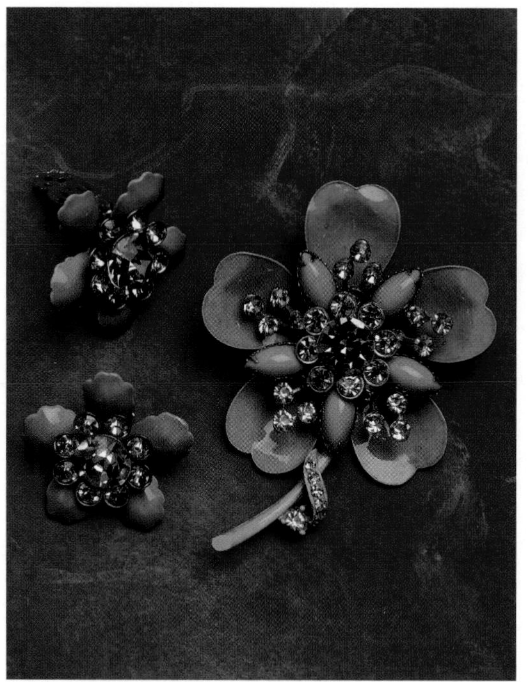

Floral brooch and earrings. Blue enameled petals, green enameled stem set with icy-blue rhinestones. Flower set with icy-blue domed glass marquise-cut stones. The brooch is 2¼" x 3" and the earrings are 1¼" in diameter. Late 1950s to early 1960s. Unmarked. $75.00 – 115.00.

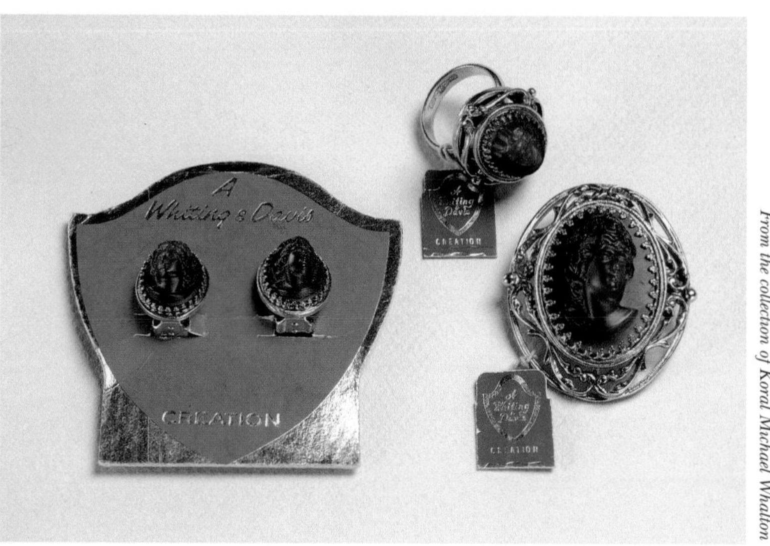

From the collection of Koral Michael Whalton

Whiting and Davis parure with original earring card and tags. The ring, brooch, and earrings are Victorian-style, gold plated with prong-set tortoiseshell plastic molded cameos. The brooch is 2" l x 1¾" w and the earrings are ¾". Only the earrings and ring are marked — which is why you should never break-up sets! $250.00 – 300.00.

From the collection of Koral Michael Whalton

Comedy/Tragedy parure. Parure consists of two pins, earrings, and ring. All copper. 1950s. Unmarked. Each pin is 2¼" long and the earrings are 1¾" long. $175.00 – 250.00.

Reinad necklace. Excellent quality. Chromium plated. Simulated pink star sapphire cabochons. Clear rhinestone brilliants. Black enamel. Reinad is a hard-to-find name. Late 1930s to early 1940s. The center of the necklace is 1¾" wide. $375.00 – 450.00.

From the collection of Koral Michael Whalton

1940s Art Deco style Trifari choker. Rose gold plated. Prong-set diamond-cut clear rhinestones. The front links are ¾" wide. $110.00 – 175.00.

Unsigned choker with an unusual color combination of rhinestones. Oval-cut faux smoky topaz, pear-cut faux peridot, and chaton-cut faux citrine. All rhinestones are foil backed. Antiqued brass. "S" link chain. Late 1940s to early 1950s. ¾" wide. $100.00 – 200.00.

1930s fringe-style brass choker. Flowers have bezel-set faux aquamarines. Unsigned. $75.00 – 125.00.

Eisenberg rhinestone pendant necklace. Large round-cut Austrian crystal clear rhinestones. Massive pear-cut Austrian crystal drop suspended in the center of the pendant. Rhodium plated. Safety clasp with catch-chain. Marked Eisenberg. $700.00 – 800.00.

Courtesy of The Glass Spoon

1950s fringe-style rhinestone necklace. Chromium plated with prong-set clear chaton-cut rhinestones and marquise-cut domed black glass. Fishhook clasp. Unmarked. $75.00 – 110.00.

1950s fringe-style necklace. Rhodium plated with prong-set blue aurora borealis rhinestones. Unmarked. The Austrian crystals are very eye catching. This necklace has a lot of appeal. $100.00 – 145.00.

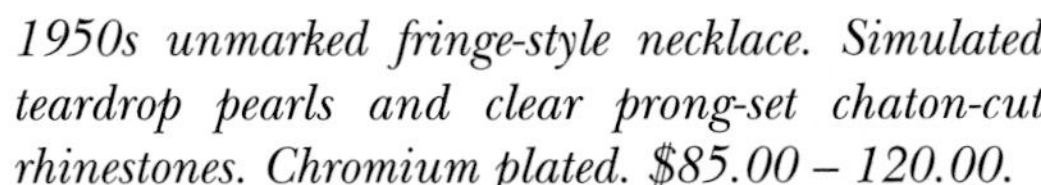

1950s unmarked fringe-style necklace. Simulated teardrop pearls and clear prong-set chaton-cut rhinestones. Chromium plated. $85.00 – 120.00.

1950s unsigned necklace. Yellow aurora borealis rhinestones, simulated pearls, and molded lemon-colored glass in oval and marquise cuts. Gold plated. $100.00 – 150.00.

Trifari necklace. Faux sapphire flowers with clear rhinestone spacers and flower centers (all prong-set). Trifanium plated (silvertone). ¼" wide. $65.00 – 90.00.

From the collection of Koral Michael Whalton

Kramer necklace in an unusual "V." Antiqued gold plate with prong-set lemon yellow rhinestones. Marked Kramer of New York. 1950s. $250.00 – 350.00.

Mid-1920s to early 1930s necklace. Silver-tone base metal. Blue sapphire and aquamarine glass. Unsigned. $65.00 – 100.00.

Bib necklace of prong-set lime, apple, and emerald green chaton-cut rhinestones. Gold plated. Marked Austria. This bib is 3¼" at the widest point. Late 1950s to early 1960s. $150.00 – 225.00.

1950s unusual Shamrock necklace. Prong-set green crackle glass cabochons with emerald green chaton-cut rhinestones. Chromium plated. Unmarked. $120.00 – 140.00.

Rhinestone choker in a bow design. Prong-set chaton-cut golden yellow rhinestones. Gold plated. Unmarked. Early 1950s. $50.00 – 75.00.

1960s faux lariat-style necklace. Clear prong-set chaton-cut rhinestones and gold-plated spiral accents. Braided chain in gold plate. Unmarked. $75.00 – 110.00.

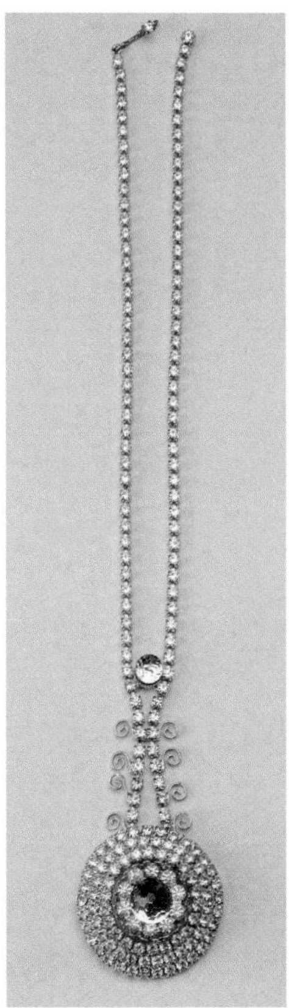

Unusual 1960s necklace. Gold plated with prong-set chaton-cut clear rhinestones. Faceted glass ball in the center of the pendant and a smaller faceted glass ball at the top of the pendant. Unmarked. $115.00 – 175.00.

Bedouin-style faux perfume bottle pendant necklace. Pewter bottle has a swirled design (2½" x 1¾"). Silver-tone rope chain. 1960s. Marked Goldette. $75.00 – 120.00.

Retro-style necklace. Foil backed blue topaz rhinestones — one large pear-cut and one smaller chaton-cut (glued in). Rhodium plated. Unmarked. $90.00 – 125.00.

Collar with gold-plated rectangles of simulated pearl and glass faux turquoise (all prong set). ¼" wide. Marked Warner. $75.00 – 95.00.

Squash blossom style necklace. Lapis blue plastic beads. Sterling plated. The pendant is 3" long x 3½" wide. 1970s. Signed Alexis Kirk. $500.00 – 650.00.

From the collection of Koral Michael Whalton

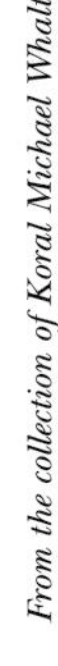

From the collection of Koral Michael Whalton

Bib necklace in gold-plated base metal set with turquoise colored plastic cabochons and crescent sections. Accented with clear chaton-cut rhinestones. Marked K.J.L. (Kenneth J. Lane). 1960s. $650.00 – 750.00.

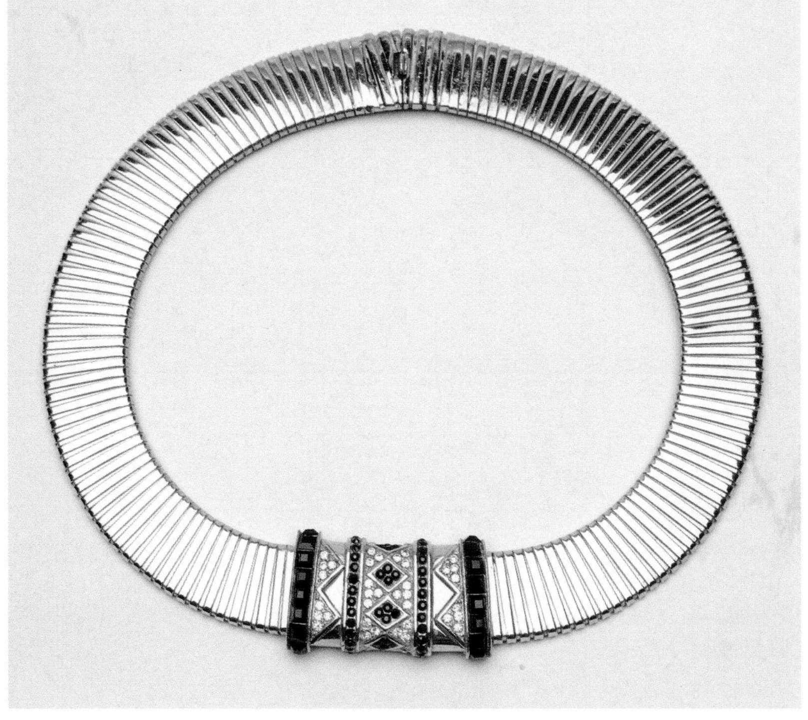

Ciner cobra-style collar set with round and square-cut black glass and clear rhinestone brilliants. Art Deco-style design. Gold plated. ¾" wide. $300.00 – 400.00.

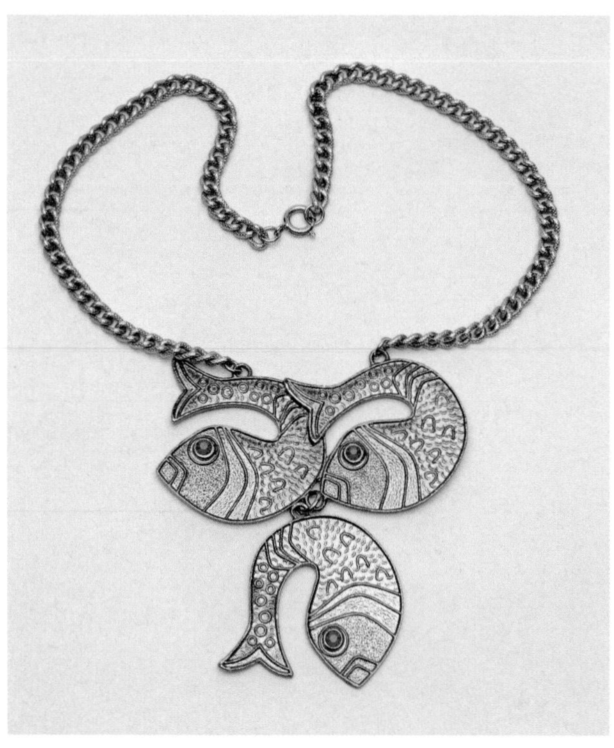

Sarah Coventry bib necklace. Lightweight bronzed gold-plate Pisces fish with bezel-set ruby red rhinestone eyes. The fish pendant section is 3¼" long. Late 1960s to early 1970s. Marked Sarah Cov. $55.00 – 85.00.

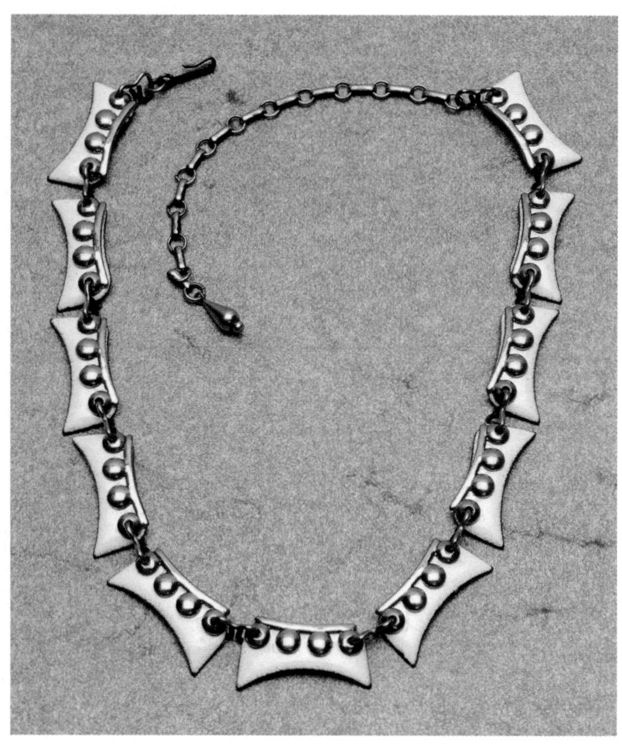

Copper necklace with white enameled links. Signed Renoir. 1950s. $125.00 – 175.00.

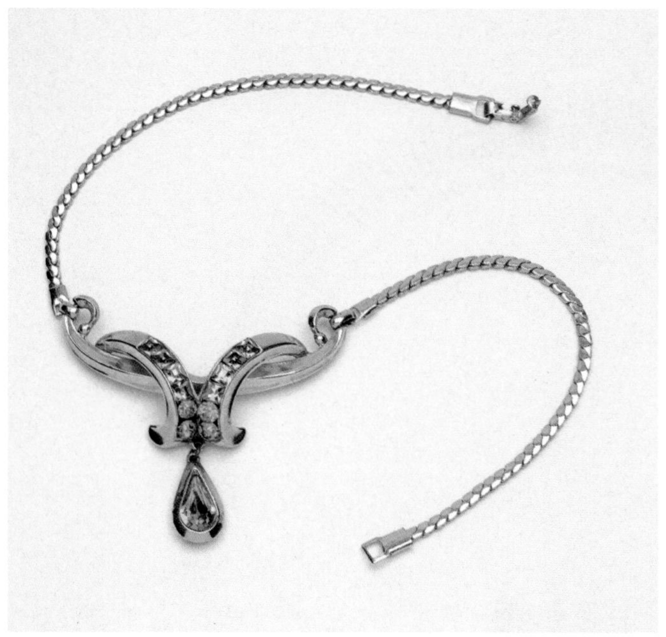

Coro 1940s dangle necklace. Gold-tone base metal with bright aqua rhinestones. $125.00 – 175.00.

Coro leaf and grape cluster design necklace. Gold tone metal. Glued-in faux citrine rhinestones. 1950s. $95.00 – 120.00.

Krementz choker. Rat-tail chain with three-dimensional roses and leaves. Rolled gold plate. $125.00 – 150.00.

Late 1940s choker. Retro-style flower and ribbon design. Amethyst and clear chaton-cut rhinestones. Gold plated. Central section is 1¼" high. Box chain. Marked Coro. $125.00 – 175.00.

Trifari necklace from the Enchantress collection. Gold-plated chains in a waterfall design. Clear rhinestone brilliants, faux Burmese ruby and emerald cabochons. The center section is 2" in diameter, and the glittering goldtone chains fall 5" below it. Original Trifari $55.00 tag from the 1960s. $175.00 – 250.00.

Emmons necklace from the Cleopatra Egyptian Queen collection. Antiqued gold tone. Chaton-cut faux citrine, peridot, and amethyst (glued-in stones). Pendant is 3¾" long. 1970s. $50.00 – 100.00.

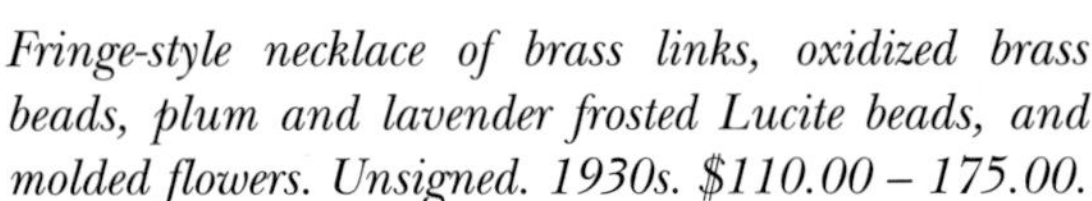

Fringe-style necklace of brass links, oxidized brass beads, plum and lavender frosted Lucite beads, and molded flowers. Unsigned. 1930s. $110.00 – 175.00.

Bolo-style necklace. Very unusual with lilac and deep purple prong-set rhinestones. Braided chain. Gold-tone base metal. Unsigned. Early 1950s. $125.00 – 175.00.

Unsigned matinee length necklace of ivory plastic beads. Gold-plated leopards with black enamel spots and green rhinestone eyes. This necklace is in a style made popular by Kenneth J. Lane and Cartier. $150.00 – 225.00.

From the collection of Koral Michael Whalton

Chanel single strand of matinee length simulated pearls (10mm baroque). The pearls are a quality color and heavy weight. They are given a rough texture to make them resemble genuine pearls. Excellent quality necklace with a decorative clasp marked Chanel with the date 1981. $700.00 – 900.00.

Matinee length single strand of simulated white pearls. Brass filigree caps and rhinestone rondellas spaced at intervals on the necklace. A heavy necklace. Unmarked. $75.00 – 115.00.

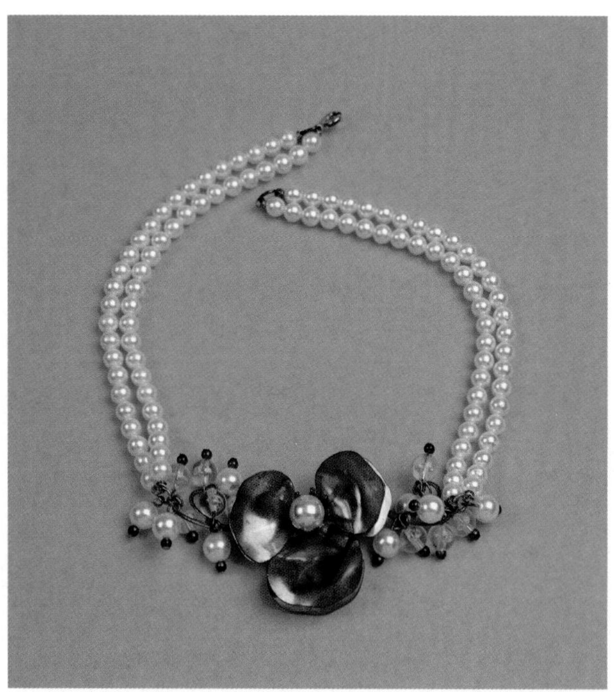

Choker of white simulated pearls. Brass flower with claw-set white simulated pearl. White simulated pearls and clear Lucite beads decorate both sides of the flower. Unmarked. $40.00 – 70.00.

Late 1950s to early 1960s triple strand bib of orange and yellow marbleized molded plastic beads. The brass beads are done in hollow pierce work. Unmarked. $45.00 – 75.00.

Double strand necklace that is light in weight. Austrian crystal aurora borealis and large iridescent papier maché beads. Brass filigree caps. Decorative clasp of the Austrian crystal beads strung on wire. 1950s. Unmarked. $75.00 – 90.00.

1930s fringe-style necklace of lightweight painted wood beads, simulated gray Tahitian pearls, Venetian glass beads, and brass filigree caps. Unmarked. $55.00 – 80.00.

Three strand bib of smoky blue and gray Austrian crystal beads, blue carnival glass beads, and simulated gray Tahitian pearls. Clasp is sterling silver plated with prong-set blue faceted glass. Unmarked. 1950s. $40.00 – 65.00.

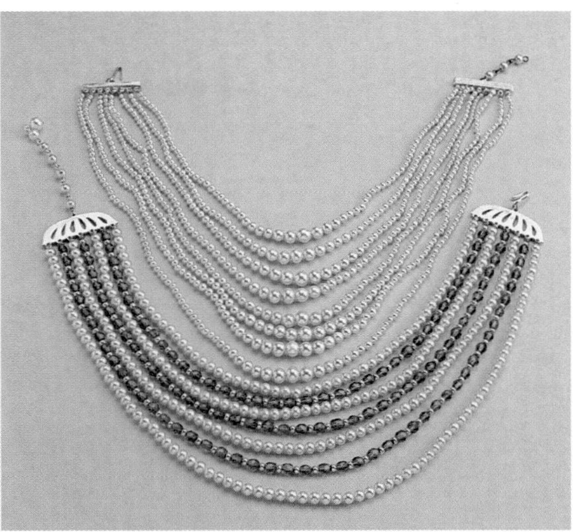

Two simulated pearl bib necklaces. Top to bottom: Bib of eight strands of graduating simulated pearls. Unmarked. Bib of seven strands of simulated pearls and smoky gray crystal beads with silver-tone bead spacers. Marked Japan. $55.00 – 80.00 each.

Late 1950s to early 1960s fringe bib. Two gold-tone mesh chains. Red and gold plastic beads, gray Austrian crystal aurora borealis beads, and brass filigree caps. Pretty gold-tone clasp with a central red bead. Unmarked. $125.00 – 155.00.

Late 1950s graduated three-strand beaded bib. Deep Prussian and royal blue molded plastic beads with Venetian glass beads. Silver-tone clasp and findings. Marked Japan. $30.00 – 45.00.

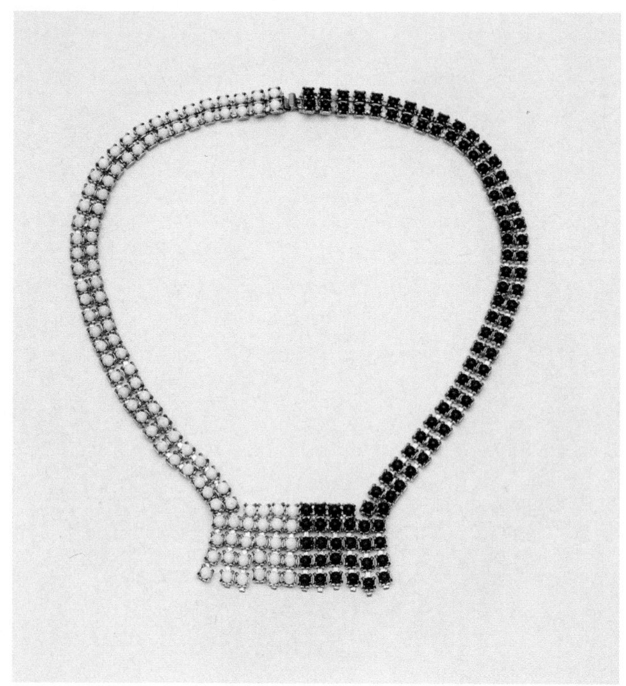

Late 1920s to early 1930s Art Deco fringe-style necklace. Chromium plated. Prong-set black and ivory composition beads. Unmarked. $100.00 – 135.00.

From the collection of Koral Michael Whalton

Miriam Haskell four strand bib of clear Austrian crystal faceted beads with antiqued brass caps and clasp. Clasp is set with clear rose monteé rhinestones. $475.00 – 550.00.

From the collection of Koral Michael Whalton

Massive Egyptian-style collar of faux white pearls and plastic beads simulating turquoise, coral, and chrysophase. Brass rondelles. For the size, this collar is extremely lightweight. Unsigned, however possibly the work of Miriam Haskell. 1960s Egyptian revival. The collar is 4" wide. $800.00 – 1,000.00.

Gilded brass filigree pendant necklace set with simulated white pearls and black glass rhinestones. Center cabochon is highly polished black mirrored metal (created to resemble hematite). Chain is set with simulated white pearls. Marked Made in West Germany. The pendant is 1¾". 1950s. $55.00 – 70.00.

Trifari collar. White enameled metal leaves and blue enameled metal flowers. Each flower is set with a tiny prong-set chaton-cut clear rhinestone. The collar is jointed so it fits comfortably at the base of the neck. 1¼" wide. Silver trifanium-plated findings. $75.00 – 125.00.

Chromium-plated mesh choker. ½" wide. Marked Volupté on a soldered-on tag. Volupté is a company which is best known for its beautiful compacts — jewelry by this company is rare. $120.00 – 180.00.

Choker of white satin cording. Gold-plated 2¼" lion pendant has green rhinestone eyes and a white glass egg in its mouth. Late 1960s to early 1970s. Unmarked. $50.00 – 75.00.

Florenza Victorian-style pendant necklace. Antiqued gold-plated pendant with black glass cabochon dangles and clear rhinestone brilliants. Central stone is a large faceted oval-cut black glass rhinestone. Suspended on a fine gold-tone chain. Pendant is 2" long. 1950s. $40.00 – 70.00.

Large 3¼" pendant necklace. Antiqued gold-tone base metal with black plastic dangling beads and black plastic oval cabochon. Glued-in clear chaton-cut rhinestone accents. Marked Celebrity Gems. Originally purchased at Macy's in the 1970s. $50.00 – 80.00.

Gold-plated King Tut pendant necklace. Blue, red, and yellow enameling on this heavy 2½" three-dimensional pendant. This pendant is unusual for the 1970s because it has not been stamped out. It was done in the "lost wax" casting method. Gold-plated link chain. Unmarked. $40.00 – 55.00.

1970s massive (4¾" x 3¼") turtle pendant necklace. Gilded brass. The turtle's legs, head, and tail move. The shell is molded imitation tortoiseshell (plastic). Yellow glass cabochon eyes. Twisted gold-plated rope chain. Unmarked. $50.00 – 75.00.

1970s pendant necklace. 3½" gold-plated lion with a silver-plated face. Olive green marquise-cut rhinestone eyes. The rhinestones are glued-in. The lions' gold body and silver face are two separate parts — the face is attached with rivets. Gold-tone twisted link chain. Unmarked. 1970s. $40.00 – 55.00.

From the collection of Koral Michael Whalton

Large 1970s pendant necklaces and circa 1980 belt buckle. Necklaces from left to right: 2½" x 4" gold-plated ram's head pendant with flesh-tone molded plastic face, marked RAZZA. $150.00 – 225.00. 3" x 2½" gold-plated lion's head pendant with flesh-tone molded plastic face, marked RAZZA. $150.00 – 225.00. The 4¼" x 2¼" gold-plated pendant of a woman is marked RAZZA. Her head and shoulders are of flesh-tone molded plastic. $150.00 – 225.00. The 5½" x 2¼" heavy, solid brass unicorn buckle has surrealistic glass eyes — white with a blue iris and black pupil, marked C. Ross 1980. $400.00 – 550.00. 3" x 2¾" gold-plated lion's head pendant with green surrealistic glass eyes with black pupils, marked TANCER-II. $150.00 – 225.00.

Hattie Carnegie Egyptian ankh pin/pendant suspended on a goldtone link chain. The pin/pendant is 3¾" long, gold plated, and has turquoise and lapis blue enamel. Faux pear-cut carnelian cabochon. Molded plastic faux lapis and turquoise beads. 1960s Egyptian revival. $200.00 – 300.00.

An unusual lariat necklace. White and gold plastic beads in imitation of Venetian glass. Gold-plated links and tassels. The four large beads at the ends of the necklace are made up of pale yellow sequins and brown glass seed beads. Unmarked. 1950s. $20.00 – 35.00.

Fancy bolo necklace on a heavy gold-tone rope chain. The 1½" in diameter bolo slide is encrusted with prong-set citrine and topaz glass cabochons and rhinestones. 3¼" long gold-tone chain tassels. Marked only with Pat. Pend. Late 1960s to early 1970s. $175.00 – 225.00.

Pendant necklaces. Left: stationary Victorian-style pendant necklace by Florenza. Antiqued gold-tone link chain, pendant, and tassel. The pendant is set with golden brown glass cabochons and black glass rhinestones. The pendant is 3½" long. $65.00 – 95.00. Right: The locket pendant is marked Whiting and Davis on the soldered on tag. Gold plated with a golden brown glass cabochon. The locket is 1½" in diameter. 1950s. $45.00 – 75.00.

Late 1970s to early 1980s American Indian-inspired pendant and wire-back earrings. 2¼" silver-tone oval set with simulated turquoise. The heart-shaped earrings are 2½" long (including wire). Unmarked. $65.00 – 80.00 set.

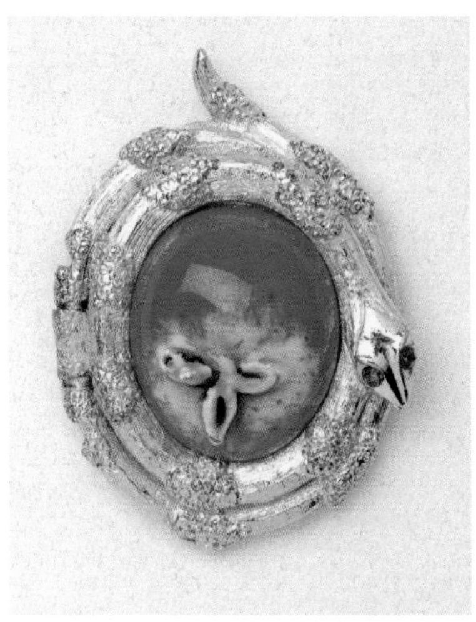

Unmarked perfume sachet pendant. Gold-tone snake with emerald green rhinestone eyes coiled around a ceramic red apple. 1970s. Sachet collecting is becoming quite popular! 2¼". $25.00 – 35.00.

From the collection of Koral Michael Whalton

Victorian revival pendant, 3¾" long x 2" wide. Antiqued gold tone with simulated pearls and smoky topaz rhinestones. Faux baroque pearl drops with brass filigree caps. Signed CoroCraft. $150.00 – 200.00.

From the collection of Koral Michael Whalton

Miriam Haskell Egyptian revival pendant. Gilded brass disk (2½" in diameter) with repoussé work. Faux coral, turquoise, and ruby glass beads, a pretty setting for the brass King Tut. $150.00 – 200.00.

Rhinestone earrings that make quite a statement! Chromium-plated earrings with prong-set chaton, pear, and baguette cut clear rhinestones. 3¼" long. 1950s. Unsigned. $115.00 – 140.00.

Stunning earrings by Arnold Scaasi. Rhodium plated with emerald-cut emerald-green rhinestones and marquise-cut clear Austrian crystal rhinestones of excellent quality. 3¼" x 2". Marked Scaasi. $175.00 – 300.00.

2¼" long earrings. Pinchbeck with fuchsia glass accents, simulated seed pearls, and tiny clear glass seed beads. Unmarked. Made in India. $45.00 – 65.00.

2¾" long dangling Sarah Coventry earrings. Gold plated with prong-set chaton-cut clear rhinestones. Marked Sarah Cov. $50.00 – 75.00.

Excellent Hattie Carnegie chandelier earrings. Austrian crystal beads and drops and prong-set chaton-cut clear rhinestones. Rhodium plated. 2¾" long. Excellent craftsmanship — these earrings are even finished and set with the rhinestones on the underside. Marked Carnegie. $175.00 – 225.00.

Three pairs of chandelier-style earrings. The earrings with the clear Austrian crystal beads are from the 1950s. 2½" long. The earrings with the yellow Austrian crystal beads are from a more recent vintage and are marked Lewis Segal California. 2¼" long. $85.00 – 110.00.

Victorian revival-style dangling earrings. Antiqued brass filigree with royal blue crystal beads. 3¾" long. Marked Kim. $75.00 – 110.00.

Unusual 1950s chandelier earrings. Gold plated with aqua chaton and marquise-cut rhinestones and aurora borealis faceted beads. Unmarked. 2" long. $85.00 – 125.00.

Whimsical 1950s earrings. Gold-plated three-dimensional teapots. Simulated claw-set pearl with loose simulated pearls on the inside of the teapot "cage." Unmarked. 1". $35.00 – 65.00.

Gold-plated oak leaves with wooden acorns. Marked Florenza. 1¾" long. 1950s. $55.00 – 75.00.

Two beautiful pairs of earrings that make the best use of Austrian crystal beads. Left: Cluster of red, pink, clear aurora borealis, and red aurora borealis crystal beads. Gold plated. 1¼" in diameter. Marked Carnegie (Hattie Carnegie). $55.00 – 75.00. Right: Gold-plated filigree with pink aurora borealis marquise-cut rhinestones and pink aurora borealis bead drops. The rhinestones are prong set. 2" long. Marked Lewis Segal California. $65.00 – 85.00.

Gilded brass circa 1910 – 1920 screw-back drop earrings. Hammered brass dangle with a red glass teardrop. 2½" long. Unmarked. $40.00 – 75.00.

Gold-tone base metal 1½" dangling earrings. Prong-set pink domed glass square. Circa 1905 – 1920. Unmarked. $35.00 – 70.00.

Late 1960s enameled Aztec birds. Silver-tone base metal bird with turquoise, rust, black, and white enamel dangling from a silver-tone fleur-di-lis. 1¾" long. Marked Art. $40.00 – 70.00.

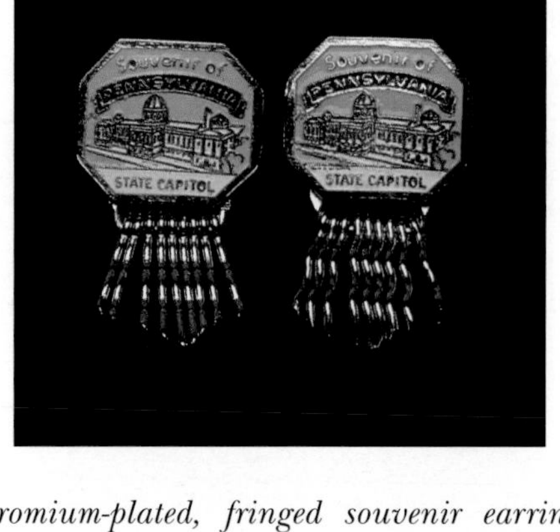

Chromium-plated, fringed souvenir earrings. Enameled picture of the Pennsylvania State Capitol. Cloisonné with turquoise, white, and navy enamel. On the front of the earrings it states "Souvenir of Pennsylvania State Capitol." Screw-backs. 1¼" long. $45.00 – 70.00.

1950s whimsical earrings. Chromium plated covered wagons with wheels that turn! Screw-backs. Unsigned. 1". $35.00 – 65.00.

1950s molded plastic Oriental-inspired earrings. Blue molded plastic with red painted hair, crown, and lips and black painted eyes and eyebrows. Simulated pearls. Note: The earrings are wearing earrings! 1¼". Chromium plated. Unmarked. $55.00 – 70.00.

Boucher silver-tone Oriental-inspired earrings. Tiny pagoda with dangling flowers. 1½". Marked Boucher 8274. $60.00 – 75.00.

From the collection of Koral Michael Whalton

1950s Eisenberg Austrian crystal rhinestone earrings. Rhodium plated with prong-set chaton and marquise-cut rhinestones in pale and royal blue. Tiny clear chaton-cut rhinestone accents. 1½" long. $175.00 – 215.00.

Whiting and Davis cameo button-style earrings. Chromium plated. 1½" in diameter. $35.00 – 55.00.

1950s pinwheel rhinestone earrings. Chromium plated with prong-set chaton-cut aurora borealis rhinestones. Central gray chaton-cut rhinestone. Unmarked. 1¼" $35.00 – 60.00.

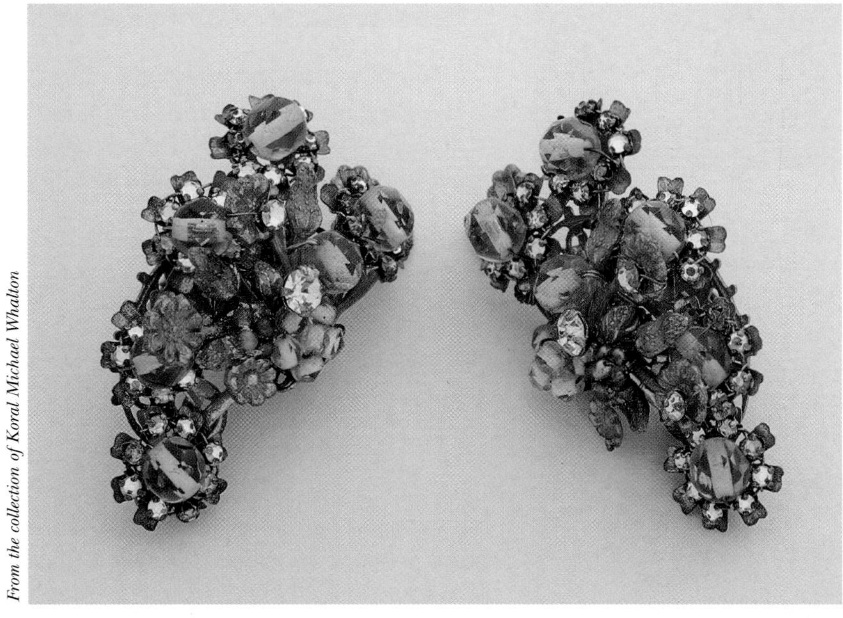

From the collection of Koral Michael Whalton

Beautiful 1950s cluster-style earrings. Gilded brass filigree with tiny gilded brass flowers, clear rose monteé-cut rhinestones, and bluish-gray Austrian crystal beads. Excellent craftsmanship. 1¾" long. Signed DeMario. $95.00 – 150.00.

1940s sterling silver Cartier/Jewels of India style earrings. Carved ruby glass fruit salad stone and two prong-set chaton-cut rhinestones. Silver filigree wirework leaves. Hallmarked sterling. ¾" long. $40.00 – 60.00.

1950s gray aurora borealis cluster earrings. These earrings are made in such a way that they will fit neatly to the shape of the wearer's earlobe (a popular style in the 1950s). Chromium plated. 1½" long. Unmarked. $35.00 – 55.00.

Retro-style 1950s earrings. Gold plated with simulated pearls and clear rhinestones. All stones are glued in. 2" long. Unsigned. $35.00 – 70.00.

1940s daisy earrings. Rose gold vermeil over sterling silver. Prong-set emerald-cut Burmese ruby rhinestones. 1¼" in diameter. Typical WWII era jewelry. Hallmarked sterling. Unsigned, resembles the work of Trifari. $65.00 – 100.00.

Antiqued gold-tone earrings with central golden yellow chaton-cut rhinestone surrounded by simulated turquoise and onyx. Screw-clip backs. 1" in diameter. Marked Hobé. $40.00 – 75.00.

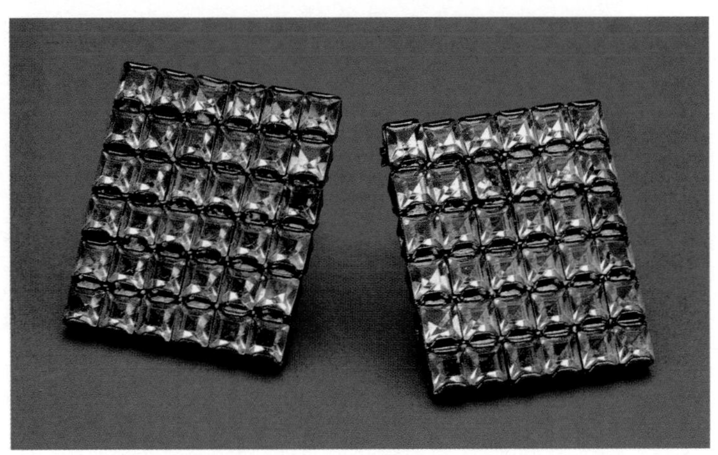

Gun-metal plated square earrings. Channel-set square-cut clear rhinestones. Marked Les Bernard. 1¼". $60.00 – 85.00.

Pair of 1950s diamond-shaped earrings. Gold plated. Prong-set foil-backed emerald, marquise, and trapezium-cut golden yellow rhinestones. Unmarked, however, was originally purchased with a Kramer for Christian Dior pin. 2¼". $45.00 – 75.00.

Two pair of gilded brass filigree earrings. Left pair: Prong-set purple Venetian glass cabochons with simulated pearls and amethyst rhinestones. Right pair: Prong-set green glass cameos with aurora borealis rhinestones. Both pair are marked W. Germany (West Germany). 1¼". (This type of jewelry is difficult to date — they are still being made in the exact same way since the 1950s.) $35.00 – 60.00.

Three pair of earrings from the 1950s. Top to bottom: Gilded brass oval-shaped earrings. Venetian glass prong-set center surrounded by glued-in simulated pearls and deep yellow rhinestones. Marked West Germany. 1½". $35.00 – 60.00. Gold-plated earrings with prong-set simulated marquise-cut topaz and simulated chaton-cut citrines. Unmarked. 1½". $30.00 – 60.00. Gold-plated leaves with prong-set marquise-cut smoky gray, chaton-cut sapphire blue, and marquise-cut topaz rhinestones. 1½". Marked Weiss. $65.00 – 80.00.

1950s button-style earrings. Silver tone with pearlized purple center and two layers of channel-set chaton-cut amethyst rhinestones. 1¼". Umarked. $35.00 – 50.00.

Pretty in pink! Rhodium-plated earrings with opaque pink glass cabochons in round, marquise, and pear-cuts, surrounded by pink chaton-cut rhinestones. All stones are prong set. 1¼". Unsigned. $45.00 – 60.00.

Late 1950s button-style earrings. Polished apple-green glass center surrounded by lime-green chaton and emerald-cut rhinestones (glued in). 1¼" Unmarked. $40.00 – 55.00.

Very appealing Judy Lee button-style earrings. Pearlized center surrounded by Austrian crystal chaton-cut rhinestones, simulated pearls, and iridescent Austrian crystal faceted beads. Silver-tone filigree backing. The beads and pearls are strung on wire and tied to the filigree backing, the rhinestones are glued on. 1¾". 1950s. $60.00 – 80.00.

Trifari seahorse pin (2¾"). The seahorse is brown enamel with green glass cabochon eye. Blue enameled seaweed. Simulated pearl bubbles. Gold plated. $175.00 – 225.00.

From the collection of Koral Michael Whalton

Trifari bubble-blowing fish pin. Orange and aqua blue enameled fish with royal blue glass cabochon eye. Simulated pearls. Gold plated. 2¾" long x 2½" high. $150.00 – 200.00.

From the collection of Koral Michael Whalton

From the collection of Koral Michael Whalton

Beautifully enameled sailfish with ruby rhinestone eye. Clear rhinestone accents. Silver-tone base metal. 2¾". $110.00 – 135.00.

Surrealistic 4¼" copper lobster brooch. Body is jointed so it can be either worn on the lapel or draped over the shoulder. Marked Rebajes. $350.00 – 475.00.

BSK 1¾" snail pin. Gold plated with a Burmese ruby bezel-set rhinestone eye. Genuine iridescent shell. $40.00 – 55.00.

Hobé starfish pin. Etched antiqued gold plate with glued-in tiny simulated seed pearls. 2¾". $65.00 – 85.00.

From the collection of Koral Michael Whalton

Seahorse pin. Gold plated with prong-set smoky gray and apple green chaton-cut rhinestones. Genuine yellow shell belly. 3" long. Signed Hobé 1965. $150.00 – 200.00.

From the collection of Koral Michael Whalton

Rare walrus brooch, 2¼" l x 1¾" w. Ivory enameled tusks. Green glass cabochon eyes. Sterling plated. Signed Hattie Carnegie and Alfred. $450.00 – 550.00.

Gold-tone 2¼" circus seal. Aurora borealis rhinestones glued onto the body and balancing on the seal's nose as a ball. Red rhinestone eye. Signed BSK. $65.00 – 80.00.

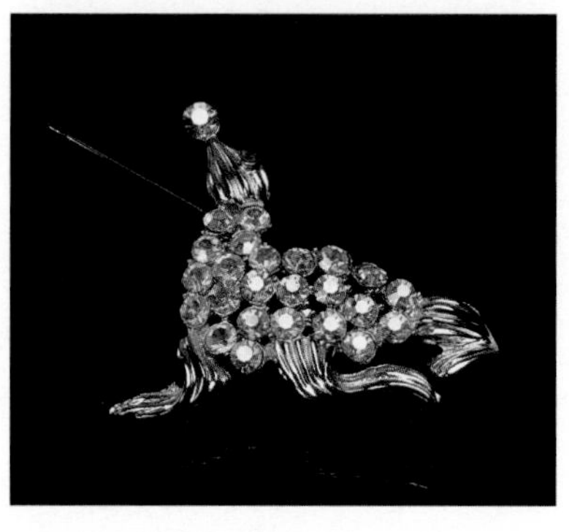

Three-dimensional etched antiqued gold-tone frog and lily pad pin. Turquoise plastic cabochon eyes. 2". Signed Hobé. $75.00 – 95.00.

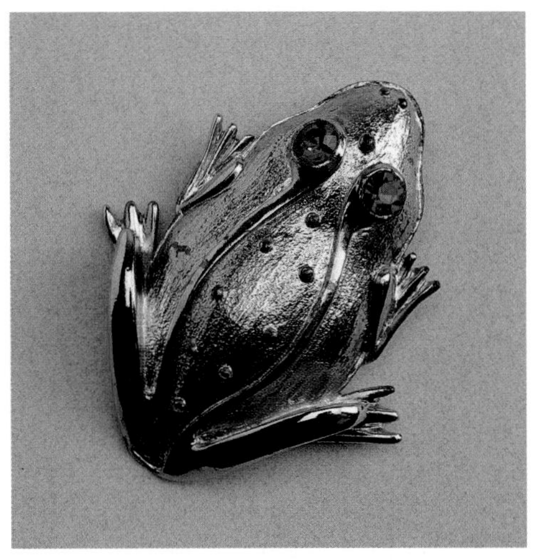

3¾" silver-tone frog. Peacock glass aurora borealis rhinestone eyes. Marked Trifari. $75.00 – 115.00.

Souvenir pin ¾". Oxidized brass frame set with tiny green, red, clear, blue, and yellow rhinestones. Center is convex glass over an enameled sailfish. Unmarked. 1930s. $40.00 – 60.00.

From the collection of Koral Michael Whalton

Frog pins. Left: HAR frog pin. Rusty brown enamel with red glass cabochon eyes. Antiqued gold tone. 1960s. 1¾" long. $125.00 – 175.00. Small unsigned frog with green enameled legs and face with white enameled back. Red glass cabochon eyes. 1¼" long. $50.00 – 75.00. Right:

From the collection of Koral Michael Whalton

Etched antiqued gold-tone turtle pin with turquoise ceramic shell. Pavé rhinestone head. Green rhinestone eyes. Marked Pauline Rader. 2½" long. 1960s. $100.00 – 175.00. Rare etched gold-plated turtle with navy blue leather shell. Green rhinestone eyes. Marked From Polly Bergen (a custom-made item Polly Bergen presented as gifts to friends). 2½" long x 1¾" wide. $650.00 – 800.00.

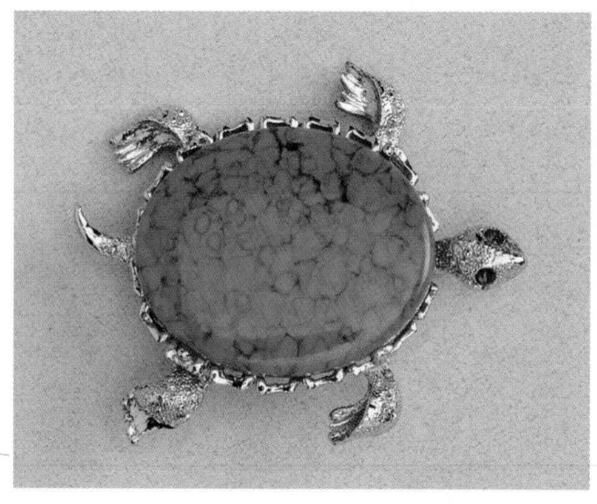

2½" gold-tone turtle. Coral ceramic shell. Green rhinestone eyes. Marked Gerry's. $45.00 – 55.00.

Large and showy salamander brooch, 4". Red glass cabochons. Blue, green, red, and clear chaton-cut rhinestones. Signed, however, the signature is illegible. $300.00 – 400.00.

Unusual Depression era grasshopper brooch. Snakeskin body and legs, leather head and neck, mother-of-pearl wings, red glass cabochon eye, green cloth tummy and pin backing. The ends of the feet are brass beads. 3¼" long. $75.00 – 100.00.

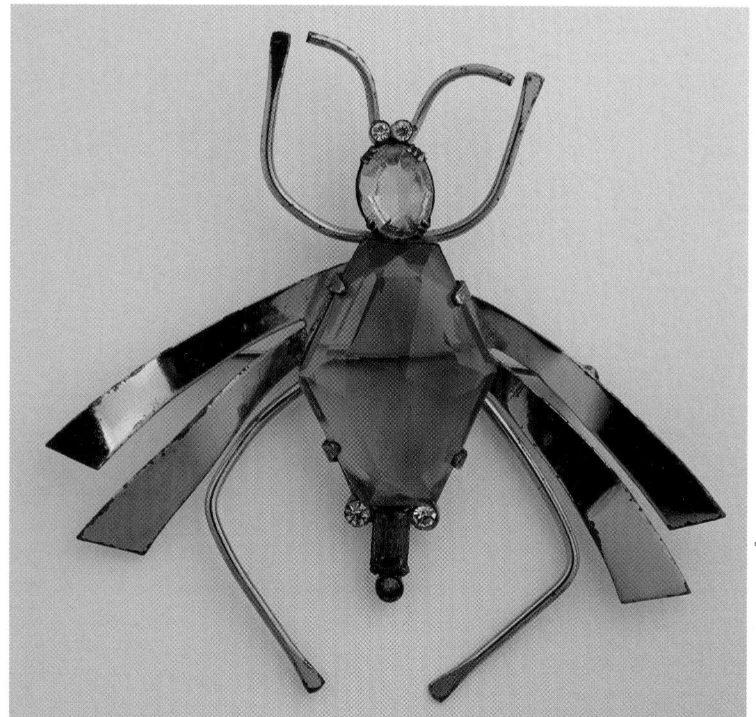

From the collection of Koral Michael Whalton

Large hornet brooch, 2¾" x 2¾". Rose gold vermeil over sterling. Clear rhinestone eyes, light green oval-cut glass head, and lozenge-cut topaz glass body. Stinger of emerald-cut sapphire glass, clear and red rhinestones. Marked Coro Sterling Craft. 1940s. $275.00 – 350.00.

A trio of rhinestone butterflies in flight. Bottom to top: Gold plated with fuchsia and aurora borealis rhinestones in chaton and marquise cuts. Marked Regency. $95.00 – 120.00. Gold plated with prong-set marquise-cut pale blue frosted glass, pale blue rhinestones in marquise and chaton cuts, and chaton-cut aurora borealis rhinestones. Marked Weiss. $100.00 – 125.00. Antiqued gold tone with glued-in lime green, lemon yellow, and golden yellow rhinestones in marquise and chaton cuts. 2¼" x 2¾". Unmarked. $85.00 – 115.00. The two butterflies on the left are courtesy of The Glass Spoon.

Butterfly pin/pendant with a 3" wingspan. Gold plated with prong-set bottle green, turquoise, emerald green, and fuchsia rhinestones in chaton and marquise cuts. Unmarked. 1960s. $55.00 – 85.00.

Large 1970s butterfly brooch, 3½" x 3½". Antiqued gold plate with glued-in lavender and plum foil-backed rhinestones in chaton and marquise cuts. Alexis Kirk (unmarked). $85.00 – 125.00.

From the collection of Koral Michael Whalton

Castlecliff dragonfly brooches, each with a 3½" wingspan and 2¼" long body. Gold plated. One dragonfly has black Lucite wings and the other has marbleized green Lucite wings. $175.00 – 225.00.

Crawler collection. Clockwise from right to left: 1950s scatter pins. Gold-plated pair of matching bugs with black enameled legs and antennae, blue enameled abdomen, and white enameled head and wigs. Sapphire blue rhinestone eyes. 1" long. Unmarked. $35.00 – 45.00 pair. Rose gold vermeil over sterling silver fly with sapphire glass oval-cut body and chaton-cut head. Tiny clear rhinestone eyes. 1¼" long. Marked Coro. 1940s. $35.00 – 50.00. 1960s unmarked bug. Brush gold plated. Simulated mabé pearl abdomen and simulated pearl head. Tiny Faux turquoise plastic beads glued on to the wings. 1¼" long. $25.00 – 40.00. Gold-tone bug with pear-cut aurora borealis rhinestones glued on to the body and wings and a chaton-cut aurora borealis rhinestone glued on to the head. Simulated seed pearl eyes. Tiny simulated seed pearl accents on the body. 1½" long. Unmarked. $25.00 – 40.00. Gold-plated stamped metal bug. Aquamarine rhinestone head, body, and eyes. All rhinestones are foil backed. 1" long. Marked Czecho (Czechoslovakia). $30.00 – 50.00. Center: Gold-plated bug with open-work wings. Head, upper layer of wings, and body are rhodium-plated with pavé clear rhinestones. The upper layer of wings move back and forth. Delicate pin of good quality. 1¼" x 1½". Unmarked. $40.00 – 60.00.

From the collection of Koral Michael Whalton

Rare Castlecliff scarab-beetle brooch, 2¼" long. Gold plated with yellow and green ceramic body. Coral oval ceramic cabochon eyes. $275.00 – 350.00.

From the collection of Koral Michael Whalton

Marcel Boucher bird of paradise brooch, 4" long. Highly detailed, excellent craftsmanship. The feathers on the head, body, and tail are realistically etched gold plate. The bird's throat and feathers have clear pavé rhinestones set in rhodium plate. The bird's floral perch has flowers of rhinestones in pastel shades of yellow, green, and lavender. Faux coral cabochon eye. All rhinestones are chaton cut and glued in. $300.00 – 400.00.

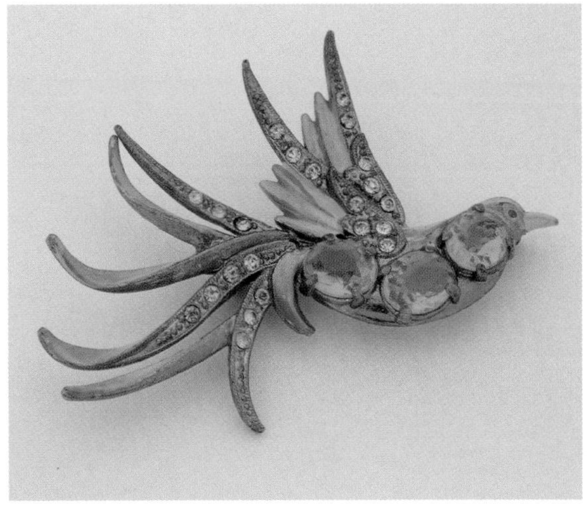

Late 1930s to early 1940s unmarked bird of paradise brooch, 3" long. Rose gold-plated base metal. Clear rhinestone brilliants on the wings and tail feathers. Tiny pink rhinestone eyes. Three oval-cut citrine rhinestones prong set on the body (unfoiled stones). Yellow and orange enamel. Bird is in a style made popular by Marcel Boucher. However, this brooch is not marked. $100.00 – 135.00.

Pair of Coro scatter pins from the 1950s. Gold plated with purple and white enamel. Tiny pink rhinestone eyes and oval-cut amethyst rhinestone bodies. The larger bird is 1¾" long and the smaller bird is 1¼" long. $35.00 – 45.00 set.

From the collection of Koral Michael Whalton

Marcel Boucher swallows. This is actually a pair of pins that can be worn as one brooch or taken apart to be worn separately. Gold plated with ruby red marquise-cut rhinestone eyes. Underside of neck and belly has a strip in rhodium plate set with clear rhinestone brilliants. Marked Boucher 9048P. Dimensions worn as one pin: 2¼" x 2½". Each pin worn separately is 2" x 2¼". Late 1950s to early 1960s. $300.00 – 400.00.

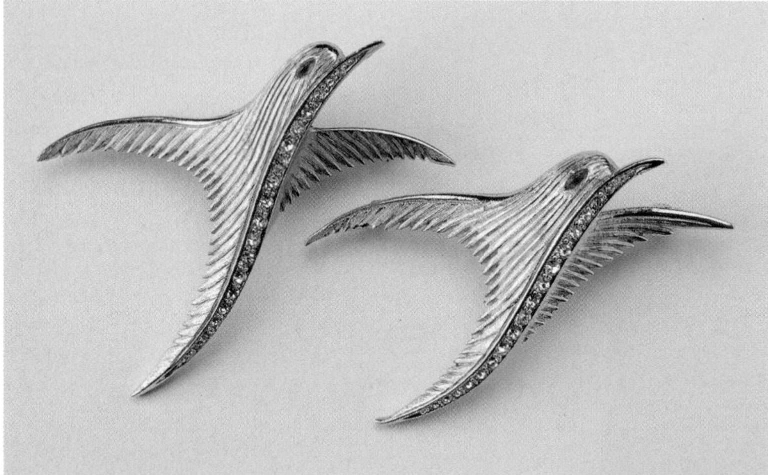

From the collection of Koral Michael Whalton

Large flamingo brooch, 4¼" long. Head, beak, and wing are silver-tone base metal set with clear rhinestone accents. The rest of the bird is gold-tone base metal. Ruby chaton-cut rhinestone eye. Unmarked. 1930s. $400.00 – 550.00.

From the collection of Koral Michael Whalton

Peacock pin with the highly detailed craftsmanship of fine jewelry. Gold plated. The feathers are realistically etched and have prong-set emerald and sapphire rhinestones. The outline of the base of the tail and the inner wing have pavé clear rhinestones set in rhodium (so they sparkle). Neck is in pavé sapphire rhinestones. Simulated pearl in the center of the flower. 3" long. Signed Jomaz. $200.00 – 275.00.

From the collection of Koral Michael Whalton

Rare 1930s penguin clips. Mr. Penguin is resplendent in top hat and cane. Pink glass oval-cut cabochon bellies. Turquoise blue enamel with white enameled eyes and feathers. Red enameled beaks, cane, ribbon on top hat, and pupils in the eyes. Golden yellow enameled feet. Clear rhinestone pavé on his feathers and her chest. Base metal. She is 1½" long and he is 1¾" long. Unmarked. $500.00 – 600.00 pair.

Collection of 1970s owls. Antiqued gold-tone owl pin/pendant with olive green ceramic belly and simulated pearl eyes. Unmarked. Late 1960s to early 1970s. 2¼". $40.00 – 50.00. Pair of Sarah Coventry gold-tone owls with iridescent yellow rose monteé cut rhinestone eyes. 1½" long. Marked Sarah Cov. $30.00 – 40.00 each. 2½" long antiqued gold-tone owl with faux tortoise-shell plastic belly. Unmarked. $40.00 – 50.00.

From the collection of Koral Michael Whalton

Bird brooch and duette collection. Top: Bird of paradise duette by Coro. Gold vermeil over sterling silver. Deep red and apple green enameled birds with clear rhinestone pavé on head and wings. Green enameled branch with enameled flowers in yellow, purple, red, and blue. Each of the flowers has a clear rhinestone in the center. Marked Coro Duette PAT. NO. 1798867 and hallmarked sterling. 1940s. 3¼" long. $275.00 – 400.00. Left: Bird of paradise mock-duette brooch. Silver-tone base metal. Pink, blue, and red enameled birds with clear rhinestone pavé on head and wings. Yellow enameled beaks and talons. Green enameled branch with enameled flowers in yellow, pink, green, and red. Each flower has a clear rhinestone in the center. Unmarked. 3¼" long. $125.00 – 175.00. Right: Cockatoo duette pin. Rhodium-plated cockatoos in pale blue and deep blue enamel. Yellow enameled beaks and talons. Red rhinestone eyes. Clear pavé rhinestone bellies. Green enameled branch. Flowers of pale blue and aqua blue enamel. Each flower has a clear rhinestone center. Unmarked. 3" l x 2½" w. $200.00 – 350.00. Bottom: Parrots mock-duette brooch. Parrots in orange and blue enamel with clear pavé rhinestone belly and beak. Gold-tone base metal. Marked with an "S" on the inside of a star (may be the work of the Colonial Manufacturing Co., Inc.), 1930s. 3" l x 2" w. $125.00 – 175.00.

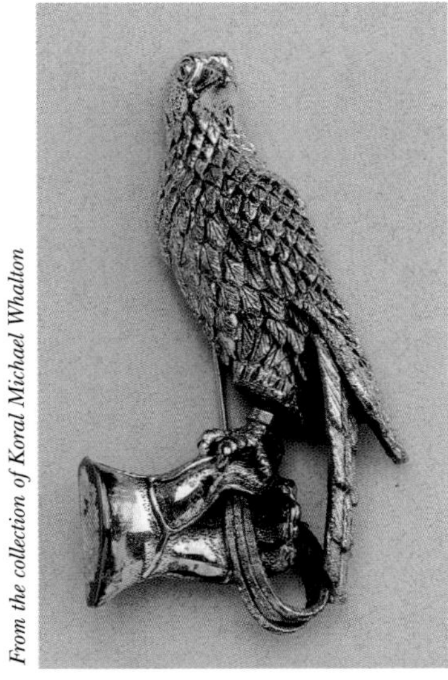

From the collection of Koral Michael Whalton

Tortolani Falconing brooch. Silver-tone base metal. 2¾" long. $175.00 – 300.00.

Pink pavé rhinestone kitty. Emerald green chaton-cut rhinestone eyes. Pink pearlized seed bead nose. Pink baguette-cut rhinestone collar. All rhinestones are glued in. Gold plated. 1¼". Unmarked. $45.00 – 60.00.

Gold-plated squirrel pin with brown molded plastic tail (simulated tortoise-shell). Clear rhinestone eyes. 2". Unmarked. $40.00 – 55.00.

From the collection of Koral Michael Whalton

Three hedgehog pins. Left to right: 1¼" gold-plated hedgehog with Burmese ruby glass cabochon eyes. Signed Boucher 9173P. $125.00 – 175.00. 1" gold-plated hedgehog with topaz rhinestone eyes. Signed Sarah (Coventry). $50.00 – 65.00. 1¾" gold-plated hedgehog with pavé rhinestone face, black rhinestone eyes and black glass cabochon nose. Unsigned. $50.00 – 65.00.

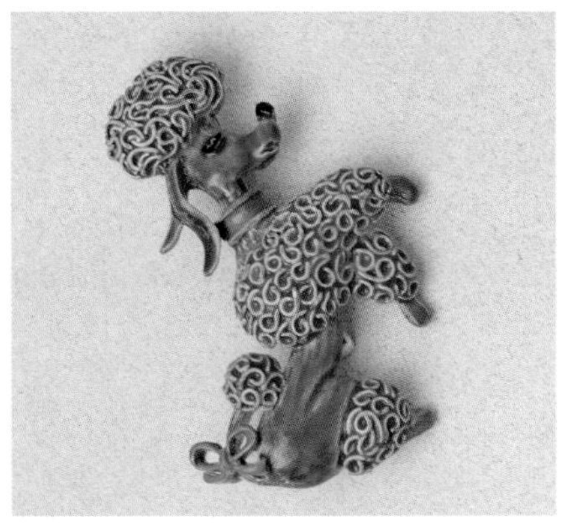

Begging poodle pin. Base metal, entire pin is done in rust colored enamel. Black enameled nose and eyes and green enameled collar and bow on tail. 1¾" tall. Marked Gerry's. $35.00 – 45.00.

Hollycraft monkey pin. Gray enameled monkey swinging from a brown enameled branch with red fruit and green leaves. Base metal. 2" x 2". 1950s. $40.00 – 60.00.

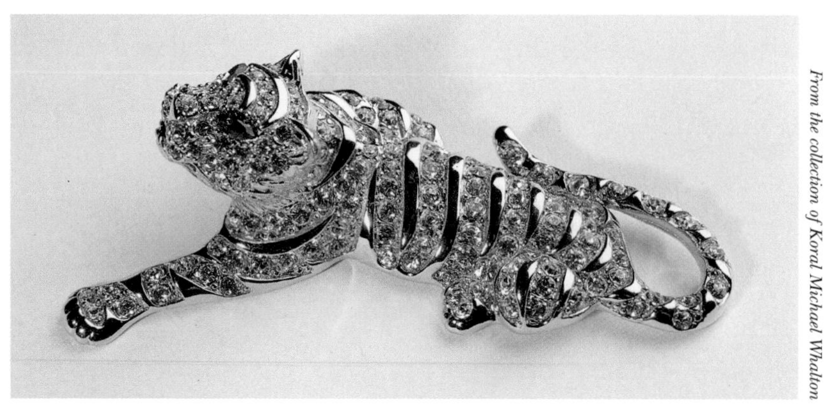

From the collection of Koral Michael Whalton

Outstanding hard-to-find Trifari tiger pin. Gold plated with clear rhinestone pavé. Smoky-gray marquise-cut rhinestone eyes. Circa 1991. 3½" long. Since this pin has been done, it has been copied by numerous other companies as well as numerous costume jewelry importers. $300.00 – 350.00.

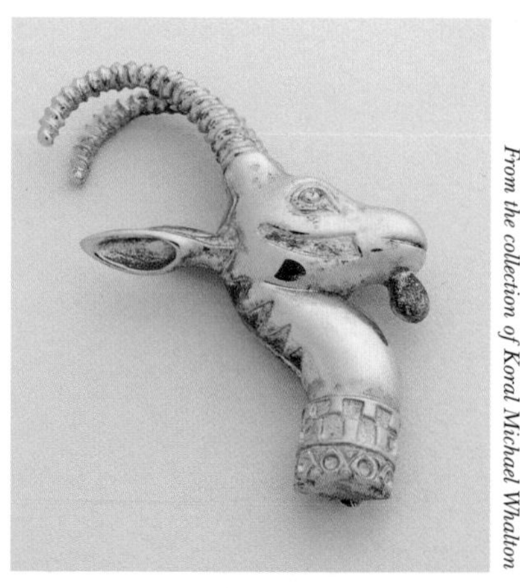

From the collection of Koral Michael Whalton

2½" African antelope pin. Gold vermeil over sterling silver. Signed Reed Barton and hallmarked sterling. $150.00 – 200.00.

From the collection of Koral Michael Whalton

Large sacred cow brooch. Gold-tone base metal with black enameling. Clear pavé rhinestone eyes and head piece. Red ruby glass cabochon in forehead. Red rhinestone accents in nose. Unmarked. 3" l x 2¼" w. $150.00 – 200.00.

Etched gold-plated tiger with black enamel stripes. 2¼" long. Marked Trifari. $150.00 – 200.00.

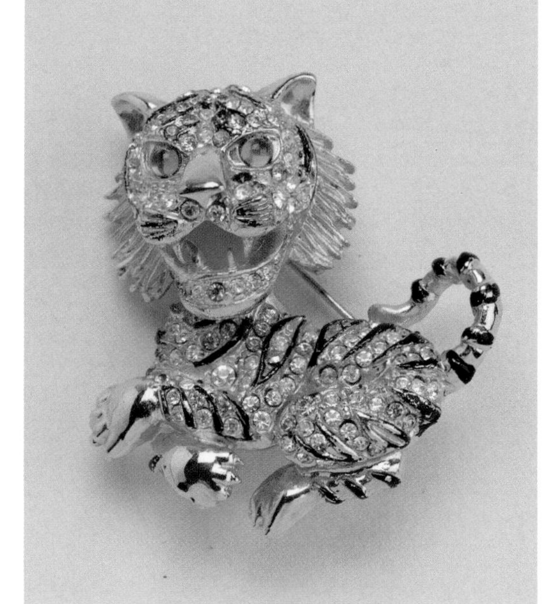

A friendly tiger? Gold-plated pin with black enameled stripes, green glass cabochon eyes, and tiny clear rhinestone accents. 2" x 2". Unmarked. 1960s. $100.00 – 125.00.

Unusual ram's head pin. Gold plated with realistic glass eyes. Probably an astrological symbol. 2¼" x 2½". Marked Florenza. This is an unusual design for Florenza, something apart from the usual Victorian style of this company's jewelry. Late 1960s or early 1970s. $100.00 – 150.00.

From the collection of Koral Michael Whalton

Taurus the bull pin. Etched gold plate with green rhinestone eye. Each of the stars has a tiny sapphire blue rhinestone center. Clear pavé rhinestone accents. 2¼" l x 1¾" w. Marked Capri. $175.00 – 200.00.

Unmarked anteater pin. Silver tone with lavender frosted plastic and lavender rhinestones. 1½" x 2". The company that made this pin copied Hattie Carnegie's original anteater pin. $70.00 – 100.00.

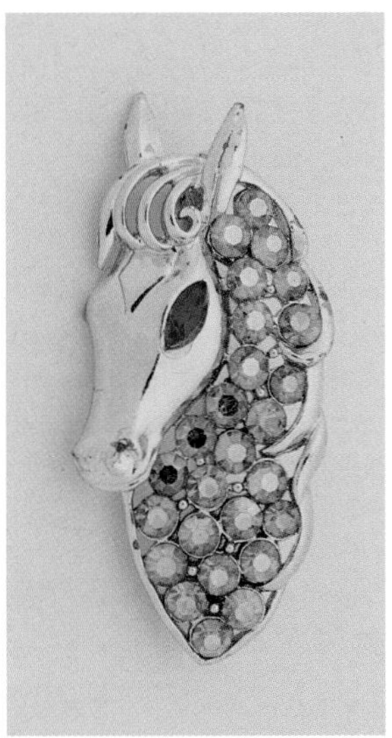

2½" horse head pin. Pavé blue aurora borealis rhinestones. Red rhinestone marquise-cut eye. Silver-tone metal. Marked Coro. $95.00 – 110.00.

From the collection of Koral Michael Whalton

The wheels turn on this covered wagon and oxen pin from the 1930s. Oxidized base metal set with pastel rhinestones in shades of pink, purple, aqua, yellow, and green. Unsigned. 2¼" long x 1¼" high. $175.00 – 200.00.

1930s Depression era horse and lucky horseshoepin. Hand-carved wood with red painted accents. Red wire bridle and reins. Unmarked. 2¾" l x 2¼" w. $40.00 – 55.00.

Horse pin collection. Top to bottom: Knight on his steed. Etched gold plate. Pavé clear rhinestones on the knight. Horse has red rhinestone eye. Red enameled shield and green and red enameled saddle. Black enameled hooves. Signed Polcini. 2¼" long x 1½" wide. $300.00 – 400.00. Race horse and jockey pin. Base metal. Brown enameled horse with black enameled hooves and bridle. Clear pavé rhinestone jockey with white enameled face and light blue enameled hat. Saddle also in pavé rhinestones. Unmarked. 1930s. 2¾" long. $175.00 – 300.00. Jumping carousel horse. Etched gold plate. Sapphire blue enameled saddle with clear rhinestone trim. Emerald green enameled harness. Clear rhinestone bridle. Marked Ciner. 2¼" long. $200.00 – 275.00.

From the collection of Koral Michael Whalton

From the collection of Koral Michael Whalton

Prima donna pin. Gold and silver-tone base metal with cream enameled face and neck. Turquoise enameled costume. Chaton-cut red rhinestone eyes and baguette-cut rhinestone nose and mouth. Clear pavé rhinestones on the ruff and collar. 2" l x 2½" w. Signed Castlecliff. $300.00 – 375.00.

From the collection of Koral Michael Whalton

1930s face with magnificent headdress. Base metal with large prong-set glass ruby and sapphires. Face has black enameled eyebrows, blue enameled eyes, and red enameled lips. Unsigned. 3" long x 2¼" wide. $275.00 – 300.00.

From the collection of Koral Michael Whalton

Three graceful Marcel Boucher ballerinas. Left to right: Ballerina with openwork tutu. Gold and silver plated with clear rhinestone accents. 1¾" long x 2" wide. Signed Boucher. Gold-plated ballerina with faux turquoise seed beads on the edge of her tutu. 1¾" x 1¾". Signed Boucher 8517. Gold-plated ballerina with etched tutu. 1¾" long. Signed Boucher 8039P. $125.00 – 175.00 each.

Tiny trio of rag doll pins. The scatter pins on the right and left are trifanium plated with ruby carved glass bodies and clear rhinestone accents. Marked Trifari DES Pat. No. 153552 (boy) and 153551 (girl). The pin in the center is sterling silver with ruby glass cabochon oval-cut face and clear rhinestone bodice, 1940s. Marked Trifari Patent No. 136079 and hallmarked sterling. Each pin is 1½" tall. $100.00 – 150.00 each.

Oriental scatter pins from the 1950s. Gold plated. Man has red enameled hat with clear rhinestone trim. Woman has black enameled collar, clear rhinestone crown and earrings. Each pin is 1" long. Unmarked. $50.00 – 75.00 pair.

Blackamoor chatelaine. Silver-tone stamped metal with black enamel. Prong-set simulated glass turquoise. Each pin is 1¾". Unmarked. 1950s. $50.00 – 75.00.

Dutch couple chatelaine. Stamped base metal, gold plated. Ruby red, emerald green, and sapphire blue glass cabochons. The cabochon faces are bezel set, the others are prong set. Clear rhinestone buttons. Each pin is 1¾" long. 1950s. Marked Coro. $75.00 – 125.00.

From the collection of Koral Michael Whalton

Disney circus brooch — a scene from the Disney movie Dumbo. Gold plated with white, blue, black, and red enameling. Marked W.D.P. (Walt Disney Productions). 2¾" long. $250.00 – 350.00.

1940s brooch/clip. Rhodium plated with green enameled leaves and golden brown enameled flower stems. Clear and gray rhinestones. Unmarked (may be the work of Pennino). 4" x 2½". In original R.H. Macy and Co., Inc. box (not shown). $150.00 – 200.00.

From the collection of Koral Michael Whalton

Rare pair of Disney Pinocchio and Jiminy Cricket clips. Pinocchio has jointed legs. Silver-tone base metal. Each 2½" long. Signed W.D.P. (Walt Disney Productions). $900.00 – 1,000.00 each.

1930s floral bouquet. Each tiny flower is silver plated and set with clear rhinestones. The larger flower is gold plated with cream enameling. The leaves are in green enamel. Stems are gold plated. On the branches behind the flowers are tiny rhinestones in pink, sapphire blue, and emerald green. 3" long. Unsigned. $175.00 – 200.00.

From the collection of Koral Michael Whalton

Beautiful 1930s enameled nosegay brooch. Gold plated with lavender, yellow, pink, orange, blue, and aqua enameled flowers. Green enameled leaves. Simulated pearl buds. Each enameled flower is set with a glued-in rhinestone which coordinates with the flower's color. Marked Coro. 2¼" wide x 3¾" long. $250.00 – 300.00.

From the collection of Koral Michael Whalton

3¼" lilac brooch. Base metal set with clear rhinestone accents. Dark green enameled leaves with light green enamel around the edges. Lilacs in purple enamel with lilac enamel around the edges. Unmarked Coro. Silver-tone base metal. Late 1930s – early 1940s. $175.00 – 225.00.

From the collection of Koral Michael Whalton

1930s lead crystal brooch. Silver-plated base metal with green enameled leaves and brown enameled stems. Tiny flowers with bezel-set rhinestones in simulated amethyst, citrine, sapphire, aquamarine, ruby, emerald, and clear. Unsigned. 2" long. $325.00 – 400.00.

Trifari iris clip/brooch. This brooch was created in the lost-wax casting method and is rhodium plated. The petals are deep blue enameled accentuated with clear rhinestones. Clear rhinestones are also set inside this three-dimensional flower with red rhinestone stamens. Marked Trifari Pat. Pend. 2¼". Late 1930s to early 1940s. $225.00 – 350.00.

From the collection of Koral Michael Whalton

Coro retro flower brooch. Gold-plated stem and outside of leaves. Flower and inside of leaves is rhodium plated with clear pavé rhinestones. Marquise-cut ruby red prong-set rhinestone stamens. 3¼" long x 2¼" wide. $350.00 – 425.00.

Coro gold-tone base metal tulip brooch. Green enameled leaves. Clear rhinestone accents. Stamens of clear marquise-cut foil-backed rhinestones are tremblers. 3¼" tall. Late 1930s to early 1940s. $95.00 – 115.00.

From the collection of Koral Michael Whalton

Gold vermeil over sterling silver floral spray brooch. Emerald-cut Burmese ruby rhinestones and clear rhinestone accents. 1940s. Signed Trifari DES. Pat. No. 137543. 3" x 3". $500.00 – 625.00.

Large nosegay brooch. Gold-plated base metal. Scrollwork design on the leaves. Each of the flowers twirls. Bezel-set pink glass cabochons. The flower petals are unfoiled light and dark pink flat rhinestones set in a gold-plated frame. Unmarked, possibly Pennino. 4½" x 3½". $300.00 – 375.00.

Eisenberg poinsettia brooch. Gold vermeil over sterling silver. Large oval-cut red glass central stone with six square-cut glass stones of the same color. Each leaf has a vein of pavé clear rhinestones. Signed Eisenberg Original and hallmarked sterling. Late 1930s – early 1940s. 3½" long x 2¾" wide. $1,500.00 – 1,800.00.

From the collection of Koral Michael Whalton

World War II era floral brooch. Gold vermeil over sterling silver. The center of each of the flowers is an oval-cut simulated amethyst. The rhinestones are unfoiled. Even though this brooch shows some signs of wear, it is still very appealing and still collectible. 3" x 4". Hallmarked sterling. $135.00 – 165.00.

Early 1930s brooch. Each gold-plated base metal leaf has a piercework vein. The leaves were crafted separately, then they were soldered together. The berries are claw-set yellow Bakelite. Unsigned. 2¾" wide. $100.00 – 150.00.

Unmarked flower brooch. Rose gold-plated base metal (stamped). Magenta prong-set plastic rhinestone. Early 1950s. 3¼". $75.00 – 100.00.

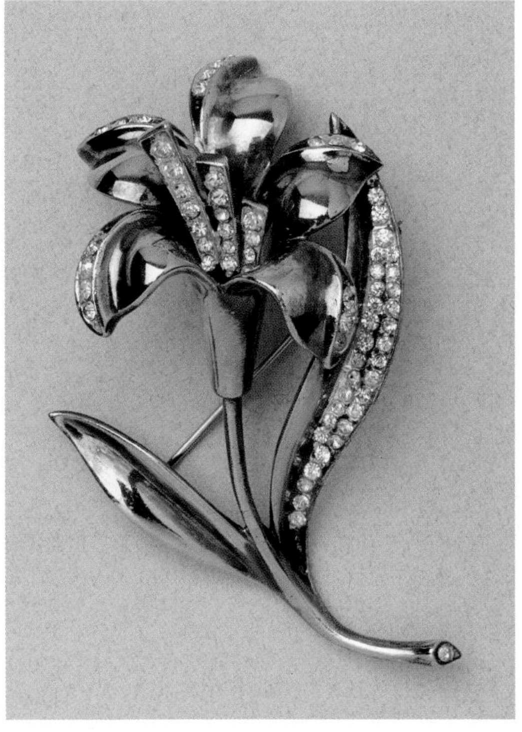

Heavy flower brooch made three dimensional by the lost-wax casting method. Sterling silver with green gold plate. Clear rhinestone accents. Curved to set prettily on the shoulder. Made in two parts and riveted together. 1940s. Hallmarked sterling. 3¼". $350.00 – 425.00.

From the collection of Koral Michael Whalton

1940s flower brooch. Gold-plated base metal. Clear rhinestones and red and aqua baguettes accent the inside of the flower. Metal stamens with red glass beads. Unmarked. 2¾" long. $175.00 – 225.00.

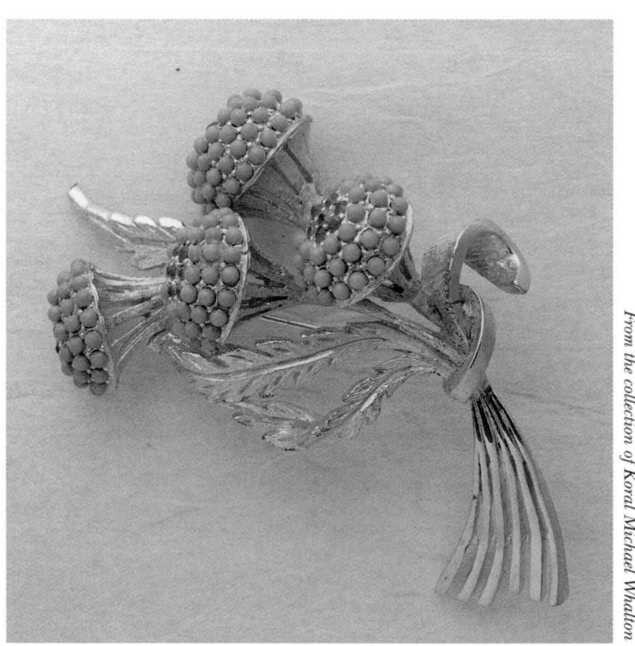

From the collection of Koral Michael Whalton

Hattie Carnegie nosegay pin. Brush gold-tone. Set with simulated turquoise beads and faux Burmese rubies. 3¼" long. $175.00 – 225.00.

1930s base metal flower brooch. Gold plated. Marquise-cut foil-backed pink, aqua, and smoky gray rhinestones. Tiny chaton-cut aqua rhinestones on the decoration holding the stems together. 4¾" long. $95.00 – 125.00.

From the collection of Koral Michael Whalton

Antiqued gilded brass double flower brooch. Simulated cream and beige baroque pearls. Clear rhinestone brilliants. 3" long. Signed Miriam Haskell. $375.00 – 425.00.

Gilded brass flower-cluster pin. Simulated baroque pearls with prong-set clear rhinestones. All rhinestones are foil-backed. 1½" x 2". 1950s. Signed DeMario NY. $125.00 – 150.00.

From the collection of Koral Michael Whalton

Flower brooch. The leaves and petals are carved mother-of-pearl. 12K gold vermeil over sterling silver. Marked Ocean Treasures and hallmarked 12K on sterling. 4½" long. $200.00 – 275.00.

From the collection of Koral Michael Whalton

Costume jewelry that mimics fine jewelry — who can tell but the experts? Exquisitely crafted rhodium vermeil on sterling silver. Simulated diamonds and pearls. Unsigned, but highly collectible — a pin of the finest quality. Hallmarked sterling. 3" long. $900.00 – 1200.00.

From the collection of Koral Michael Whalton

Ledo brooch. Rhodium-plated leaves, clear pavé rhinestones, and cobalt blue glass flower buds. Circa 1961. 2¾" long. $400.00 – 475.00.

Scarce and stunning Schiaparelli orchid brooch. Completely covered with Austrian crystal rhinestones of the highest quality — all prong-set. The rhinestones are in shades of icy blue, sapphire, and clear. Rhodium plated. 3" x 3½". Brooch is unsigned, originally bought as a set with earrings marked Schiaparelli. (Earrings not shown.) $750.00 – 900.00.

From the collection of Koral Michael Whalton

From the collection of Koral Michael Whalton

Schreiner flower pin. Prong-set sapphire blue marquise-cut rhinestones and simulated turquoise beads. Gold plated. 2¾" long. $150.00 – 200.00.

1940s three-dimensional leaf and flower-bud brooch. Excellent design. Rose and yellow gold vermeil over sterling silver. Two oval-cut simulated sapphires (unfoiled). 2¼" x 4¼". A World War II era brooch. Hallmarked sterling. $175.00 – 215.00.

Weiss flower pin with Austrian crystal rhinestones of excellent quality. Flower petals of deep magenta marquise and pear-cut rhinestones. The center of the flower is in pale pink chaton-cut rhinestones. Stem of baguette-cut brown rhinestones. Leaves of bottle green marquise and pear-cut rhinestones. All rhinestones are prong set. Gold plated. 1950s. 3½". $100.00 – 145.00.

1950s floral brooch. Flower petals of lavender marbleized Venetian glass marquise-cut stones. Leaves of pink marquise-cut rhinestones. Flower center and accents of fuchsia chaton-cut rhinestones. Flower buds are baguette-cut fuchsia rhinestones. Stems of gold-plated wire. Unsigned. $60.00 – 85.00.

Enameled flower pin. The shiny petals are realistically shaded — olive green at the edges fading to a deep brown towards the flower's center. The center is japanned with prong-set peridot rhinestones. 2¼" in diameter. Unmarked. 1950s – 60s. $35.00 – 55.00.

Three flower pins. Left to right: Flower of turquoise and white glass. Marquise-cut petals and leaves. Chaton-cut center. All prong set. Gold plated. Unmarked. Antiqued gold-tone flower with etched stem. White plastic prong-set rhinestones in marquise and chaton-cuts. Smaller white chaton-cut stones are glued in. Unmarked. Flower of black and white glass. Marquise-cut leaves and petals. White glass cabochon center. Gold plated. Unmarked. All pins are from the 1950s – 60s. $40.00 – 60.00 each.

Enameled flower by Art. Bright pink enameled petals with orange edges. Olive green enameled leaves and stem. The leaves have golden yellow rhinestone accents. The flower stamen is pavé apple green rhinestones. All the rhinestones are glued in. 2½" long. 1960s – 70s. $45.00 – 85.00.

Large leaf pin. Gold plated with prong-set harvest colored rhinestones in orange, brown, and golden yellow. Pear, marquise, oval, and emerald cuts. 2¾" x 3¼". Marked Napier. $175.00 – 225.00.

Kramer leaf pin. Gold-tone metal. Simulated topaz marquise-cut cabochons. The cabochons are glued in. Mid 1950s to early 1960s. $55.00 – 80.00.

1960s swirled wheat pin/pendant. Heavy antiqued gold-tone. Oval-cut simulated tortoiseshell cabochon. 2½". Marked U.S. Pat. No. 3509734. (Patent applied for by Henry B. Lederer, Atlantic Beach, NY. Filed June 14, 1967. Patented May 5, 1970 – appeared in Official Gazette on the same date.) $75.00 – 90.00.

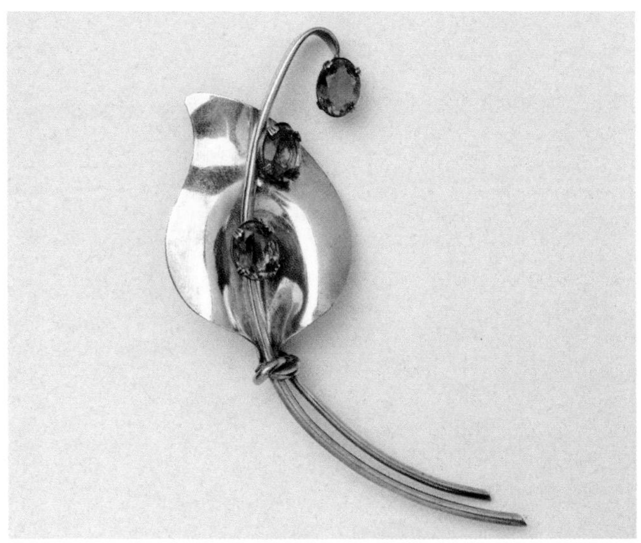

1940s sterling leaf brooch. Gold vermeil leaf and rose gold vermeil stem. Three prong-set oval-cut simulated amethysts. 3¾". Signed K. KEDLER, a very rare mark. $150.00 – 200.00.

Sandor Goldberger enamel brooch with perching bee. Stamped brass with sky blue enameled outer petals. Center of flower is enameled in russet brown. Yellow and black enameled bee. 2" in diameter. Marked Sandor Co. $145.00 – 175.00.

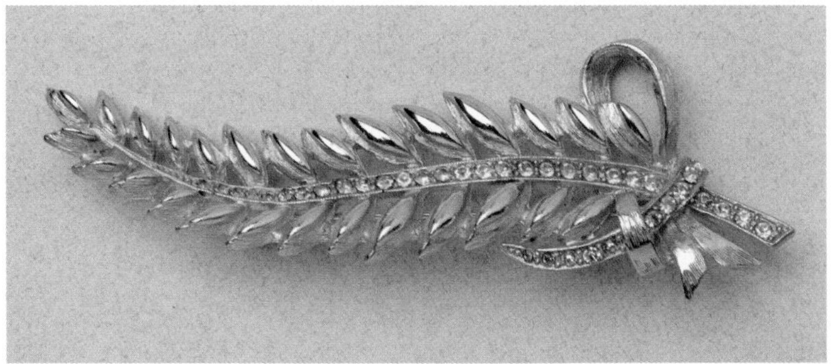

DeNicola leaf brooch. Gold plated with pale blue rhinestone vein and ribbon. 3¾" long. DeNicola is a rare name. $200.00 – 245.00.

Karu-Arke leaf pin. Antiqued bronze with glued-in chaton-cut aquamarine, aqua aurora borealis, sapphire, and sapphire aurora borealis rhinestones. $100.00 – 135.00.

Coro leaf pin. Silver-tone metal with glued-in pink rhinestones and pink aurora borealis rhinestones. Iridescent glass marquise-cut cabochons. 2¼". Mid 1950s to early 1960s. $55.00 – 75.00.

Stamped silver-tone base metal nosegay pin. The center of each flower has a turquoise molded plastic rose. A lightweight brooch from the 1950s. 3". Unmarked. $55.00 – 80.00.

Unusual 1930s bouquet brooch. Silver-tone pot metal with periwinkle-blue enameled leaves and bow. Three-dimensional pink celluloid flowers with sapphire-blue rhinestone centers. Rhinestones are glued in. Imaginative use of materials! 3¾". Unsigned. $175.00 – 225.00.

Heavy Coro free-form flower brooch in a spoke design. Etched silver-tone base metal. Emerald-cut glass sapphire and five icy blue emerald-cut rhinestones. All stones are foil backed and glued in. 2¼" x 2¼". $75.00 – 125.00.

Beautiful late 1920s to early 1930s basket brooch. Rose gold plated base metal. Oval-cut prong-set Austrian crystals of excellent quality (not foil backed). Basket is set with emerald-green stones. The flowers are garnet, Burmese-ruby, citrine, amethyst, sapphire, and aquamarine rhinestones. 2½". Unmarked. $200.00 – 250.00.

Late 1930s to early 1940s basket brooch. Silver-tone base metal. The basket's base is enameled in turquoise blue and set with clear rhinestone brilliants. The flower buds are pink, blue, and green plastic cabochons. Blue and white enameled flowers and green enameled leaves. Clear rhinestone accents. 2¼". Unsigned. $150.00 – 200.00.

1930s pea pod brooch. Silver-tone pot metal. The sides of the pea pod are clear baguette-cut rhinestones. The tip, leaves, and stem are pavé tiny clear chaton-cut clear rhinestones. All the rhinestones are foil backed. The peas are green glass beads strung on wire. Marked with an arrow piercing the letter S. 2¾". $200.00 – 275.00.

Coro functional doorknocker brooch designed by Adolph Katz. Gilded brass set with sky blue oval and round-cut cabochons, red and topaz square-cut rhinestones, red round-cut cabochon, and clear chaton-cut rhinestones. 2¾" l x 1½" w. $200.00 – 250.00.

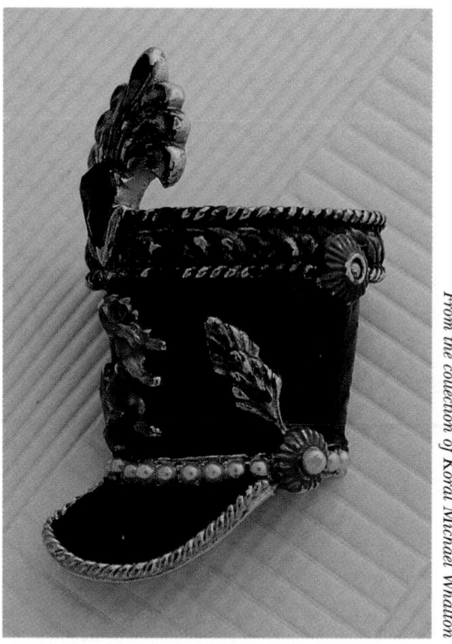

Band conductor's hat pin. Blue, black, green, orange, yellow, and red enameling. Simulated seed pearls and pear-cut amethyst rhinestone. Gold plated. Signed Art. 2" long. $125.00 – 200.00.

Collection of crowns. Top: 1940s gold-plated Trifari crown pin and earrings. Simulated pearls. $125.00 – 145.00. Left: 1950s crown scatter pin. 1¼". Gold plated with prong-set golden yellow and clear chaton-cut rhinestones. $20.00 – 30.00. Unmarked crown, probably Trifari. Gold plated with red glass oval-cut cabochons with clear and red chaton-cut rhinestones. 2". $150.00 – 200.00. Crown "scatter" pin, 1", 1950s. Gold plated with prong-set chaton-cut emerald green and clear rhinestones. $20.00 – 30.00. Pair of B. David crown earrings. Rhodium plated with prong-set baguette, chaton, and marquise-cut rhinestones and simulated pearls. 1¼" long. $75.00 – 100.00. Center crown with red cabochons courtesy of The Glass Spoon.

From the collection of Koral Michael Whalton

A royal grouping! From left to right and top to bottom: 1¾" crown with gilded brass wire work in a style made popular by Hobé. Pastel colored rhinestones in aqua, lavender, and pink. Emerald-cut, chaton-cut, and marquise-cut rhinestones. Simulated pearl accent at the top of the crown. Signed Original by Robert. $150.00 – 255.00. A 1½" version of the famous Trifari crown. Gold plated with oval-cut emerald-green and sapphire-blue cabochons, ruby-red baguettes, and emerald-green, clear, and ruby-red chaton-cut rhinestones. Marked Trifari. $150.00 – 250.00. 1940s gold-plated crown, set with clear chaton-cut rhinestones. 2¼" wide. Marked Trifari Pat. Pend. $125.00 – 225.00. 1¾" antiqued gold-tone crown by Jeanne. Emerald, ruby, citrine, and sapphire rhinestones. $110.00 – 145.00. 1" x 1½" rhodium-plated Boucher crown with pavé clear rhinestones, clear rhinestone baguettes, and simulated pearls. Marked MB 5388. $175.00 – 275.00. Nice silver-plated fleur-de-lis crown. Four simulated pear-shaped pearls. 1¾" x 3". Signed Tortolani. $150.00 – 250.00. Silver-tone base metal Ralph Lauren crown with lion perched on top. 1½" tall. $45.00 – 60.00. Tiny Sarah Coventry rhodium-plated crown with royal blue enameled accents. Clear rhinestone brilliants. 1" x 1". $30 .00 – 40.00. Crown collecting, as you can see, has become quite popular!

Watch-fob pendant/brooch. Antiqued gold tone. Edge of brooch is set with simulated pearls and clear chaton-cut rhinestones. The portrait is hand-enameled porcelain. 2¾" long. Signed BSK on the back of the metal and Limoges on the back of the porcelain. $175.00 – 250.00.

From the collection of Koral Michael Whalton

Watch-fob brooch. Gold vermeil over sterling silver. Edge of brooch set with clear and sapphire blue chaton-cut rhinestones. The center is porcelain with hand-painted enamel flowers and signed with an "H." 2¾" long. The brooch itself is signed Nettie Rosenstein and hallmarked sterling. $250.00 – 350.00.

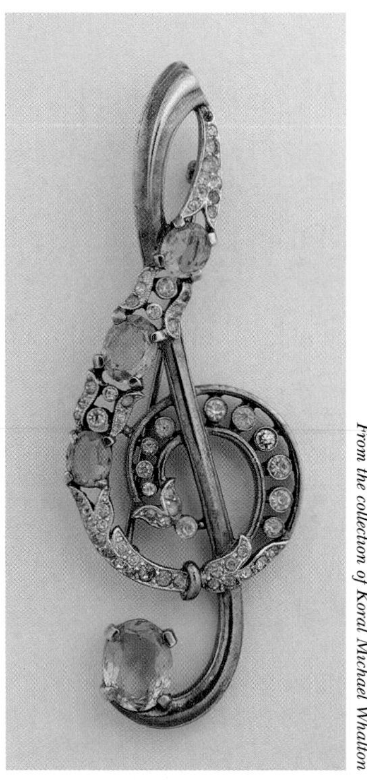

From the collection of Koral Michael Whalton

Trifari treble cleft. Rose gold plate. Clear rhinestone accents and oval-cut pastel pink and blue rhinestones. The larger rhinestones are not foil backed. 3¼" long. $250.00 – 375.00.

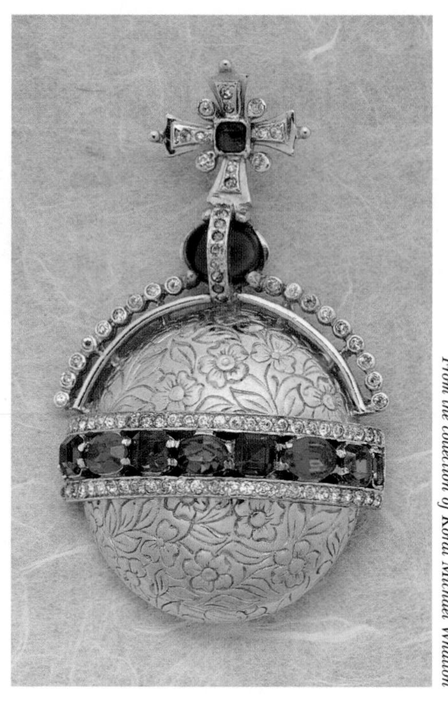

From the collection of Koral Michael Whalton

Mazer royal orb pin. Circa 1953. A pin designed in celebration of the coronation of Queen Elizabeth II. Gold plated. Rhodium-plated insets with clear pavé rhinestones. In the center of the Maltese cross (at the top of the orb) is a square-cut sapphire blue rhinestone. Below the cross is an amethyst glass cabochon. Encircling the orb is a belt of sapphire, Burmese ruby, and emerald rhinestones in oval and emerald cuts. Signed Mazer Bros. 3" long x 1¾" wide. $500.00 – 600.00.

1920s turban pin. Antiqued gold-tone pot metal with prong-set golden yellow rhinestones. The center is molded plastic. Unsigned. $55.00 – 75.00.

Victorian revival brooch. Antiqued gilded brass with intricate design work. Oval-cut unfoiled large simulated aquamarines. 2½" x 2½". Early 1930s. Unmarked. $200.00 – 275.00.

Sash pins, circa 1905 – 1910. Each is made of heavy brass. Left pin is 2" x 3½" with three bezel-set foil-backed sapphire glass stones. Middle pin is a 1¼" x 2½" rectangle with a vine design done in repoussé. Bezel-set coral glass cabochon. Right pin is 1½" x 2½" with fancy leaf and scroll design done in repoussé. Large bezel-set antique square-cut simulated citrine. Marked G.C.H. $95.00 – 125.00 each.

Circa 1910 – 1920s lace pin. Gilded brass set with oval-cut simulated amethyst (unfoiled). 1¼" x 1½". Unmarked. $75.00 – 95.00.

1930s cushion brooch. Bezel-set oval and round-cut rhinestones in sapphire and aquamarine (foil backed). Gilded brass. 2½" x 2½". Unmarked. $175.00 – 250.00.

Circa 1900 – 1910 brooch. Gilded brass with repoussé work. Large garnet glass oval-cut stone (unfoiled). 2¾" x 3½". Unsigned. $125.00 – 200.00.

Large 1930s pot metal brooch. Gold plated. Large oval-cut foil-backed amethyst glass stones. All prong set. Signed, however the mark is illegible. 1¾" x 3½". $75.00 – 125.00.

Trifari swirl pin. Glued-in simulated pearls and clear baguette-cut rhinestones (foil backed). Gold trifanium plated. 2¼" long. $65.00 – 85.00.

From the collection of Koral Michael Whalton

Etched gold-tone bouquet. Simulated pearls. Rhodium-plated accents set with clear rhinestones. Marked Boucher 7775P. 2¼" wide. $125.00 – 175.00.

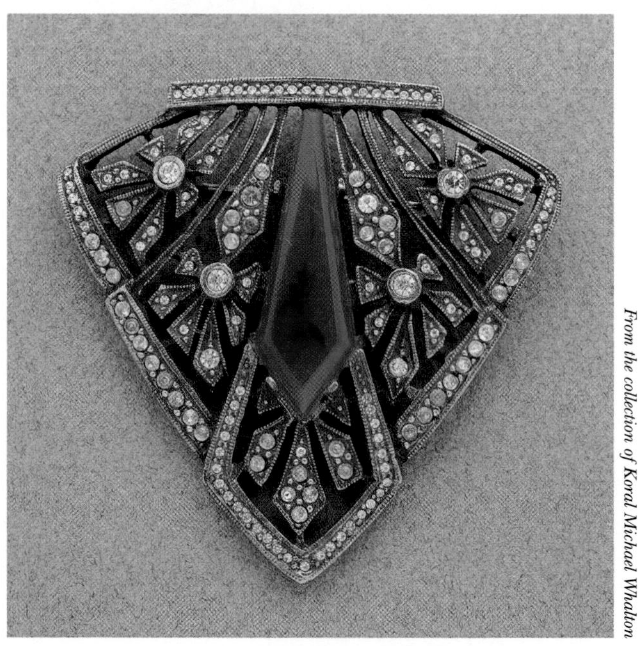

From the collection of Koral Michael Whalton

Deco-style brooch by Les Bernard. Antiqued gold tone with clear rhinestone accents and an amber colored molded plastic center stone. 2½" x 2½". $200.00 – 275.00.

Brooch in a gold-plated swirl design with large simulated pearls. 1960s. 1¾" x 2½". Faux pearls are ¾" in diameter. Unsigned. $75.00 – 100.00.

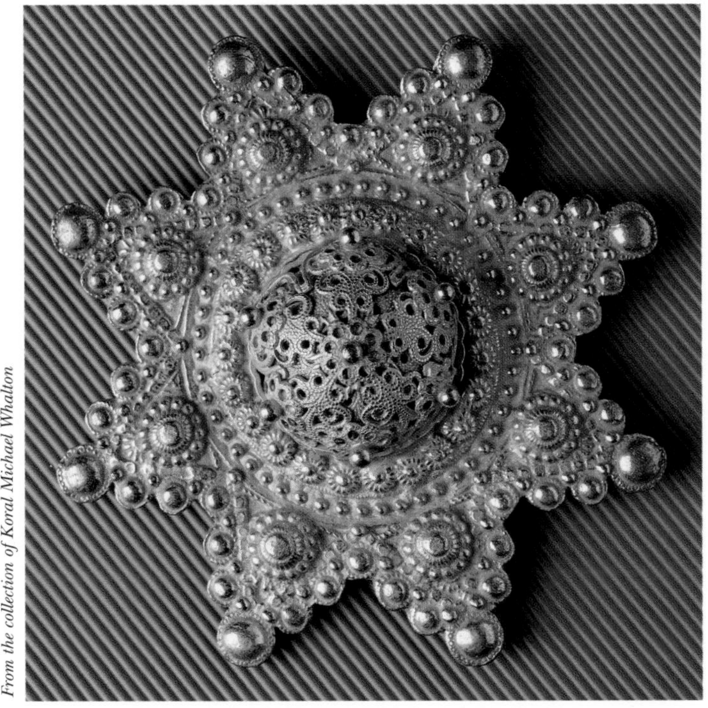

From the collection of Koral Michael Whalton

Extremely rare Adele Simpson sachet brooch. Gilded brass star with Middle Eastern influence. Shown front and back with the sachet opened. Marked Adele Simpson C-771-4905 (hand signed – etched into the metal). 3½" in diameter. $1,000.00 – 1,200.00.

From the collection of Koral Michael Whalton

Pair of Jomaz pins. Left pin: Gold-plated peacock. Clear pavé rhinestone head, neck, and body. Tail feathers in blue and green enamel with prong-set sapphire blue rhinestones. 2¼". $250.00 – 325.00. Right pin: Gold- and rhodium-plated daisy with pavé clear rhinestones. 2½" in diameter. $200.00 – 275.00.Both from the 1960s.

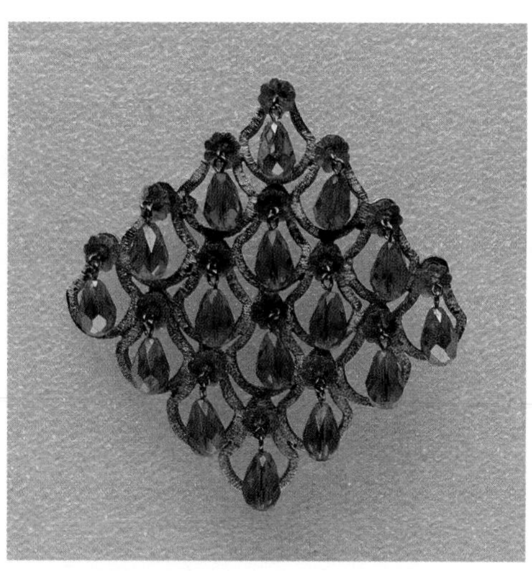

Vendome pin. Gold tone with fuchsia pink Austrian crystal aurora borealis dangling teardrop beads. 1950s. 2½" x 2½". $125.00 – 175.00.

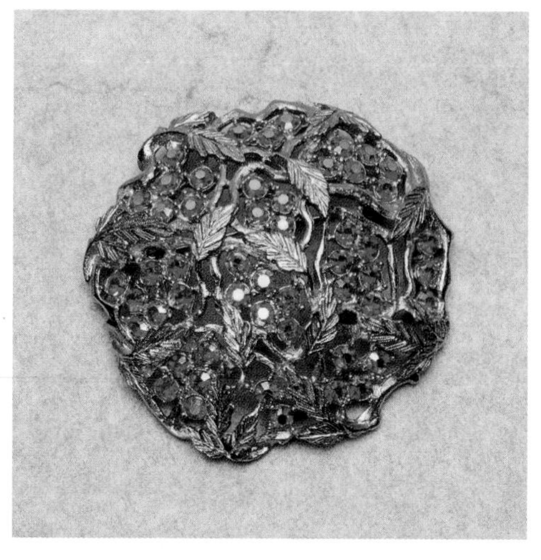

Grapevine brooch. Gold-tone metal vines and leaves with aurora borealis rhinestone grapes (the rhinestones are glued in). Late 1950s to early 1960s. Marked Sarah Cov. 2¼" x 2¼". $65.00 – 95.00.

From the collection of Koral Michael Whalon

Kenneth J. Lane — large brooch that makes a statement! Gold plated with pavé clear rhinestones. Four deep blue molded plastic ridged ovals. Signed K.J.L. (Kenneth J. Lane). 1960s. 3¼" x 3¼". $300.00 – 450.00.

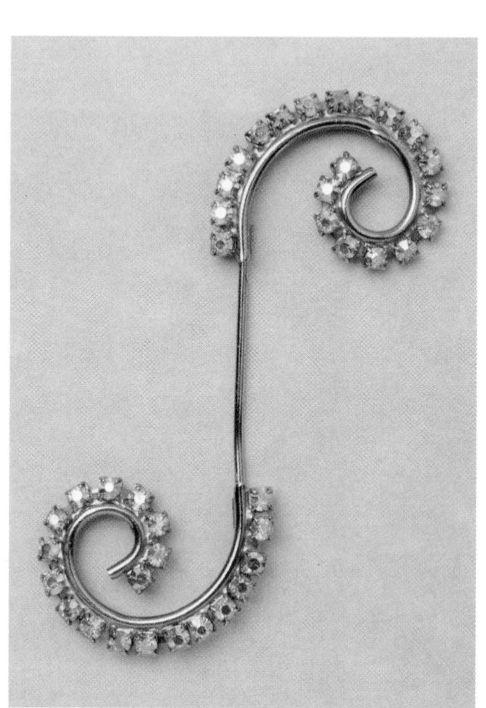

1950s hat/jabot pin. Gold-plated swirl design with prong-set Austrian aurora borealis rhinestones. One end screws into the pin shaft. Unsigned. $45.00 – 65.00.

Unsigned centipede-style brooch from the 1950s. Frosted purple glass marquise-cut rhinestones, and pink round and marquise-cut cabochons. The spine is clear and aurora borealis prong-set rhinestones. Gold plated. 3¼". $50.00 – 65.00.

Brooch of superior quality. The foil-backed glass stones are stunning. Five large pink oval-cut rhinestones, lime green marquise and chaton-cut rhinestones, and golden yellow chaton-cut rhinestones. All rhinestones are prong set. Gold plated. 1950s – 1960s. Unsigned — probably a designer brooch. 2¼" x 2¼". $175.00 – 225.00.

From the collection of Koral Michael Whalton

Unusual Austrian crystal cushion brooch. Multicolor glass stones, unfoiled. Large rose-cut faux citrine, fuchsia and amethyst rhinestones. Smaller chaton-cut rhinestones in pink and pale blue. Marquise-cut rhinestones in pink, sapphire, light green, pale yellow, sky blue, amethyst, and emerald green. All rhinestones are prong set. Note there are as many diverse settings as stones! Unsigned, but fabulous! 2¾" x 2". $190.00 – 250.00.

Large and flashy rhinestone-encrusted cushion brooch. Gold plated. The outer edge of the brooch is done in prong-set deep turquoise marquise-cut rhinestones. The center is done in a conglomeration of the following rhinestones: blue chaton cut aurora borealis, sapphire blue rose cut, pale blue chaton cut, lime green marquise cut, and marquise-cut glass simulated turquoise. 1950s. 3¼" in diameter. Unmarked. $225.00 – 275.00.

Florenza pin. Antiqued gold tone with simulated pearls and frosted purple glass cabochons. Chaton-cut rhinestones in lavender, amethyst, and emerald-green. All stones and simulated pearls are glued in. 1¾". Late 1950s to early 1960s. $40.00 – 65.00.

Rhinestone pyramid pin. Silver-tone base metal. Prong-set pale yellow chaton and marquise-cut rhinestones (unfoiled). Small prong-set chaton-cut aurora borealis rhinestones (foil backed). 1950s. 2¼" x 2¼". Unmarked. $70.00 – 85.00.

1950s cushion-style flower brooch. Center of the flower is smoky gray rhinestones in a cluster setting. First layer of flower petals is bottle green marquise-cut rhinestones. Bottom layer is smoky gray marquise-cut and bottle green chaton-cut rhinestones. The marquise-cut stones are the only ones that are not foil backed. All rhinestones are prong set. Gold plated. 2¼" x 2¼". Unsigned. $55.00 – 80.00.

1950s cushion pin in shades of brown. Deep brown marquise-cut rhinestones, chaton-cut golden brown rhinestones, and smaller chaton-cut aurora borealis rhinestones. Three large brown simulated mabé pearls in the center. The pearls and rhinestones are prong set. Gold plated. Unsigned. 2" x 2". $40.00 – 55.00.

Pinwheel cluster brooch. Antiqued gold-tone metal with simulated pearls, apple green rhinestones, Venetian glass beads, aurora borealis rhinestones, pear-cut tourmaline domed glass, topaz pear-cut rhinestones, apple green prystal beads, and antiqued gold-tone flowers. 2½" x 2½". 1950s. Unmarked. $55.00 – 70.00.

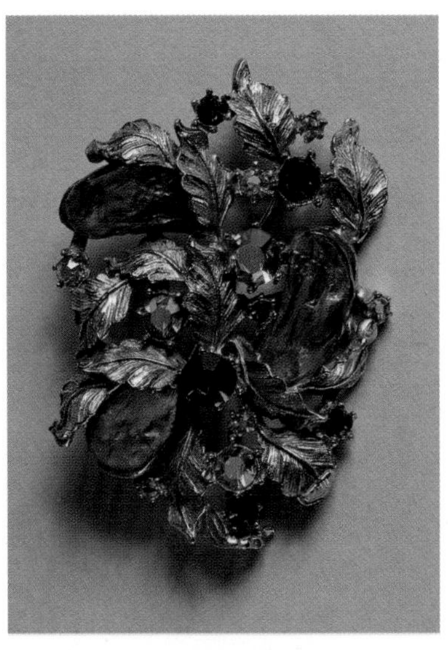

HAR pin with gold-plated leaves intertwined with three golden brown pearlized "beans." Aurora borealis and deep brown rhinestones. Faux prong settings. (Prongs are there, but they are not used to hold the stone in place. Instead, the stones are glued in.) 2¼" x 2¾". 1950s – 1960s. $75.00 – 95.00.

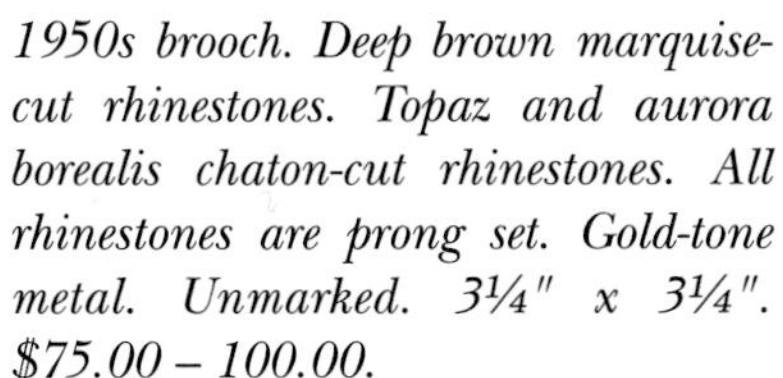

1950s brooch. Deep brown marquise-cut rhinestones. Topaz and aurora borealis chaton-cut rhinestones. All rhinestones are prong set. Gold-tone metal. Unmarked. 3¼" x 3¼". $75.00 – 100.00.

From the collection of Koral Michael Whalton

Schreiner filigree oval brooch/pendant. Gold plated. Blue topaz, peridot, and amethyst rhinestones, all set inverted (a Schreiner signature technique). Faux amber oval-cut cabochon in the center (glass). Marked Schreiner New York. 2½" long x 2¼" wide. $275.00 – 350.00.

Regency cushion brooch with rhinestones in harvest colors. Rhinestones are in pear, marquise, chaton, and oval cuts. All rhinestones are of excellent quality and all are prong set. Antiqued brass. 2" x 2½". Signed Regency Jewels. $110.00 – 135.00.

From the collection of Koral Michael Whalton

Collection of Maltese crosses. Left to right, top to bottom: Emmons gold-tone filigree Maltese cross. Marquise-cut and chaton-cut rhinestones in orange. Chaton-cut rhinestones in olive green. 2¼" in diameter. $75.00 – 100.00. Florenza antiqued gold-plated Maltese cross pin/pendant. Large round-cut brown rhinestone in the center and four pear-cut rhinestones in the same color. Four black pear-cut rhinestones and clear chaton-cut rhinestone accents. 2¾" in diameter. $150.00 – 190.00. Gold-plated Maltese cross with red enamel and red velvet. Red rhinestones, simulated seed pearls, turquoise glass beads, and central turquoise glass cabochon. Marked Art. 2" in diameter. $95.00 – 120.00. Accessocraft Maltese cross. Antiqued gold plate in a knobby design with a large antique square-cut bottle green glass rhinestone center (unfoiled). 2½" in diameter. $300.00 – 375.00. Large pavé rhinestone Maltese cross. Large green cabochon in the center encircled by smaller green glass cabochons. Gilded brass. Signed K.J.L. (Kenneth J. Lane). 2¾" in diameter. $325.00 – 400.00.

Large Oriental inspired brooch. Gold plated with green plastic used to imitate carved jade. The central design is an openwork swan or crane. 1950s – 1960s. The top of the brooch is 2½" in diameter and the drop is 1½" in diameter, the whole brooch is 4¼" long. Signed Hattie Carnegie. $275.00 – 375.00.

Nugget-style star brooch. Antiqued gold-tone base metal. Center is a large green glass round-cut rhinestone (foil-backed). 3" x 3¾". Marked Capri. 1960s. $70.00 – 90.00.

From the collection of Koral Michael Whalton

More Maltese crosses! Left to right, top to bottom: Regency Maltese cross pin. Gold plated with large chaton-cut sapphire blue central rhinestone. Smaller sapphire chaton-cut rhinestones and light blue marquise-cut rhinestones cover the rest of the pin. All rhinestones are prong set. 2" in diameter. $125.00 – 175.00. Weiss antiqued silver-tone Maltese cross pin. 2" in diameter. Twisted rope design frame. Sapphire blue rhinestones in chaton and marquise cuts. Sky blue aurora borealis marquise-cut rhinestones. All rhinestones are glued in. 1960s. $115.00 – 140.00 Silver-tone Weiss Maltese cross pin. Round and oval-cut black glass cabochons, simulated pearls, and pale gray rhinestones. All prong set. 2¼" in diameter. 1960s. $125.00 – 150.00.

1960s asymmetrical star pin. Gold plated with prong-set rose-cut simulated citrine. The rhinestone is unfoiled. 2" x 3¼". Marked Van S Authentics 2477. $110.00 – 125.00.

Unusual pin in a coral branch design. Gold plated. Concave glass center with watermelon tourmaline colors. The tips of the branches are set with clear rhinestones. Unsigned. 1¾" x 2". 1960s. $50.00 – 75.00.

Late 1930s to early 1940s clip/brooch. Retro floral spray. Gold plated. Oval-cut unfoiled rhinestones of excellent quality in amethyst, ruby, sapphire, aquamarine, and citrine. Tiny prong-set clear rhinestone accents. 4" long. Unmarked. $225.00 – 375.00.

From the collection of Koral Michael Whalton

Retro swirling ribbon brooch. Gold-plated base metal. Large oval-cut simulated citrine (foil backed). Six oval-cut simulated emeralds (unfoiled). Clear rhinestone accents. Late 1930s – early 1940s. Unsigned. 2" wide x 3¼" long. $250.00 – 375.00.

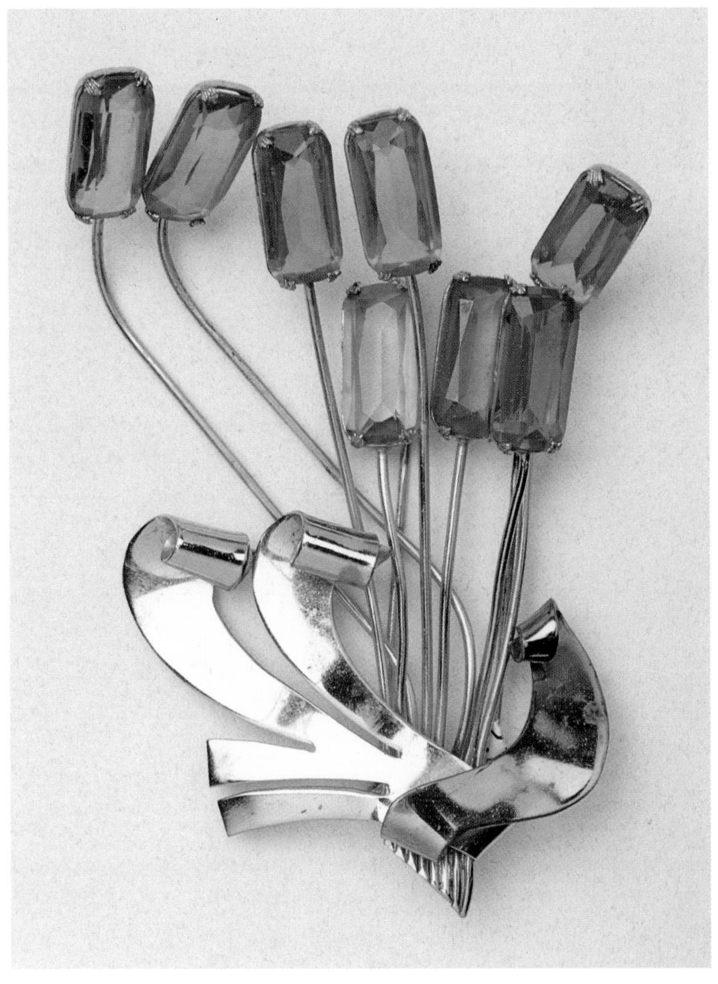

Large retro clip/brooch. Rose and yellow gold plated. Eight rectangular-cut faux topazes. All stones are prong-set and unfoiled. Marked Coro. 2¾" x 4". 1940s. $150.00 – 200.00.

From the collection of Koral Michael Whalton

Ralph DeRosa retro floral clip/brooch. Two rectangular-cut simulated Burmese rubies. Clear rhinestone accents. Gold vermeil over sterling. Marked R. DeRosa and hallmarked sterling. 1940s. 2¼" wide x 2¾" long. $650.00 – 725.00.

Floral spray brooch in original box. Rose gold-plated flowers and bow. Yellow gold-plated stems. The center of each flower is rhodium plated with clear rhinestones and larger central red rhinestones. 3½". Unsigned. $75.00 – 100.00. This brooch has been passed down through three generations of the Author's family.

Etched gold-plated bow. Black molded plastic beads and tear drop, simulated pearls, and rhinestone rondelle. Marked Hattie Carnegie. 2½" x 3½". $125.00 – 150.00.

Retro bow brooch. Gold vermeil over sterling silver. Large square-cut simulated topaz. The brooch has tiny piercework bows. 1940s. 2½" x 3¼". Marked Reja and hallmarked sterling. $200.00 – 300.00.

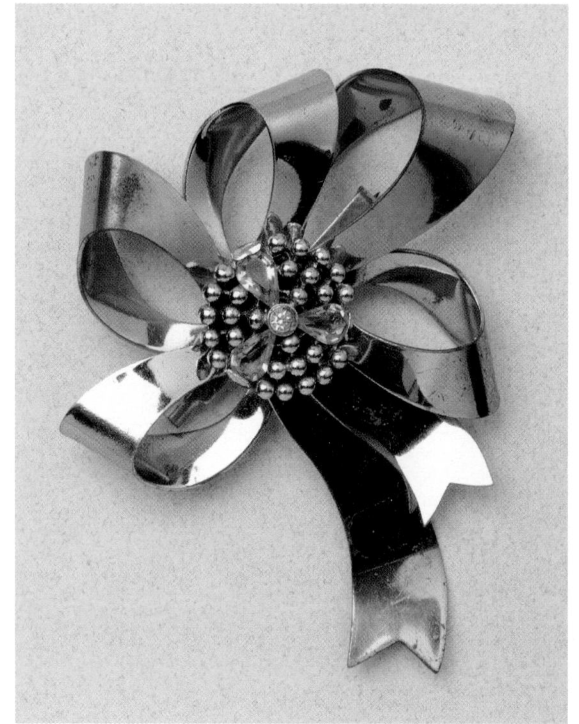

Early 1940s bow with moveable ribbons and streamers. Three lime green pear-cut rhinestones accent the center which has silver beading. Ribbon in yellow gold-plated metal, silver-plated metal, and copper. Unsigned. 2¼" x 3¼". $130.00 – 175.00.

From the collection of Koral Michael Whalton

1930s flower brooch. Pavé rhinestone stem, leaves, and flower center. Petals are foil-backed marquise-cut amethyst, citrine, emerald, sapphire, and ruby rhinestones (prong set). Silver-tone pot metal. Unsigned. 3½" long. $225.00 – 300.00.

1930s pot-metal brooches. Top to bottom: Floral brooch with clear pavé rhinestones on stems and leaves. Antique square-cut simulated aquamarine flowers (unfoiled). Unmarked. 2¾" x 3¾". $225.00 – 300.00. Floral brooch tied with a bow — a popular 1930s design. Prong-set marquise-cut clear rhinestones (foil backed). Clear pavé rhinestones on stems, leaves, and bow. Unsigned. 2½" x 4". $150.00 – 225.00.

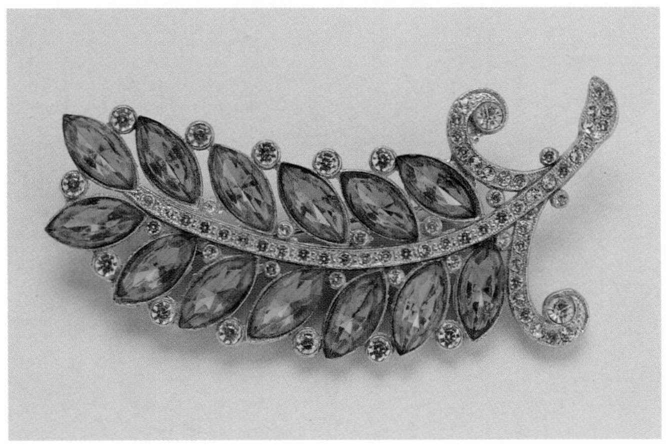

1930s leaf brooch. Turquoise colored glass marquise-cut rhinestones (foil backed). Clear pavé rhinestones on stem and leaves. Silver-tone pot metal. 3½" long. Unsigned. $150.00 – 225.00.

From the collection of Koral Michael Whalton

1930s feather brooches. Top: Silver-tone base metal with clear pavé rhinestones and blue rose-cut glass aquamarines. Unsigned. Each brooch is 3¾" long. Bottom: Silver-plated base metal with clear pavé rhinestones and blue glass moonstone cabochons. $175.00 – 250.00 each.

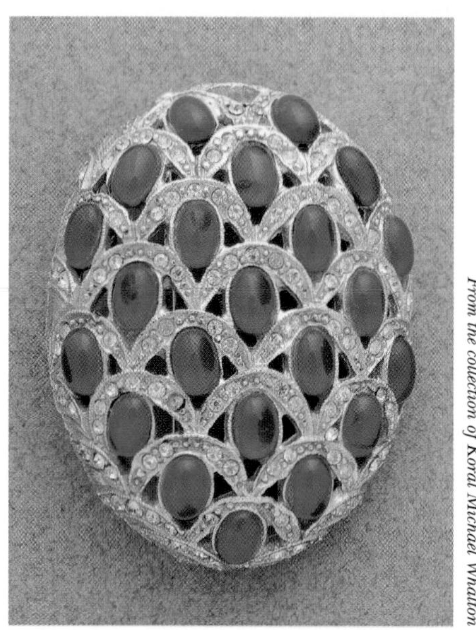

From the collection of Koral Michael Whalton

Oval cushion pin. Rhodium plated with clear pavé rhinestones and red glass oval-cut cabochons. Marked Les Bernard Inc. 1¾" long x 1¼" wide. $200.00 – 250.00.

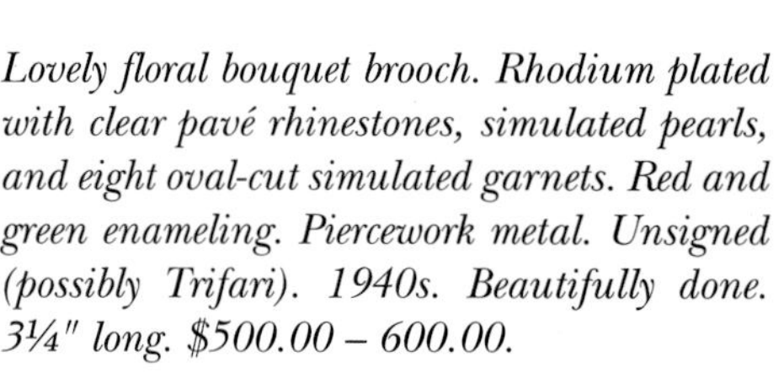

Lovely floral bouquet brooch. Rhodium plated with clear pavé rhinestones, simulated pearls, and eight oval-cut simulated garnets. Red and green enameling. Piercework metal. Unsigned (possibly Trifari). 1940s. Beautifully done. 3¼" long. $500.00 – 600.00.

From the collection of Koral Michael Whalton

From the collection of Koral Michael Whalton

1930s pot-metal flower brooch. Lucite rhinestones in plum and clear. The plum rhinestones are prong set and the rest are glued in. Unsigned. 4" long. $130.00 – 175.00.

From the collection of Koral Michael Whalton

1930s wreath brooch. Pink and deep plum oval-cut rhinestones and clear pavé rhinestones (all foil backed). Base metal. Unsigned, but resembles some of the early work done by Eisenberg. 2" x 3". $225.00 – 275.00.

From the collection of Koral Michael Whalton

Trio of clear Austrian crystal rhinestone brooches. Left to right: Eisenberg. Rhodium plated. 2¼" l x 1½" w. Ribbon loop set with clear chaton and emerald-cut rhinestones. 1950s. Has original box (not shown). $350.00 – 475.00. Eisenberg brooch in a twist design. Pear and chaton-cut clear rhinestones. Top: large rhinestone is tapered oval cut. 3" long. 1950s. $425.00 – 525.00. Grape cluster brooch. Clear chaton, marquise and pear-cut rhinestones. Rhodium plated. Stem and vine in clear pavé rhinestones. Marked Weiss. 1950s. 2½" l x 1½" w. $175.00 – 225.00.

Trio of clear rhinestone brooches. Left to right: Late 1930s Eisenberg (script "E") brooch set with high quality, clear Austrian crystal rhinestones. 2" x 2¼" spoke and ribbon design. $500.00 – 650.00. Eisenberg Ice brooch in a swirled leaf design. Rhodium plated. Foil-backed rhinestones. 2" x 2½". A newer Eisenberg from the 1980s. $200.00 – 275.00. Pavé brooch. Free-form floral spray with ribbon. Rhodium-plated set with high quality clear Austrian crystal rhinestones. Marked, but illegible. Possibly Eisenberg. $700.00 – 825.00.

Massive 1930s leaf brooch, 3½" x 5½". Pavé clear Austrian crystal rhinestones with larger pear and marquise-cut clear rhinestones. All rhinestones are of excellent quality. Unsigned Eisenberg. $800.00 – 1,000.00.

From the collection of Koral Michael Whalton

Three Eisenberg Original clips. All Eisenberg jewelry must be seen in person to be believed — the stones are always of the most fantastic quality. The ever-present, large Austrian crystal rhinestones with the highest refractive quality. Eisenberg jewelry is almost always recognizable on sight without even looking for the mark! Left to right: 3¼" long clip with emerald, star, chaton, marquise, and oval-cut rhinestones. Silver-tone base metal. Marked Eisenberg Original with the number 3. 1930s to pre-war 1940s. $600.00 – 800.00. 2½" clip of predominantly oval-cut rhinestones with pear, five-facet, and marquise-cut rhinestones at the top. The large stones are all prong-set and the small accent stones are bezel-set. Signed Eisenberg Original and hallmarked sterling. 1940s. $600.00 – 800.00. Massive clip set with seven large tapering oval-cut rhinestones and small chaton-cut rhinestone accents. Silver-tone base metal. 3½" long. Marked Eisenberg Original and the letter "N." 1930s to pre-war 1940s. $900.00 – 1,200.00.

From the collection of Koral Michael Whalton

1940s brooch of a free-form leaf tied with a bow. Sterling silver with clear chaton-cut rhinestones on the vein and stem. One large antique square-cut rhinestone of excellent quality (unfoiled). 3½" long. Hallmarked sterling. \$200.00 – 300.00.

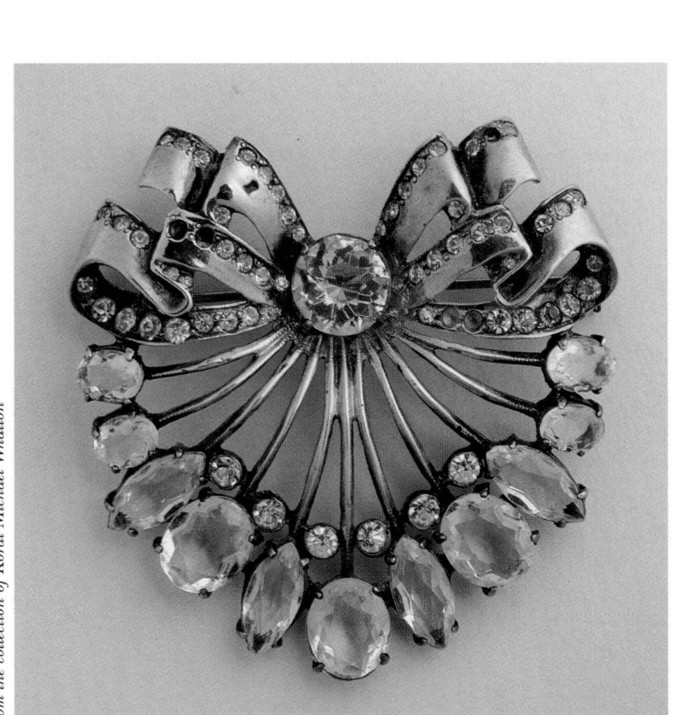

From the collection of Koral Michael Whalton

Eisenberg sterling silver bow/fan brooch. Pale aquamarine blue unfoiled rhinestones in marquise, oval, and round cuts. Small clear rhinestone accents. Marked Eisenberg Original and hallmarked sterling. 2½" x 2½". Late 1930s to early 1940s. \$1,000.00 – 1,200.00.

Rhodium-plated brooch with clear pavé rhinestones, clear marquise-cut rhinestones and large central pear-cut glass sapphire. All stones are prong set (including the tiny pavé rhinestones). The quality look of genuine jewelry! Signed Polcini. 1¾" x 2¼". \$225.00 – 300.00.

1950s pin done in the Art Nouveau style. Pewter with round and oval-cut sapphire blue glass cabochons. Marked Made in Austria. 2" x 2". \$65.00 – 85.00.

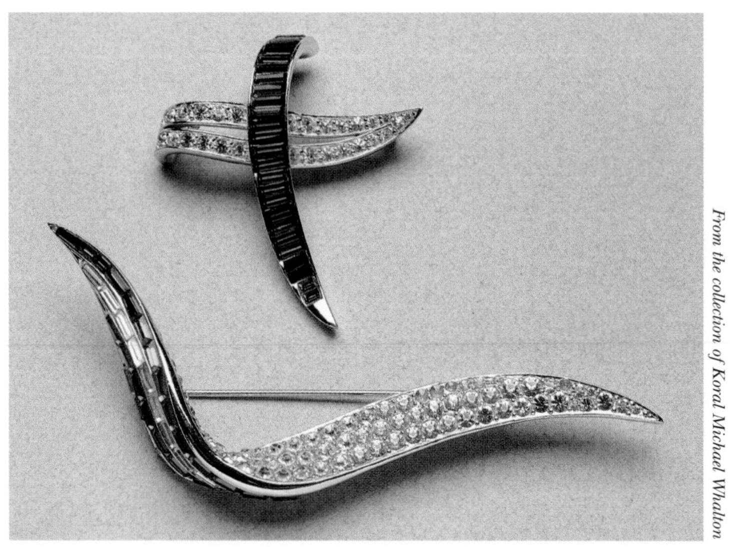

From the collection of Koral Michael Whalton

Top to bottom: Boucher "X" brooch. Rhodium plated. Half of the "X" is clear pavé rhinestones and the other half is sapphire blue rhinestone baguettes. 2¼" x 2". Marked Boucher 6565. $375.00 – 425.00. Art Moderne feather brooch. Rhodium plated. One side is done in clear pavé rhinestones and the other side is done in sapphire blue and clear baguettes. Marked Jaclyn Canada 8027. 4½" long. $325.00 – 400.00.

1930s pin. Oxidized silver-tone base metal filigree. Pink and clear chaton-cut rhinestones and aqua marquise-cut rhinestones (all prong set). Unmarked. $55.00 – 80.00.

From the collection of Koral Michael Whalton

1950s Eisenberg wreath pin. Rhodium plated. Prong-set clear and sapphire blue chaton-cut Austrian crystal rhinestones of excellent quality. 2½" x 2". $400.00 – 500.00.

Breathtaking fur clip. Pavé clear rhinestones with glass cabochon blue moonstones and clear marquise-cut rhinestones. All stones are of excellent quality. Rhodium plated. Mid-1930s. 2¼" x 2¾". Unmarked, but an extremely desirable piece. $450.00 – 600.00.

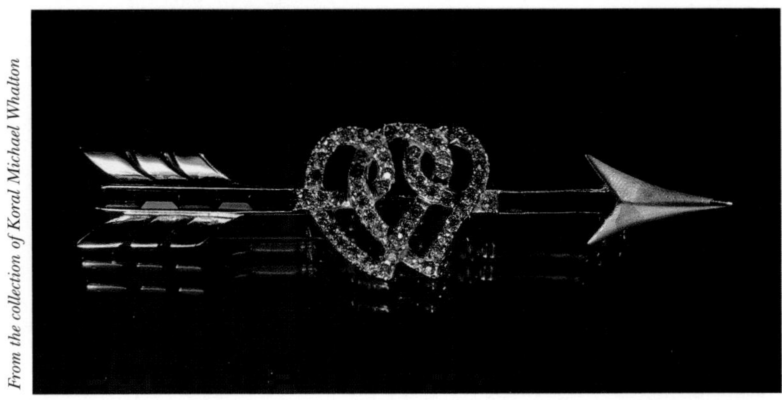

From the collection of Koral Michael Whalton

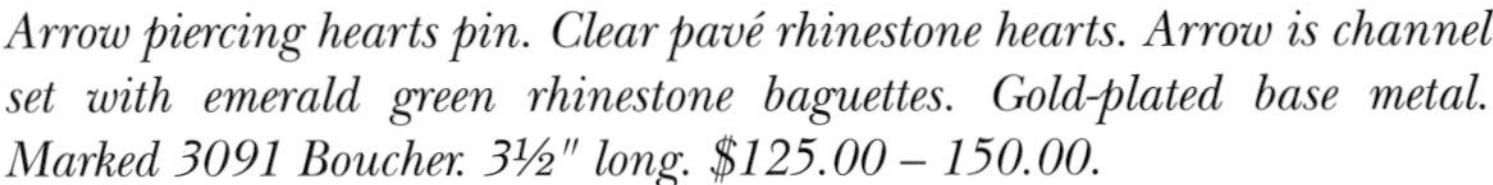

Arrow piercing hearts pin. Clear pavé rhinestone hearts. Arrow is channel set with emerald green rhinestone baguettes. Gold-plated base metal. Marked 3091 Boucher. 3½" long. $125.00 – 150.00.

From the collection of Koral Michael Whalton

Hobé cameo pin. Chromium plated. Pale yellow and clear chaton-cut rhinestones and smoky gray marquise-cut rhinestones. Cameo of carved mother-of-pearl. 1950s. 1¾" l x 1½" w. $150.00 – 225.00.

From the collection of Koral Michael Whalton

Four Miriam Haskell pins. Left to right and top to bottom: Simulated seed pearl flower with tiny white seed bead veins. Prong-set central chaton-cut pink rhinestone surrounded by simulated pearls. 1¾" in diameter. Antiqued silver-tone filigree crescent pin. Simulated baroque and seed pearls. 2". Antiqued gilded brass filigree cushion pin. Simulated pearls and prong-set chaton-cut clear rhinestones surrounded by tiny gilded brass stamped flowers. 2½" in diameter. Round gilded brass filigree pin. Three emerald-cut pink rhinestones. Pink glass beaded flowers with rhinestone rose monteé-cut centers. 1¾" in diameter. $125.00 – 175.00 each.

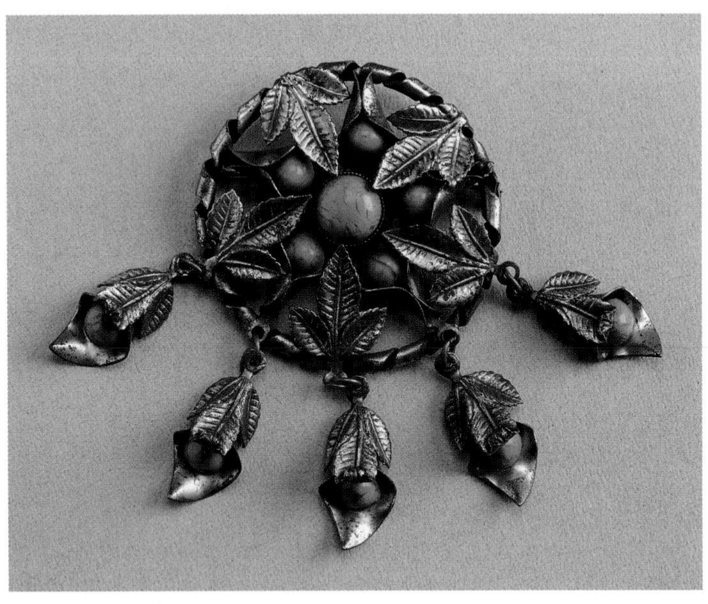

Silver-tone base metal pin with glass simulated turquoise. 2½" in diameter round pin with silver-tone leaves and five drops makes this pin a total of 4" long. Unsigned, possibly Middle Eastern. $75.00 – 125.00.

Victorian style Scottish agate pin. Silver-tone metal set with genuine agate. Signed Miracle. 2" in diameter. $70.00 – 90.00.

1950s crescent pin. Chromium plated. Blue and apple green pear-cut rhinestones and chaton-cut aurora borealis rhinestones. All rhinestones are prong set. Beautiful color combination. 3¼". $75.00 – 100.00.

Sarah Coventry abstract cushion brooch. Rhodium plated with clear chaton-cut rhinestones (glued in). $55.00 – 75.00.

Lisner question mark pin. Rhodium plated. Rhinestones in pastel shades of green, blue, yellow, pink, lavender, and aurora borealis. All prong set. 2½" long. $85.00 – 115.00.

Art Deco-style pin. Rhodium plated with glued-in clear rhinestone accents. Four black plastic cabochons. Five triangular dangles with clear rhinestones. 2¼" x 3¼". Marked Sarah (Sarah Coventry). Sarah Coventry is becoming more collectible as the years go by. $65.00 – 95.00.

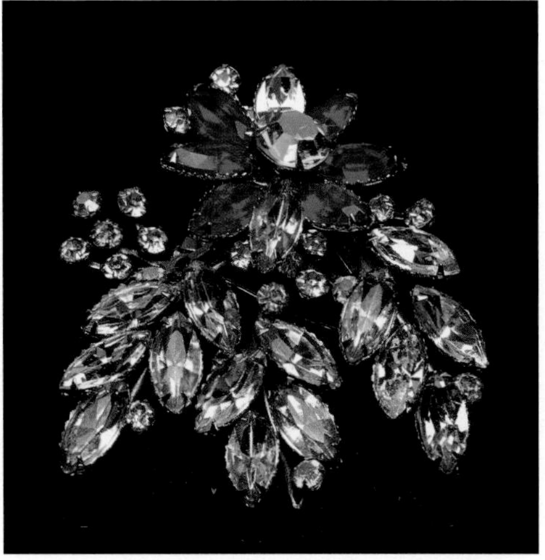

1950s floral brooch. Silver-tone stamped metal with prong-set clear marquise and chaton-cut clear and aurora borealis rhinestones, red marquise-cut rhinestones, and one large aurora borealis chaton-cut rhinestone in the middle of the flower. 2¾". Unmarked. $75.00 – 90.00.

Grouping of clear rhinestone brooches. Left to right and top to bottom: Beautiful, three-dimensional bow brooch with a tiny cluster of flowers in the center. Rhodium plated with clear chaton-cut and baguette rhinestones. 2¼" wide. Signed Mazer and 22. $300.00 – 400.00. 1950s Eisenberg pin. Rhodium-plated swirl with chaton, round rose, and marquise-cut rhinestones. All rhinestones are prong set. Signed Eisenberg in block letters. $125.00 – 175.00. Large and heavy brooch. Rhodium plated with clear emerald, chaton, oval, and marquise-cut rhinestones. All rhinestones are glued in. 3" in diameter. Signed Coro. $95.00 – 115.00. 1950s leaf brooch. Silver-tone with glued-in marquise and chaton cut rhinestones. 3" long. $75.00 – 100.00. Beautiful 1930s pin. Silver-tone base metal with emerald, chaton, and square-cut rhinestones of excellent quality. All rhinestones are glued in. Unsigned. $90.00 – 115.00. Rhodium-plated grapevine and grapes pin/pendant. Chaton and marquise-cut rhinestones. All rhinestones are prong set. 2¼" x 2¼". Marked Krementz. $100.00 – 125.00.

1950s star pin. Chromium plated. Prong-set amethyst rhinestones in pear, chaton, and emerald cuts. Lavender chaton-cut accents. 2". Unmarked. $35.00 – 60.00.

Judy Lee floral brooch. Silver-tone stamped metal. Simulated baroque pearls, marquise-cut clear rhinestones, and chaton-cut aurora borealis rhinestones. 1950s. 4" x 2½". $80.00 – 110.00.

Two black enameled pins set with black glass rhinestones. The round spoke design pin is 2½" in diameter and is unmarked. The feather pin is marled Weiss. 2½" long. $65.00 – 155.00.

Coral enameled ribbon-star. Chaton and marquise-cut smoky brown topaz rhinestones (glued in). Unmarked. Late 1950s to early 1960s. 2½" in diameter. $50.00 – 70.00.

Lisner fleur-di-lis pin. White enameling with chaton-cut black glass rhinestones. 2¾" long. 1950s. $75.00 – 90.00.

From the collection of Koral Michael Whalton

Weiss square pin. Gun-metal plated. Covered in prong-set rhinestones in shades of ice blue, sapphire blue, Prussian blue, and royal blue. Rhinestones and glass cabochons in every cut imaginable! 2" x 2". $225.00 – 300.00.

From the collection of Koral Michael Whalton

1950s iridescent circle pin. Gun-metal plated. Prong-set chaton-cut red rhinestones and marquise-cut red aurora borealis rhinestones. All rhinestones are Austrian crystal of the finest quality. The pin is 2¾" in diameter and signed Sherman (a Canadian company). $100.00 – 175.00.

Karu-Arke pin. Japanned square with branches encircling rhinestones in shades of golden yellow and aurora borealis. All rhinestones are glued in. 2". $50.00 – 70.00.

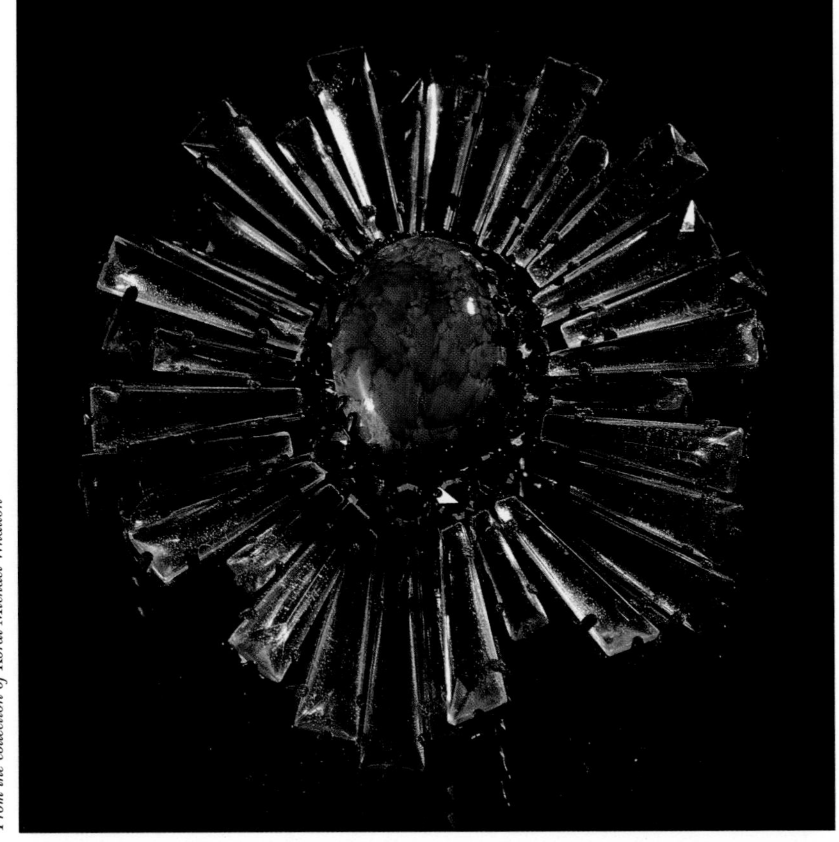

From the collection of Koral Michael Whalton

Schreiner keystone-ruffle pin. Gun-metal plated. Prong-set keystone-cut clear rhinestones. Tan and purple marbleized ceramic cabochon in the center surrounded by inverted-set smoky brown topaz rhinestones. 3¼" long x 2¾" wide. $300.00 – 375.00.

From the collection of Koral Michael Whalton

Miriam Haskell barbaric ham bone brooch. Gilded brass filigree, glass simulated coral, and glass simulated bone chips. The two ham bones are genuine bone (however, doubtfully from the ham!). 4½" long. $400.00 – 600.00.

From the collection of Koral Michael Whalton

Hattie Carnegie cluster brooch. Unusual color combination. Large round star-cut orange rhinestone in the center surrounded by coral glass beads and coral glass oval-cut cabochons, simulated pearls, purple round rose-cut rhinestones, and clear chaton-cut rhinestone accents. Gold plated. 2¼" in diameter. $300.00 – 425.00.

From the collection of Koral Michael Whalton

Robert DeMario cluster wreath. Gilded brass filigree, gilded brass leaves, black glass faceted teardrops, and black glass seed beads. 2½" x 3". $275.00 – 350.00.

From the collection of Koral Michael Whalton

Miriam Haskell chandelier brooch. Gilded brass filigree, rose monteé cut clear rhinestones, three clear Lucite accents set with clear chaton-cut rhinestones, and three crystal chandelier drops with gilded brass caps. Very unusual! 4" long x 2¼" wide. $600.00 – 700.00.

From the collection of Koral Michael Whalton

DeMario leaf cluster pin. Gilded brass leaves with tan enameling. Prong-set chaton-cut smoky topaz rhinestones. 2½" x 2". Signed Robert DeMario New York. $200.00 – 300.00.

From the collection of Koral Michael Whalton

Eisenberg sterling brooch and clip. Left: 2½" x 2½" cornucopia brooch. Gold vermeil over sterling silver. Six prong-set triangular-cut topaz rhinestones across the top and one large one in the center. Bezel-set clear rhinestone chaton-cut accents. Unfoiled rhinestones. Signed Eisenberg Original (7) and hallmarked sterling. Right: 3" long x 2½" wide spoke design clip. Gold vermeil over sterling silver. Seven oval-cut light golden topaz foil-backed rhinestones across the bottom and a larger one in the center. Two star-cut deep golden topaz rhinestones at the top. Chaton-cut clear rhinestone accents. Signed Eisenberg Original (34) and hallmarked sterling. $1,000.00 – 1,200.00 each.

Courtesy of The Glass Spoon

Unsigned 1950s bracelets. Left: Gold-plated bracelet with tapering lozenge-cut purple rhinestones and chaton-cut aurora borealis rhinestones. Small lavender chaton-cut rhinestone accents. All rhinestones are prong set. $90.00 – 125.00. Right: Stunning wide rhinestone bracelet. Gold plated with prong-set chaton-cut rhinestones in deep purple, lavender, and purple aurora borealis. Unsigned, but probably a designer piece. $200.00 – 300.00.

Miriam Haskell bracelet. Four strands of light and bright aqua crystal beads. Gilded brass filigree clasp set with bright aqua glass beads and prong-set rhinestones in coordinating color. Safety catch chain. $250.00 – 350.00.

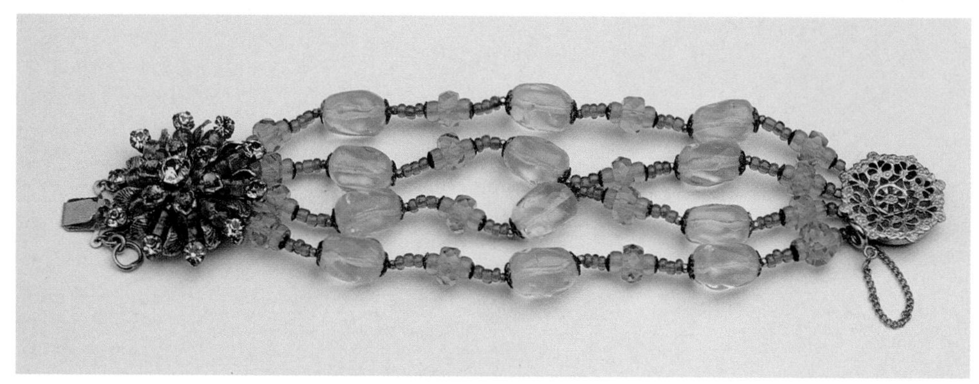
From the collection of Koral Michael Whalon

From the collection of Koral Michael Whalton

Stunning Elsa Schiaparelli bracelet. Five strands of emerald green Austrian crystal beads. Fancy 2" wide floral clasp with a cluster of the same beads and flower petals of marquise-cut aurora borealis rhinestones. The clasp is chromium plated. Safety catch chain. Marked Schiaparelli. 1950s. $500.00 – 600.00.

From the collection of Koral Michael Whalton

Unsigned Eisenberg bracelet from the 1930s. Gold vermeil over sterling silver. Round rose-cut golden yellow unfoiled rhinestones and clear rhinestone accents. ¼" wide. Hallmarked sterling. $500.00 – 600.00.

Unusual 1950s bracelet. Molded plastic three-dimensional spiraled circles in beige with gold (they look like miniature wedding cakes!), beige pear-cut frosted glass, and chaton-cut peach aurora borealis rhinestones. Gold plated. Unsigned, but probably a designer piece. 1¼" wide. Safety catch chain. $100.00 – 200.00.

Unsigned 1950s bracelet. Gold-plated scroll-work design with glued-in red aurora borealis chaton-cut rhinestones. Safety catch chain. 1" wide. Resembles work done by Coro. $55.00 – 80.00.

1950s chunky, funky bracelet. Gold plated with ceramic and glass simulated lapis lazuli, jade, onyx, carnelian, crysophase, turquoise, and amethyst. 1¼" wide. Unsigned, but a fun bracelet! $80.00 – 115.00.

1950s fancy link bracelet. Antiqued gold and silver tone. Blue aurora borealis rhinestones and plastic turquoise seed beads (all glued in). 1" wide. Unmarked. $80.00 – 110.00.

Beautiful Emmons bracelet. Antiqued gold-tone links with purple and green unfaceted glass squares and rectangles. ¾" wide. $100.00 – 175.00.

Two unusual 1950s bracelets. Top: Gold plated with turquoise molded plastic set with clear rhinestone accents. 1" wide. Marked Trifari. $90.00 – 150.00. Bottom: Gilded brass filigree bracelet set with turquoise molded plastic flowers, brass flowers, simulated pearls, lavender chaton-cut rhinestones, and aqua pear-cut rhinestones. All rhinestones are glued in. 1" wide. Signed Art. $70.00 – 90.00.

A bracelet that mimics the real thing! 1" wide gold-plated nugget bracelet with prong-set oval-cut simulated garnets (unfoiled). Safety catch chain. Marked Panetta. $200.00 – 300.00.

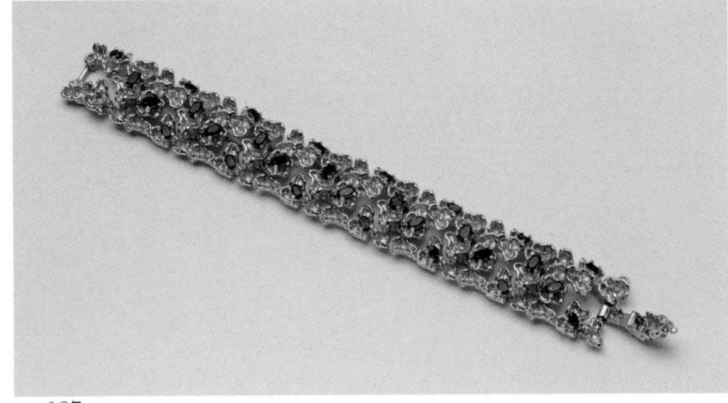

1950s bracelet with gold-plated etched links of flowers and leaves. Emerald-cut deep green rhinestones and chaton-cut apple green rhinestone flower centers. All rhinestones are prong set. Unmarked. $60.00 – 75.00.

Victorian-style chunky slide bracelet. Gilded brass filigree disks set with pearlized squares, chaton-cut emerald and amethyst rhinestones. Gilded brass fluted beads. Even the underside is finished beautifully with designs etched into the brass disks. Safety catch chain. 1¾" wide. Unmarked. 1950s. $150.00 – 225.00.

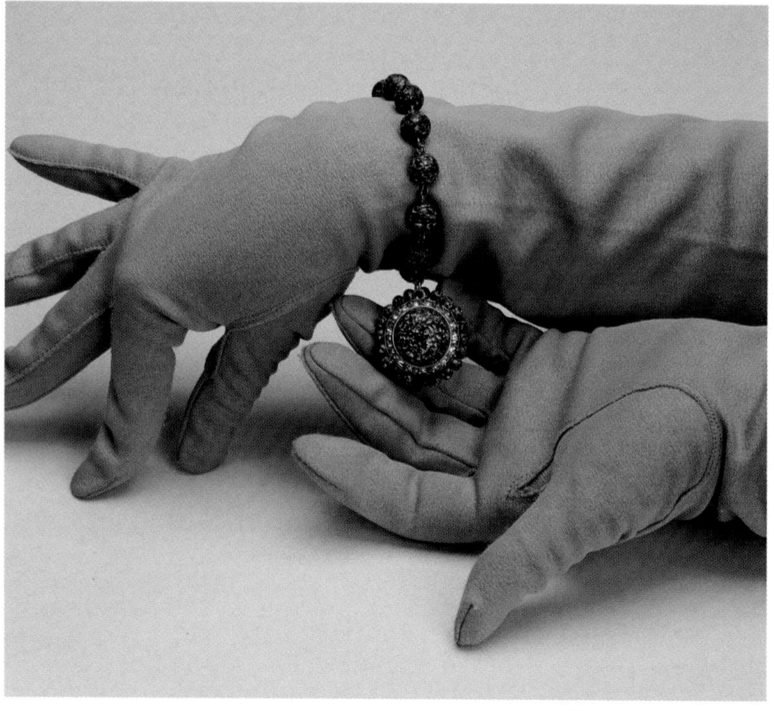

Unusual mottled composition beads and charm decoration adorn this bracelet. The charm has channel-set clear chaton-cut rhinestones. Late 1950s to early 1960s. Unsigned. $45.00 – 65.00.

1950s beaded bracelet. Seven strands of brown glass beads and brown simulated pearls. Fancy decorative push-slot clasp set with a cluster of copper-tone beads and brown glass beads. $75.00 – 115.00.

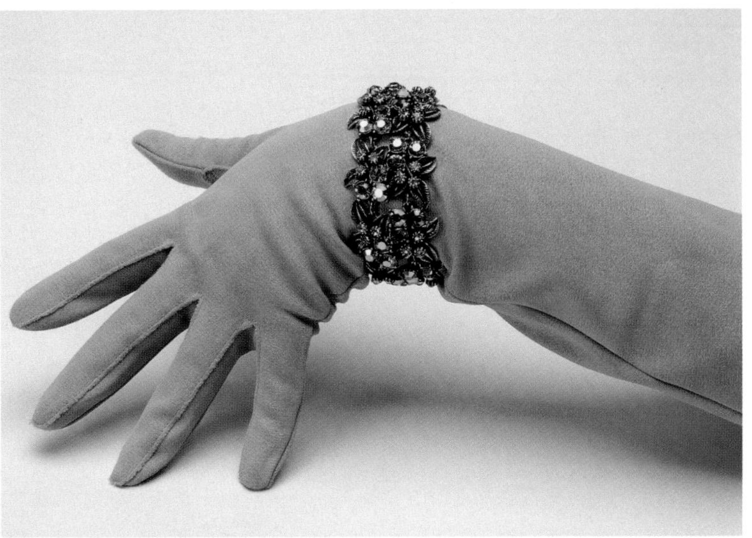

Beautiful 1950s antiqued gold-tone leaf design bracelet. Tiny three-dimensional leaves set with blue aurora borealis chaton-cut rhinestones and tiny yellow chaton-cut rhinestone accents. All rhinestones are glued in. 1½" wide. Marked Florenza. $125.00 – 150.00.

From the collection of Koral Michael Whalton

A fun 1950s bracelet! Gold tone with molded and painted plastic faces of many countries. Red rhinestone chaton-cut accents (glued in). 1¼" wide. Unsigned. $150.00 – 225.00.

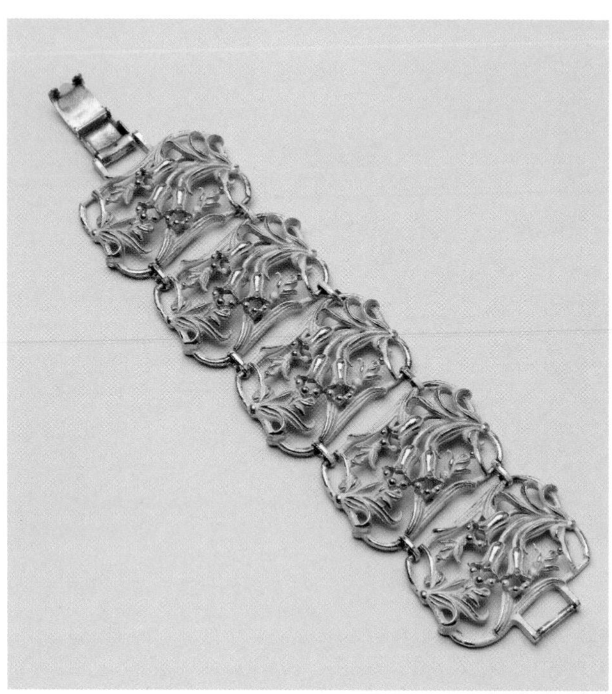

Karu 2" wide link bracelet. Gold plated with ivory enameling. Floral open work design. $90.00 – 125.00.

From the collection of Koral Michael Whalton

Antiqued gilded brass link bracelet. Brass filigree accents set with glass jade, emerald, and amethyst cabochons, fuchsia pink glass cabochon, simulated seed peals, blue enameled center with a chaton-cut blue topaz rhinestone, oval and chaton-cut amethyst rhinestones, oval and chaton-cut citrine rhinestone, and opaque square-cut blue and red glass. All stones and accents are prong set. Safety catch chain. ¾" wide. 1950s. Unsigned, probably French. $200.00 – 300.00.

Very unusual and highly collectible Chinese version of Snow White and the Seven Dwarves. Bracelet of silver-tone filigree wirework. Each figure is hand-carved from bone and then hand painted. 1¼" wide. Marked China. $500.00 – 600.00.

From the collection of Koral Michael Whalton

Three chunky 1950s bracelets. Top to bottom: Gilded brass links set with plastic simulated amber and chaton-cut topaz rhinestones. 2" wide. Unmarked. $125.00 – 200.00. Gold-plated bracelet with Oriental and Indian flair. Center link has a red molded plastic Oriental face. 1½" wide. Unsigned. $110.00 – 175.00. 1950s antiqued gold-plated bracelet. Four domed Lucite confetti ovals. Red sections with gold glitter and shell-chip confetti. 2¼" wide. $125.00 – 200.00.

From the collection of Koral Michael Whalton

Two 1950s chunky bracelets. Top to bottom: Antiqued gold-tone filigree-style heavy bracelet with simulated glass jade and turquoise, purple pear-cut Venetian glass, and simulated seed pearls. 1½" wide. Unmarked. $210.00 – 310.00. 1½" wide bracelet of gilded brass oval-shaped links. Bezel-set amethyst Venetian glass cabochons and chaton-cut amethyst rhinestones. Safety catch chain. Unmarked, probably French. $350.00 – 475.00.

From the collection of Koral Michael Whalton

Spectacular 2½" wide bracelet. This one should be called the "everything but the kitchen sink" bracelet! Gilded heavy brass with three-dimensional filigree. The center link has a large blue scarab and tiny simulated coral beads. The next two links have glass carved scarabs in simulated jade and amethyst. The rest of the links have Venetian glass, simulated seed pearls, green glass intaglios, blue oval-cut rhinestones, emerald-green glass cabochons, simulated opal cabochons, amethyst glass cabochons, and one square-cut simulated amber stone. The bracelet has gilded brass ghekos, griffins, dragons, gargoyles, Pegasus, Zeus, fleur-di-lis, twisting vines, and flowers. Safety catch chain. A real show stopper! The back is even finished prettily! Unmarked, probably French. $1,200.00 – 1,500.00.

Emmons silver-tone Egyptian revival bracelet. Inverted square-cut plastic simulated lapis lazuli, black plastic seed beads. 1¼" wide. $100.00 – 175.00.

German silver-tone cobra-style bracelet. Prong-set clear Austrian crystal rhinestones. 1" wide. Chromium plated. Marked Made in West Germany. $125.00 – 200.00.

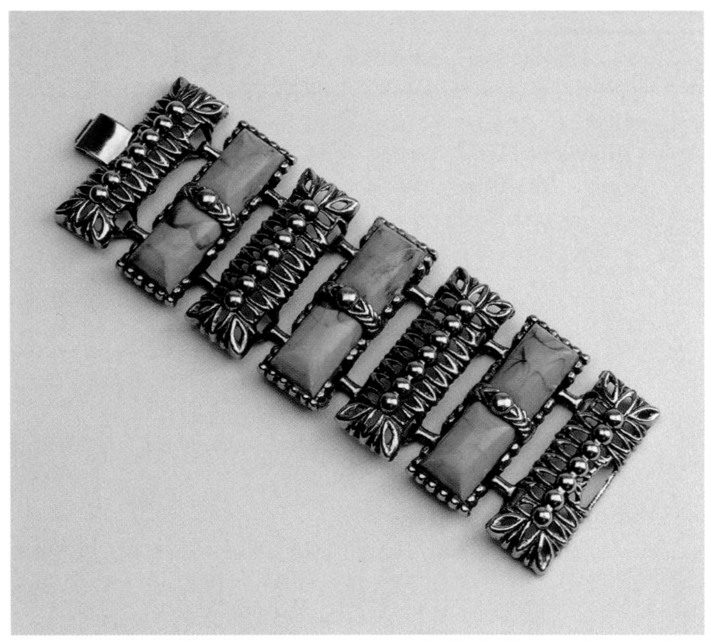

2¼" wide chunky bracelet from the late 1950s to early 1960s. Silver-tone base metal set with plastic simulated turquoise. $150.00 – 225.00.

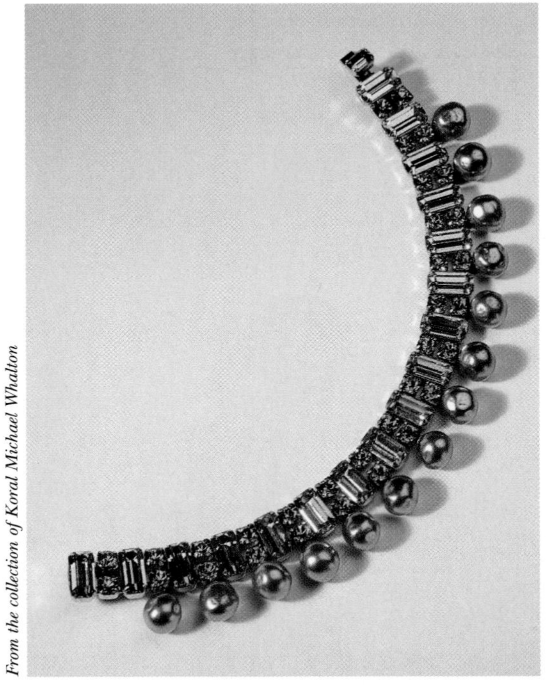

From the collection of Koral Michael Whalton

Elegant Albert Weiss bracelet from the 1950s. Emerald-cut and chaton-cut lavender rhinestones. Simulated gray Tahitian baroque pearls. Chromium plated. ¾" wide. Marked Weiss. $175.00 – 250.00.

Trifari bracelet. Silver-tone Trifanium-plated pear-shaped links. Each link is set with a pear-cut white iridescent plastic stone. ¾" wide. Late 1960s. $50.00 – 75.00.

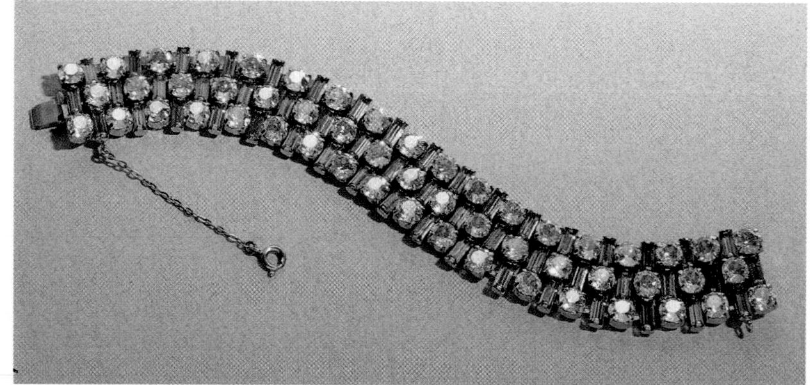

From the collection of Koral Michael Whalton

Beautiful 1¾" wide 1950s rhinestone bracelet. Prong-set chaton-cut aurora borealis rhinestones and sapphire blue baguettes. Chromium plated. Safety catch chain. Unmarked, probably a designer piece. $125.00 – 225.00.

Courtesy of The Glass Spoon

Two 1950s bracelets that make the best of apple green glass! Top to bottom: ¾" wide gold-plated chain-link bracelet. Apple green Venetian glass, apple green prystal beads, and apple green rhinestones. All stones, glass, and beads are prong set. Unmarked. $75.00 – 110.00. Hattie Carnegie bracelet with three stands of apple green, yellow, and beige Venetian glass beads. Push-slot clasp is set with a large round rose-cut apple green rhinestone. $125.00 – 175.00.

From the collection of Koral Michael Whalton

Gold-plated heavy chain link bracelet. Bright green and royal blue plastic beads. Unmarked, possibly Kenneth J. Lane. ¾" wide. $175.00 – 225.00.

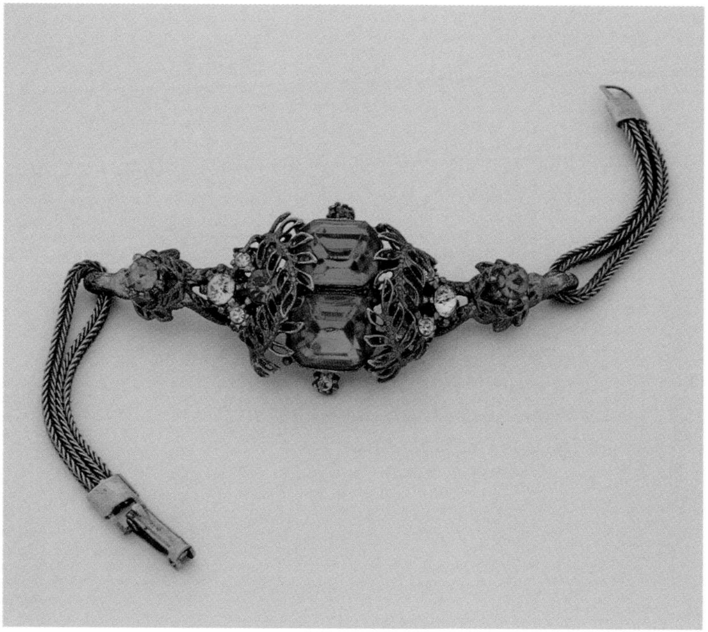

1930s silver-tone base metal bracelet. Center section is silver-tone filigree leaves set with two large aqua emerald-cut rhinestones, pink, lavender, and clear chaton-cut rhinestones (all foil backed). Unmarked. The center section is 1" wide. $125.00 – 175.00.

Gold-plated chain-link bracelet with suspended charm. The charm is gold plated and is 1½" long x 1" wide. On one side of the charm is a three-dimensional gold-plated vase with prong-set rhinestone flowers. Pink, aqua, sapphire, amethyst, ruby, and topaz rhinestones. The other side of the charm is a star with a prong-set ruby red rhinestone center. Safety catch chain. 1950s. Marked Barclay on the bracelet's clasp. $175.00 – 225.00.

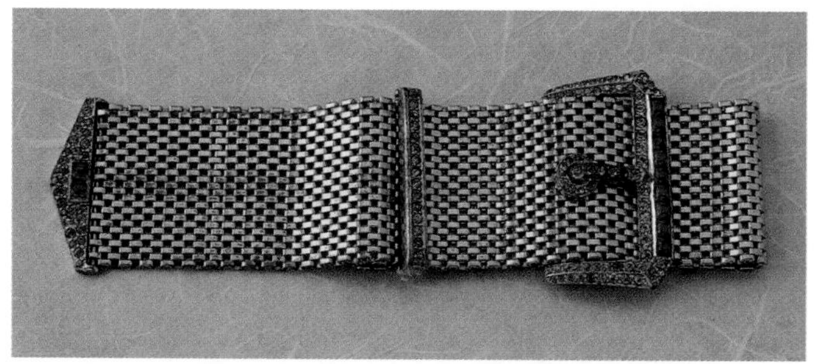

Art Deco style 1930s belt buckle bracelet. Gold-plated base metal with channel-set square-cut Burmese ruby rhinestones. Clear rhinestone accents. Unmarked. Unusual design. 1¼" wide. $165.00 – 215.00.

From the collection of Koral Michael Whalton

1950s Coro charm bracelet on original card. Gold-plated chain-link bracelet with three-dimensional charms depicting the sights of New Orleans. Has charms representing the St. Louis Cathedral Jackson Square, Absinthe House, an iron lace balcony, Mardi Gras, the French market, and Pirates Alley. The original card reads "New Orleans by Coro." $100.00 – 175.00.

From the collection of Koral Michael Whalton

Brush-tone silver and gold-plated hinged cuff. Unusual honeycomb pattern. 1" wide at the widest point of the bracelet. 1960s. Marked Jomaz. $225.00 – 325.00.

Very unusual Vendome snake cuff. This cuff opens to reveal a hidden watch! Each rigid link has two intertwining snakes with ruby-red rhinestone eyes. Silver-tone base metal. 1" wide. 1950s to 1960s. $300.00 – 400.00.

1930s piercework Art Deco cuff. Gold plated. 1¾" wide. Emerald green and clear chaton-cut rhinestones. Has an unusual patented spring hinge closure. Marked with an R and Pat. 1994826. (Patent description: Licensed to George K. Lowe, Providence, RI. November 26, 1934. Assigned to D.M. Whatkins, Co., Providence, RI. Appeared in Official Gazette on March 19, 1935.) $200.00 – 300.00.

Rose gold-plated hinged cuff with a three-dimensional flower and ribbon design. Safety catch chain. Unsigned, however may be the work of Whiting and Davis. 1¾" wide. $110.00 – 175.00.

From the collection of Koral Michael Whalton

Elegant Trifari double flower cuff. Rose gold plated set with clear chaton and baguette cut rhinestones (glued in). 1¾" wide at the widest point. Early 1940s. Marked Trifari Pat. Pend. $300.00 – 400.00.

From the collection of Koral Michael Whalton

Victorian revival snake cuff. Antiqued gold plated with tiny faux turquoise seed beads and red and clear rhinestones (all glued in). The snakes are 1¼" wide. Safety catch chain. Unmarked, however may be made by Art. $300.00 – 400.00.

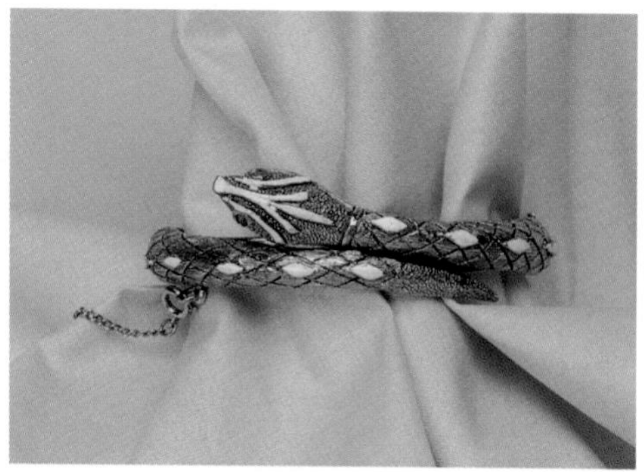

Snake cuff. Antiqued gold plated with white enameling and orange rhinestone eyes (glued in). The opened mouth has a red enameled forked tongue. The snake is ¾" wide at the widest point on the bracelet. Safety catch chain. Unmarked, however may be made by Art (made by the same company as the Victorian revival snake at left). $200.00 – 300.00.

From the collection of Koral Michael Whalton

Four 1960s cuffs. Top left: Unsigned ¾" wide gold-plated cuff with neon red enamel. Geometric design. $110.00 – 200.00. Top right & bottom left: two identical ¾" wide gold-plated cuffs. Three-dimensional spiny design. Both marked Alexis Kirk. $125.00 – 210.00. Bottom right: ¾" wide gold-plated cuff with turquoise enameling. Three-dimensional spiny design. Marked Alexis Kirk. $135.00 – 225.00.

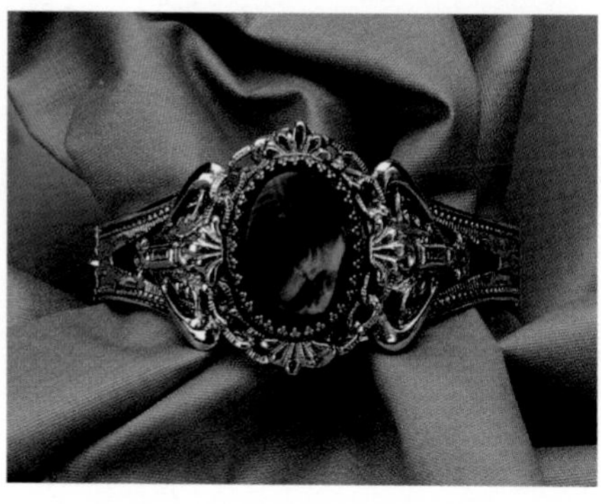

Whiting and Davis Victorian-style cuff. Rhodium plated. Fancy filigree open-work design with a prong-set black and purple marbleized Venetian glass oval-cut stone. The cuff is 1½" wide in the front and tapers to ½" in the back. The cuff is finished prettily in the back as well as the front. $125.00 – 175.00.

Excellent expansion bracelet. Chromium plated with prong-set simulated pearls and clear marquise and emerald-cut Austrian crystal rhinestones of fine quality. 1" wide. 1950s. Unmarked. $75.00 – 125.00.

Large scarab cuff. Gold plated with a royal blue molded plastic scarab beetle. Enameled decorations in the front and back of the bracelet in lime green, emerald green, royal blue, turquoise blue, and golden yellow. The cuff is 2" at the widest point. Signed Thomas Fattorini Ltd. Regent Street. Birminghami. $120.00 – 145.00.

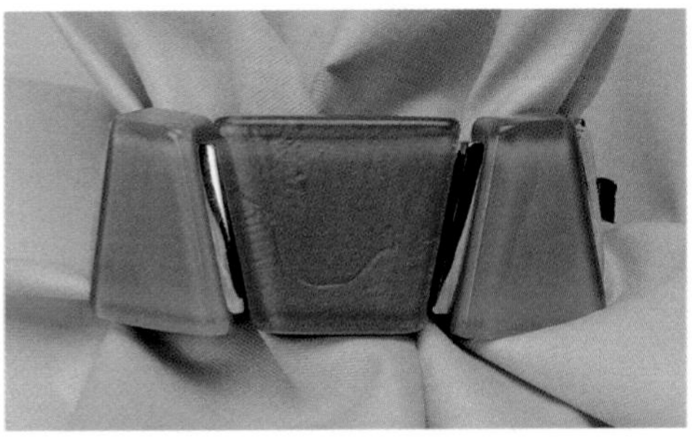

1970s Trifari cuff. Three Lucite geometric sections in lavender, aqua, and turquoise. Chromium plated. 1¼" wide at widest point on cuff. Signed Kunio Matsumo and marked Trifari. $70.00 – 95.00.

Two sweetheart expansion bracelets with original red velvet and gold box. The box states "The Carmen adjustable bracelet. Original quality. Patented May 23, 1898, Feb. 5, 1901. Made only by the D.F. Briggs Co. Attleboro, Mass." Gold plated. One bracelet has an etched gold heart and the other has a bezel-set red glass heart. Each bracelet is only marked with Pat. Pend. Passed down through the Author's family. $100.00 – 125.00 each.

World War II era brooches from left to right: Stylized 4½" floral spray with clear, lime green and fuchsia rhinestones. Hallmarked sterling. 3¼" retro floral brooch with five amethyst glass (unfoiled) rhinestones. Marked SterlingCraft by Coro. The 3" flower brooch is tied with a bow and has a lozenge-cut green glass rhinestone and clear rhinestone brilliants. Hallmarked sterling. The leaf brooch is tied with a bow and has four chaton-cut sapphire blue glass unfoiled rhinestones. Hallmarked sterling. All brooches are from the 1940s. $65.00 – 100.00 each.

From the collection of Koral Michael Whalton

Massive Tortolani heavy sterling-plated zodiac bracelet and pendant necklace. Highly detailed craftsmanship — three dimensional with all the signs of the zodiac represented. Extremely rare. The pendant is 3½" x 2¾" and the hinged cuff is 2" wide. $1,000.00 – 1,200.00. (This set was originally purchased in 1957 at the Detroit Hilton for over $200.00.)

From the collection of Koral Michael Whalon

Jerusalem silver filigree cross pendant on a box chain with matching earrings. Intricate silver wire work. Bezel-set sapphire glass stones. Cross pendant is 3½" long x 2" wide and the earrings are 1¼" in diameter. Unmarked. $1,000.00 – 1,200.00.

Italian silver piercework crown gauntlets with matching brooch and earrings. Highly detailed craftsmanship. Genuine bezel-set lapis lazuli cabochons. This parure blurs the line between costume and fine jewelry (this is often called bridge jewelry). Marked Peruzzi Florence and hallmarked silver 800. The gauntlets are 1¾" at the widest point, the brooch is 2¾" in diameter, and the earrings are 1" in diameter. $1,200.00 – 2,000.00.

From the collection of Koral Michael Whalon

Mexican sterling fringe-style necklace with black enamel work. Box push-slot clasp. Marked and hallmarked Mexican Sterling 78-36. $200.00 – 300.00.

1940s Mexican sterling mask pin and earring set. Carved obsidian masks. The pin is 1¼" and the earrings are ¾". Not marked or hallmarked. $125.00 – 175.00.

Collection of 1950s Siamese sterling. Sets from left to right: Fan pin, oval-shaped clip-on earrings, and link bracelet with white enamel. The 1¼" x 2½" pin and 1" earrings are marked Made in Thailand. The 1" wide white enameled bracelet is marked Siam and hallmarked sterling. Unusual flip ring — one side has golden yellow enamel and the other side has gray enamel. Puffed drop earrings in golden yellow enamel. The 1" wide ring is marked Siam and hallmarked sterling. The 1¾" long earrings are not marked. Pin and puffed drop earrings in black enamel. The 1½" x 2" pin is marked Siam and hallmarked sterling and the 1½" long earrings are not marked. Siamese sterling jewelry is found not only in these colors, but are also found in pale blue, navy blue, and red enamel as well. Rarely found is the same jewelry in gold plate. Earrings $40.00 – 100.00 pair, pins $75.00 – 120.00 each, bracelet $100.00 – 135.00, flip ring $45.00 – 75.00.

From the collection of Koral Michael Whalon

Large, showy 3¾" flower brooch. Marked (but is illegible) and hallmarked sterling. $250.00 – 325.00.

1960s 2¼" x 2¼" floral brooch crafted by Italian designer Guglielmo Cini. Marked and hallmarked Sterling by Cini. $150.00 – 175.00.

Dogwood bloom brooch. 1½" x 1½". Marked Ballou and hallmarked sterling. $55.00 – 75.00.

4½" daffodil brooch. Large simulated pearls in the center of the flower and bud. Hallmarked sterling (in a palette). 1940s. $75.00 – 100.00.

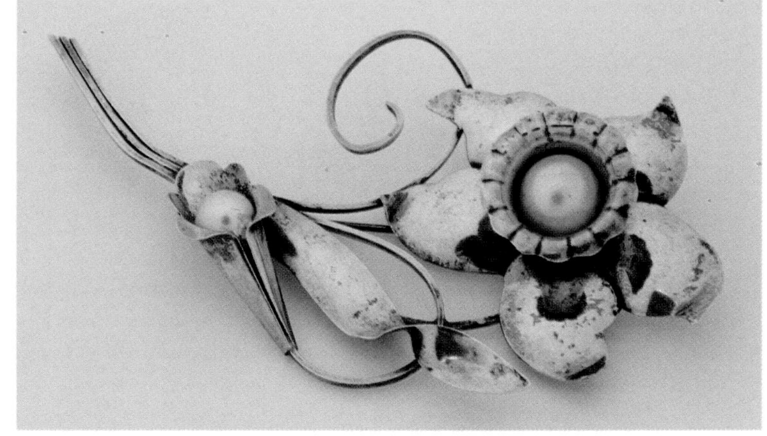

4½" pussy willow brooch. Marked Mexico and hallmarked sterling. 1940s. $65.00 – 95.00.

Sterling silver parrot chatelaine pins with green agate bodies. One pin is 2" long and the other is 1½" long. Marked Mexico and hallmarked sterling. $85.00 – 120.00.

From the collection of Koral Michael Whalton

Two 1950s Renoir palette pins. Each is 4¼" long. One palette is sterling silver and the other is copper. The copper palette is marked Renoir and the silver one is marked Sauteur Renoir and hallmarked sterling. $100.00 – 150.00 sterling, $75.00 – 100.00 copper.

Pair of 2½" street lamp scatter pins. Three dimensional with citrine rhinestones representing the candle's flame. Marked Lang and hallmarked sterling. $45.00 – 60.00 each.

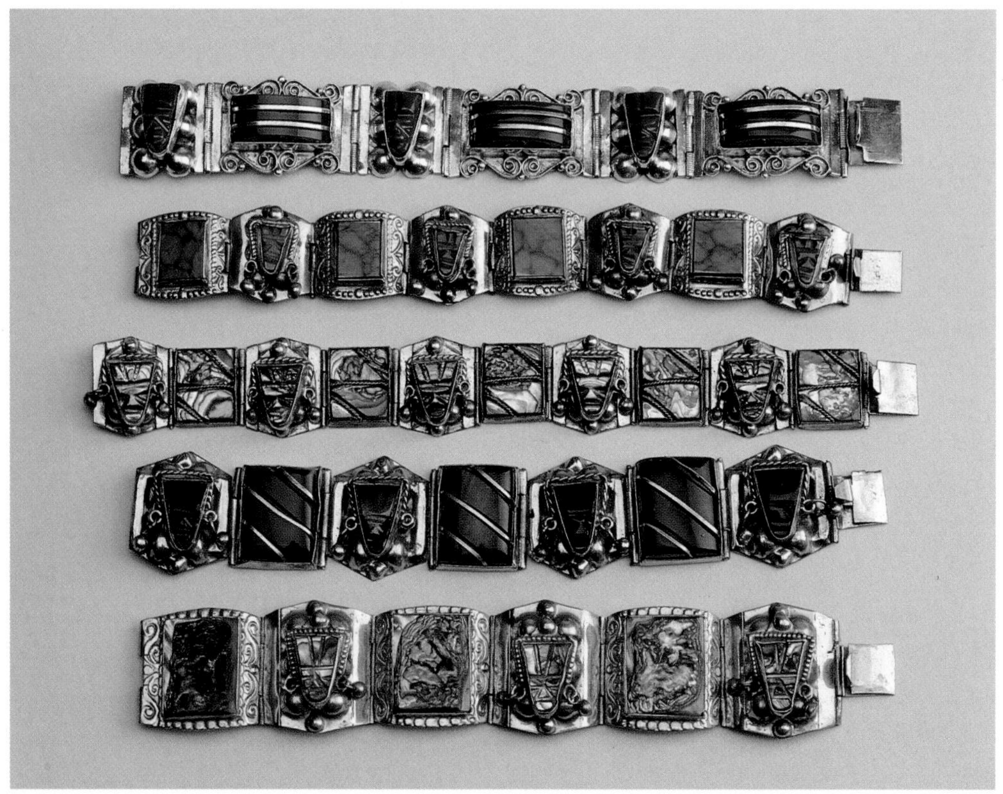

Grouping of sterling silver mask-link bracelets. Top to bottom: Mask-link bracelet with carved opaque green glass. 1" wide. Marked Mexico and hallmarked sterling. Sterling silver mask-link bracelet with faux turquoise (glass). Each mask is wearing silver earrings. 1" wide. Marked Hencho en Mexico (Made in Mexico). Mask-link bracelet with carved mother-of-pearl. Each mask is wearing silver earrings. 1" wide. Marked Taxco 925 Mexico. Mask-link bracelet with carved obsidian. Each mask is wearing silver earrings. 1" wide. Marked Hencho en Mexico. $200.00 – 300.00 each.

Unmarked sterling silver dangle earrings. Screw back. Prong-set emerald-cut smoky gray glass. 1940s. 1" long. $75.00 – 100.00.

Sterling silver bracelet made in Mexico. Links of repoussé work leaves and carved agate. 1¼" wide. $175.00 – 200.00.

Piercework cuff with etched flower basket designs. Bezel-set genuine amethyst cabochons. Hallmarked and marked Silver China Bee. ¾" wide. $250.00 – 300.00.

Dainty silver piercework link bracelet with prong-set genuine cultured pearls. The circular links are ½". Hallmarked sterling 1940s. $100.00 – 125.00.

1¼" wide, heavy link bracelet. Excellent craftsmanship. Marked Antonio, Taxco (in a crown logo) and hallmarked silver with an eagle logo and Made in Mexico ZZ 627). Antonio Pineda opened for business in 1941 and is still in operation in Taxco, Mexico, today. $400.00 – 500.00.

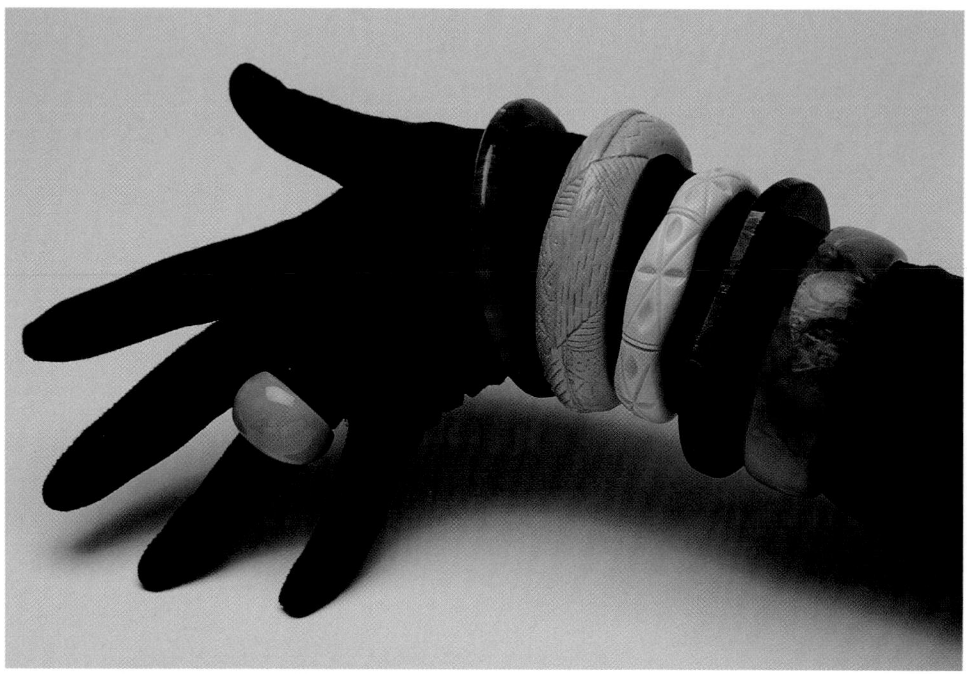

Bakelite bangles and ring. Marbleized brown and gold, ivory and carved golden yellow. The ring is ¾" wide and the bangles range in width from ¼" to ¾". Carved golden yellow bangle $65.00 – 130.00. Carved ivory bangle $60.00 – 100.00. Other bangles $35.00 – 60.00. Ring $25.00 – 45.00. (The carved golden yellow bangle looks to have been made from a "home kit.")

From the collection of Koral Michael Whalton

Ceramic tribal face with Lucite horns in the headdress. The headdress is felt with dyed rabbit fur. Red felt earrings. The face has blue painted eye shadow, black painted eyelashes, and red painted lips. 3¼". 1940s. Unmarked. $175.00 – 275.00.

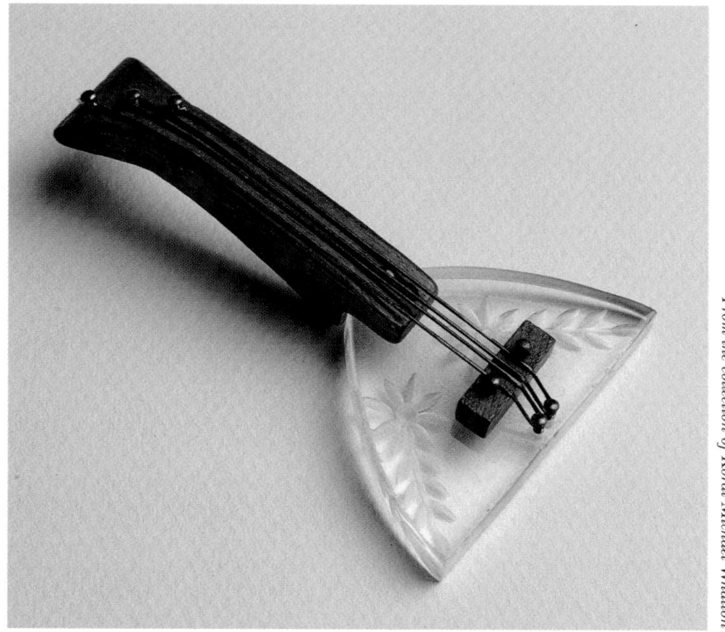

From the collection of Koral Michael Whalton

Wood and Lucite balalika. The strings are made of wire. The Lucite is undercarved. 3½" long. Unsigned. $95.00 – 175.00.

Courtesy of The Glass Spoon

1940s ceramic faces. Left to right: Ceramic lady wearing a Lucite floppy hat with a felt flower. 3¼". Right: Unusual geometric Lucite pin in amber and clear with a green ceramic face. Tribal influence. 3¾". Unmarked. $175.00 – 300.00.

Courtesy of The Glass Spoon

Collection of Lucite insects and animals. The fox has a red Bakelite head. All are carved and under carved. $175.00 – 250.00 each.

Courtesy of The Glass Spoon

Clear Lucite with a red Bakelite dog and horse. $165.00 – 250.00 each.

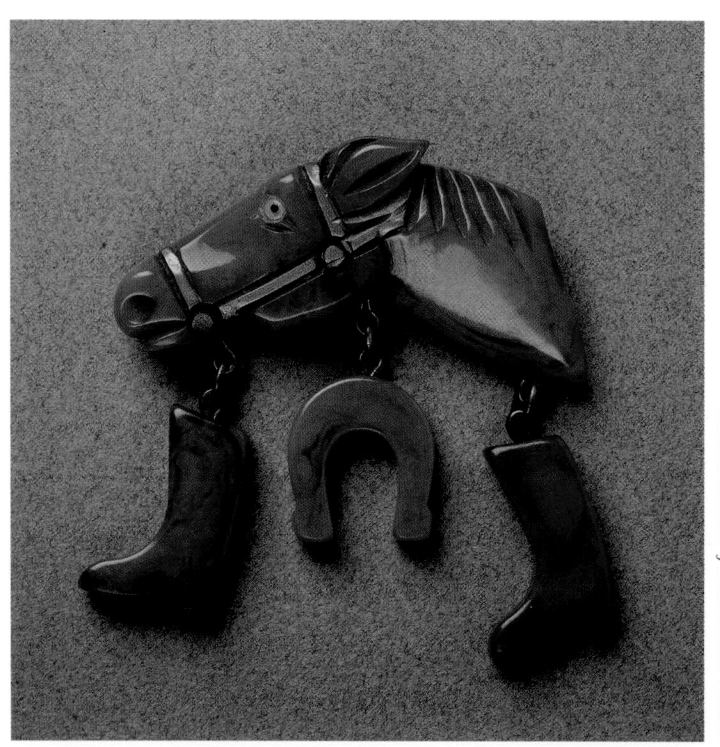

From the collection of Koral Michael Whalton

Carved Bakelite horse with dangling horseshoe and cowboy boots. The bridle is painted gold and the eyes are yellow with black pupils. A deep brownish-red color. 2½" x 2¾". Unmarked. $175.00 – 250.00.

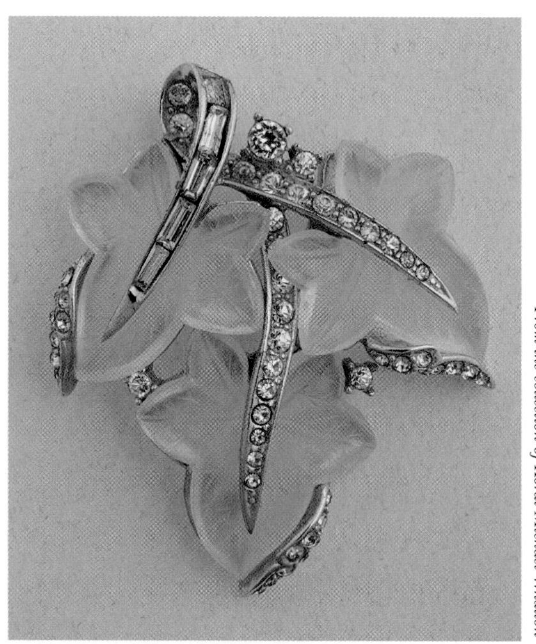

From the collection of Koral Michael Whalton

Boucher Lucite maple leaves. Rhodium plated with chaton and baguette-cut clear rhinestone pavé. The Lucite leaves have etched veins. 2" x 2¼". Marked Boucher 6428. $275.00 – 350.00.

From the collection of Koral Michael Whalton

Scallop shell clip/brooch and earring set. Rhodium plated with chaton-cut and baguette clear rhinestones. Clear Lucite. The clip/brooch is 1½" x 1½" and the earrings are ¾" x ¾". Marked Trifari - Pat. Pend. $500.00 – 600.00 set.

Celluloid fringe necklace. Sky blue Celluloid chain with a fringe of the same type of flowers. Each of the flowers has a pink plastic center. Green Lucite leaves. An extremely lightweight necklace. $75.00 – 100.00.

Two early plastic cameos. Left to right: Under-carved Lucite with black Bakelite carved cameo, 2" x 2½". Gilded brass pendant with cream celluloid and black Bakelite carved cameo, 2" x 2½". Lucite square cameo $175.00 – 250.00, cameo pendant $175.00 – 275.00.

Simulated tortoise-shell cube-beaded choker. Gilded brass beads and chain. $70.00 – 100.00.

Tutti-fruitti! Necklace of plastic and glass fruits and leaves. Gilded brass push-slot clasp with prong-set yellow plastic. Marked Austria. $150.00 – 200.00. Top left pin: Celluloid flowers with Bakelite and wooden fruit. Green glass leaves. Unmarked. 2¾" long. $75.00 – 110.00. Painted celluloid fruit basket pin. 1½" x 2¼". $50.00 – 75.00.

Two expandable bracelets one with a matching pair of earrings. The set on the left is composed of plastic daisies and beads strung on elastic cording. The earrings were once clip-ons and they were changed to pierced wire backs. 1950s. $55.00 – 85.00. The expandable bracelet on the right has green celluloid leaves and ivory carved Bakelite flowers. Mid-1940s to early 1950s. $55.00 – 80.00.

Unusual 1930s Depression era bracelet. Gilded brass chain with gilded brass beads, purple Lucite molded buttons, and marbleized turquoise Catalin molded buttons. 1¼" wide. Unmarked. $125.00 – 150.00.

Brightly colored plastic tutti-fruitti expandable necklace and earring set. Plastic fruit, leaves, and beads strung on elastic. Author bought this set new in 1986. $60.00 – 75.00.

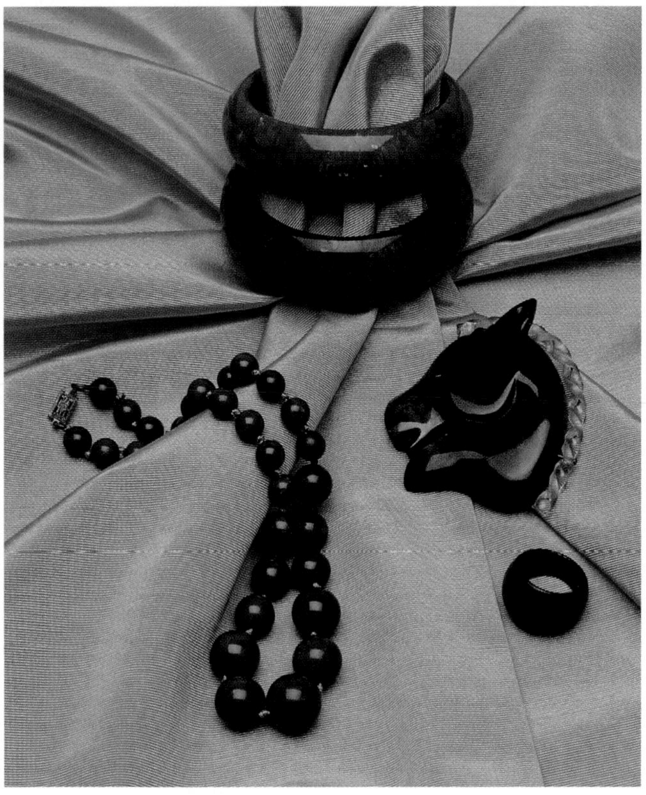

Mix and match green marbleized Bakelite. The 2¾" horse brooch has a clear Lucite mane. $175.00 – 250.00. Two bangle bracelets: one is ¾" wide and the other is 1" wide. $35.00 – 60.00 each. A short necklace of Bakelite marbleized beads. The cord between each of the beads is knotted. The largest bead is ½" in diameter. Gilded brass push-slot clasp. $40.00 – 65.00. ¾" wide ring. $25.00 – 45.00. The horse pin is courtesy of The Glass Spoon.

Butterscotch Bakelite bangle with a carved rose design. 1¾" wide. $200.00 – 300.00. Pair of butterscotch lady bug scatter pins. Carved bodies with chocolate brown painted faces and spots. Green rhinestone eyes. Metal prong legs. $100.00 – 150.00 pair. Bangle courtesy of The Glass Spoon.

A collection of red early plastics. 1" wide, red deeply carved Bakelite bangle bracelet. $175.00 – 250.00. A pin of red piercework molded leaves and stems. Catalin. $65.00 – 80.00. Molded red Catalin lobster pin with black painted eyes. 2¾" long. Marked only with the number 3. $75.00 – 115.00. The bangle is courtesy of The Glass Spoon.

Courtesy of The Glass Spoon

Beige celluloid bangle with aqua rhinestones. ¾" wide. $125.00 – 250.00.

Lucite fruit collection. The earrings are amber Lucite set with golden yellow rhinestones. Base metal stems and leaves with green enameling. 1¼". Unmarked. $25.00 – 50.00. Fuchsia apple with fuchsia rhinestones. Base metal stems and leaves with green enameling. Unmarked. 2". $50.00 – 100.00. The apple pin is courtesy of The Glass Spoon.

1950s glass and Lucite cushion pin. Gold plated with green Lucite caps and iridescent blue beaded centers. The centers are a cluster of iridescent blue Austrian crystal flat, flower-shaped beads. Unsigned. 1¾" in diameter. $50.00 – 65.00.

From the collection of Koral Michael Whalton

3" x 4¼" brooch with green celluloid stems and leaves. Yellow and purple ceramic flowers. Unmarked. $300.00 – 400.00, if perfect or in excellent condition.

Oriental inspired drop earrings. Green marbleized Bakelite with gold-plated Oriental design. 2¾" long. Unmarked. $100.00 – 150.00.

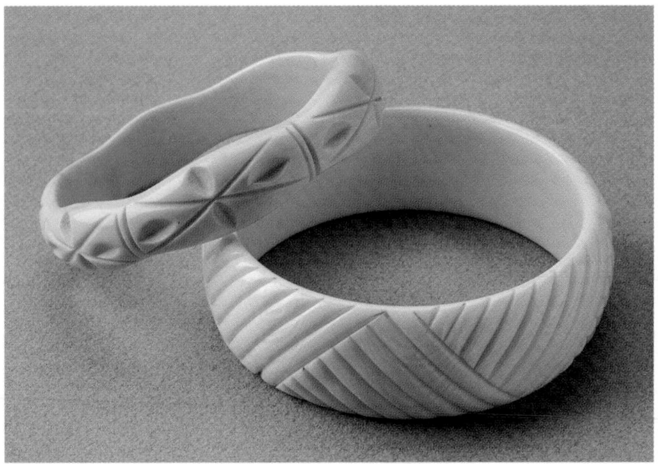

Two carved Bakelite ivory bangles. The geometric diagonal striped bangle is 1" wide. $150.00 – 250.00. The other bangle is ½" wide and has a carved geometric design. $60.00 – 100.00.

Courtesy of The Glass Spoon

Butterscotch and black ribbon brooch and bracelet set. Catalin and Bakelite. $450.00 – 575.00.

From the collection of Koral Michael Whalton

Carved, marbleized green Bakelite snapping turtle brooch with a carved wooden shell. Black painted eyes. 2" x 3". $175.00 – 250.00.

Celluloid abstract floral earrings. Pale green leaf, white stems and flowers, aurora borealis rhinestone accents. 1950s. 1¾" long. Marked West Germany. $35.00 – 50.00.

Unusual 1950s fringe-style dangle earrings. Blue pearlized plastic pear-shaped center with prystal beads in olive green, golden yellow, royal blue, and aqua blue. Pale green celluloid flower with silver-tone bead in the center. 2" long. Unsigned. $30.00 – 55.00.

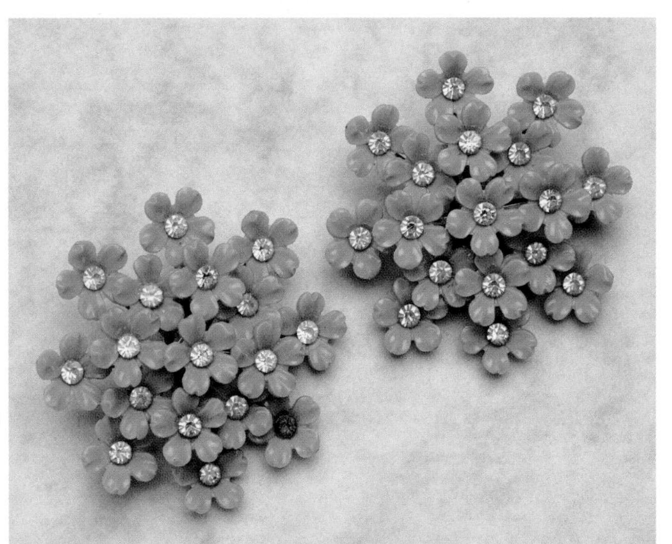

1950s Coro flower cluster earrings. Blue plastic flowers with clear rhinestone centers. 2¼" in diameter. $40.00 – 75.00.

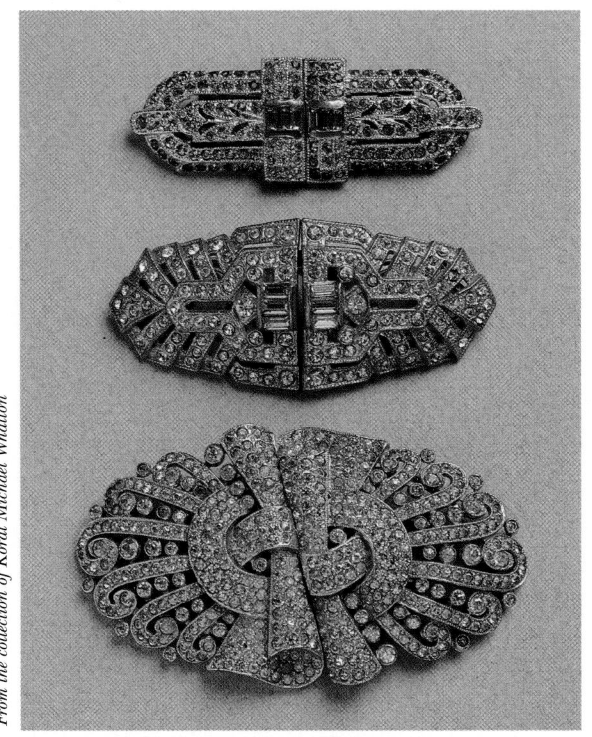
From the collection of Koral Michael Whalton

Trio of Art Deco duettes. Top to bottom: Silver-tone base metal set with clear rhinestone brilliants and clear baguettes. 2½" long. Marked Coro Duette Pat. No. 1798867, Pat. No. 1852188. 1930s. $200.00 – 275.00. Gold-tone base metal set with clear rhinestone brilliants and clear baguettes. 2¾" long. Marked Coro Duette Pat. No. 1799867, Pat. No. 1852188. 1930s. $225.00 – 300.00. Fancy rhodium-plated duette. Clear pavé rhinestones. Marked Clip Mates Trifari 25. 3" long x 1¾" wide. 1930s. $275.00 – 325.00.

1930s dress clips. Gilded brass with prong-set pear, inverted square, and chaton-cut rhinestones in pink and clear. Each clip is 2¼" long. The back of the clip is marked PAT. 1852188. (Patent description: Brooch/clasp. Applied for by Elijah A. Phinney South Addelborough, RI and assigned to George H. Fuller and Son Pawtucket, RI. Filed on February 17, 1931. Appeared in the Official Gazette on April 5, 1932.) $110.00 – 170.00 pair.

1930s dress clips. Silver-tone base metal set with simulated coral oval and round-cut cabochons, pink oval-cut rhinestones, and clear chaton-cut accents. Each is 2¼" high x 2" wide. The back of the clip is marked PAT. 1801128. (Patent description: finding for clasps. Applied for by Anthony E. Waller Providence, RI on September 8, 1930. Appeared in Official Gazette on April 14, 1931.) $125.00 – 200.00 pair.

1970s Elton John style glasses. The frames are light turquoise enamel set with pear-cut aqua rhinestones and ivory and turquoise plastic accents. Antiqued goldtone. Rose tinted glass. Marked Christian Dior on the frames and on the arms. Hallmarked 1/10 – 12K G.F. (gold filled) on the arms only. $900.00 – 1,100.00.

From the collection of Koral Michael Whalton

Uncirculated Florenza key chain from the 1950s. Gold plated with the tassel tips ending in aurora borealis rhinestones. One end unscrews in order to slide keys onto it. 2½" long. The original paper tag is still attached — one side says "Florenza" and the other says, "Original Design." $50.00 – 75.00.

From the collection of Koral Michael Whalton

1930s base metal fur clip. Four large aqua pear-cut rhinestones, four smaller aqua chaton-cut rhinestones, one tiny green chaton-cut rhinestone, and central clear rhinestone. All rhinestones are unfoiled. Unmarked. 2¾" x 2½". $150.00 – 225.00.

Beautifully crafted brass and cloisonné belt buckle. Turquoise, purple, royal blue, white, and red enameling. Circa 1905. 1¾" x 3¼". Unmarked. $100.00 – 175.00.

Collection of jeweled belt buckles (one with a matching brooch). Top left: Gilded brass three-piece belt buckle with golden yellow glued-in rhinestones. 1¾" x 6½". Top right: Gilded brass three-piece belt buckle with golden orange glued-in rhinestones. 2" x 6" Center, bottom: Copper three-piece belt buckle in a leafy design with matching brooch. Tourmaline striped glass cabochons, all bezel-set. The buckle is 2¼" x 5" and the brooch is 1¾" x 2¼". Buckles $75.00 – 100.00 each, set $85.00 – 115.00.

Gold-plated watch fob with bezel-set pink paste stones in pear and oval cuts. Unmarked. $45.00 – 75.00.

From the collection of Koral Michael Whalton

Very rare War era Statue of Liberty ring. Sterling silver with bezel-set red, clear, and blue rhinestones. An excellent example of the popular collectible patriotic jewelry. Marked Patent Applied for C and R (possibly Cohn and Rosenberger) and hallmarked sterling. $400.00 – 550.00.

From the collection of Koral Michael Whalton

Hard-to-find Eisenberg sterling silver ring. Bezel-set clear rhinestones. 1" wide across the top. Marked with the Eisenberg Original "E" (not the script "E"). 1940s. $800.00 – 1,000.00.

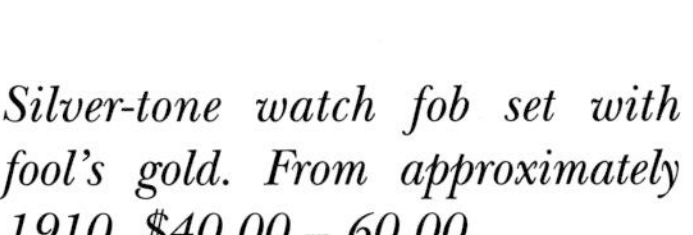

Silver-tone watch fob set with fool's gold. From approximately 1910. $40.00 – 60.00.

Newer Collectibles

Costume jewelry purchases from the 1980s to present.

Many antique jewelry collectors often overlook the many sensational jewelry items being offered today for sale. In the 1980s there was a boom in the costume jewelry industry. Many of the companies and designers that offered imaginative and beautiful jewelry in the 1980s were short-lived and have become increasingly collectible. Many collectors had the foresight to purchase these items and have seen the value increase dramatically in just a few short years. Many of the 1980s collectibles include, but are not limited to Kirk's Folly, Catherine Stein, Laurel Burch, Monet for Yves St. Laurent, Wendy Gell, Les Bernard, J. Gladstone, Butler and Wilson (a British company), as well as many companies who have been around since before the 1980s: Monet, Anne Klein, Napier, Givenchy, Capri, Kenneth J. Lane, Erwin Pearl, Christian Dior, Trifari, Stanley Hagler, Arnold Scaasi, and Ciner.

Some of these designers combined the best attributes of the past eras with new and imaginative ideas as well as new materials. Creative combinations of wood, paper, papier maché, glass, mirrors, wood, and rhinestones were used in the 1980s to make a whole new genre of craft jewelry. Many of these pieces were left unsigned. Jewelry by J. Gladstone gave a whimsical attitude to jewelry. Gladstone's purposely mismatched earrings were often constructed of combinations of plastics, papier maché, rhinestones, and sometimes bronze. These large and often quite funky jewelry items are the very essence of the 1980s!

The 1990s: Many of today's newest collectibles include Karl Lagerfeld, Kenneth J. Lane (and his designs for Avon), Princess Michaela, Joan Rivers, Mary Beth Burchardt for Pell and Disney, Elizabeth Taylor for Avon, Ciner, Vivienne Westwood, Arnold Scaasi, Ian St. Gielar, Iradj Moini, Thelma Deutsch, David Mandel, Larry Vrba, Robert Sorrell, Chanel, Isabel Canovas, and Nolan Miller.

Even the choosiest of today's collectors would do well to collect the larger-than-life and breathtaking designs by Robert Sorrell. Mr. Sorrell designs couture jewelry for Thierry Mugler and designed jewelry for the movie *To Wong Foo, Thanks for Everything, Julie Newmar* starring Patrick Swayze, Wesley Snipes, and John Leguizamo. Each jewelry item is marked "Sorrell" and is produced in limited quantities. Robert Sorrell's astounding color combinations bring a smile to the face and make the jewelry a joy to wear as well as to collect.

Joan Rivers's Classics Collection is indeed classic as well as classy. This "do everything" lady has designed scrumptious jewelry that often takes inspiration from the genuine gems worn and collected by royalty. Many of Joan's jewelry items have a Fabergé style due to the inspiration of her own personal collection and love of Fabergé.

Mary Beth Burchardt has been designing jewelry not only for Pell but also for Disney and Precious Moments. Currently available exclusively through Disney are Tinker Bell, Sorcerer Mickey, and Cinderella with Jiminy Cricket and Pinocchio currently in the works. Each of these pins are highly detailed and are plated in 24KT gold and hand set with Swarovski Austrian crystal rhinestones. Timmy is available through the Precious Moments Chapel. Mary Beth's (MBB) jewelry for Pell is redesigned from Pell's original 1940s molds and is plated in 24KT gold and hand set with Swarovski Austrian crystal rhinestones.

Ian St. Gielar is another new name to keep an eye on. The jewelry is tagged and marked with the collector in mind — each jewelry item is signed and numbered. St. Gielar jewelry is considered by collectors and wearers as works of art. The jewelry is all hand crafted and limited to six items per design. St. Gielar's jewelry has been seen worn by Whoopi Goldberg and Morgan Fairchild among others.

Please note, the jewelry in this section will not be given values. Many of these items are still in production and thus may be purchased new. Prices are determined by manufacturer or designer.

Beautiful antique gold-tone set done in the Art Deco style. Clear rhinestones and simulated coral cabochons. Elizabeth Taylor for Avon. Earrings are 1¾" long and the pin is 1½" x 2¾".

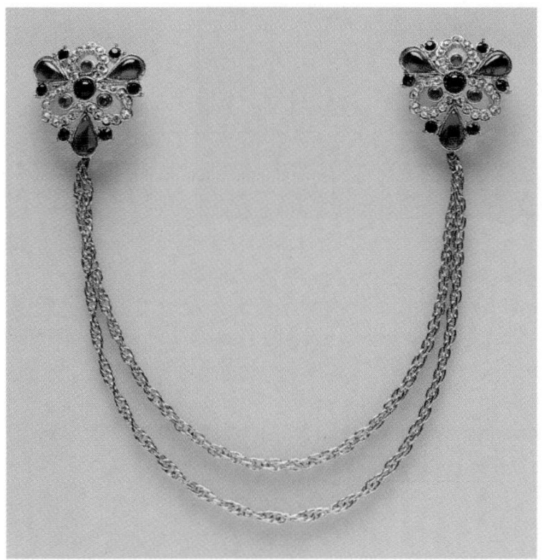

Chatelaine pin by Sphynx. Gold plated with simulated ruby and onyx cabochons. Clear rhinestone brilliants. 1980s. Pins are 1¼" x 1¼" and the chain is 7½" long.

Elegant tassel set in simulated onyx beads. Antique gold-tone set with clear rhinestones. The pierced earrings are 3" long. The matinee length necklace has a tassel that is 4¾" long. From Avon's Cafe Society Collection. Marked Avon.

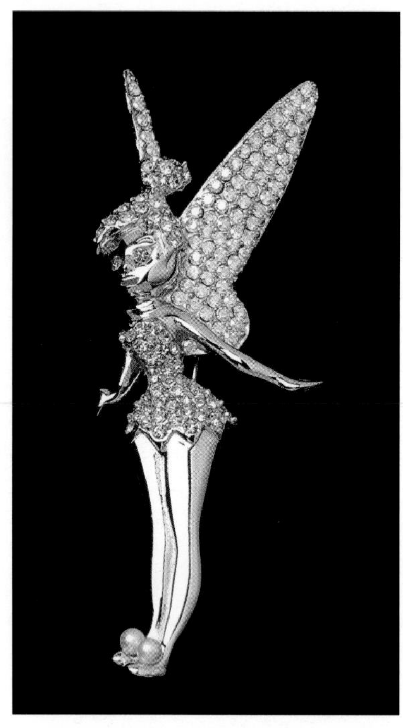

Tinkerbell pin designed by Mary Beth Burchardt for Disney. 24k gold plated and hand set with Swarovski Austrian crystal rhinestones in aurora borealis, peridot, and sapphire. Red enameled mouth. Simulated pearls on shoes. Pin is 3¼". Marked MBB and ©Disney.

Jewelry designs by Craft. Gold-plated sea shell pin and earrings set with simulated pearls and simulated onyx cabochons. Pin is 4" long, the earrings are 1¾" in diameter. Brush gold-tone pin set with simulated onyx cabochons, clear chaton-cut rhinestones and white ceramic cabochons is 2¾" x 2¾".

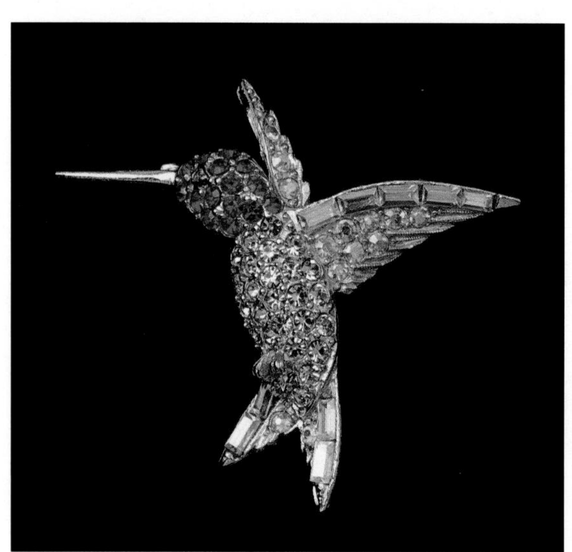

*Redesigned gold-plated ruby-throated hummingbird pin by Mary Beth Burchardt for Pell. Swarovski Austrian crystal rhinestones in aurora borealis, peridot, and ruby. 24k gold plated, 2" x 2¼". Marked MBB and Pell.**

*Pin-wheel pin redesigned by Mary Beth Burchardt for Pell. 24k gold plated and hand set with Swarovski Austrian crystal rhinestones and a central simulated pearl. Channel set baguettes in fuchsia, red, peridot green, lavender, sapphire blue, and citrine. Clear chaton-cut rhinestone brilliants. 2½" in diameter. Has 1¼" matching earrings (not shown). Marked MBB and Pell.**

** These pins are made from Pell's original 1946 molds.*

Enameled jewelry by Craft. Pin and earrings set in brush gold tone with orange enamel set with simulated pearls, peridot green and amethyst square-cut rhinestones. 3½" long. Pin is 2" x 2" and the earrings are 2¼" long. Brush gold-tone drop earrings in white enamel set with simulated pearls and fuchsia, peridot green, and sapphire blue rose-monteé cut rhinestones.

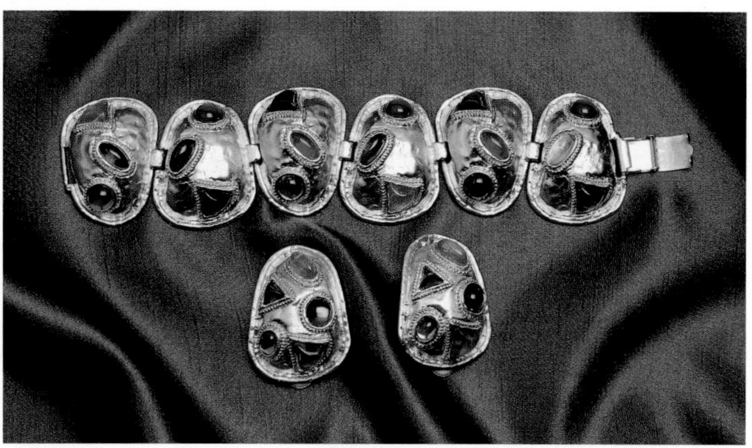

Brush gold-tone chunky bracelet and earrings set. Simulated ruby, sapphire, citrine, and amethyst abstract-cut cabochons. The earrings are 1¾" long and the bracelet is 1¾" wide. Marked Les Bernard.

Sterling silver-plated western-style concha necklace with black leather cording. Simulated turquoise, coral, agate, and onyx. Each concha is approximately 1¾". Marked Laurel Burch. Early 1990s.

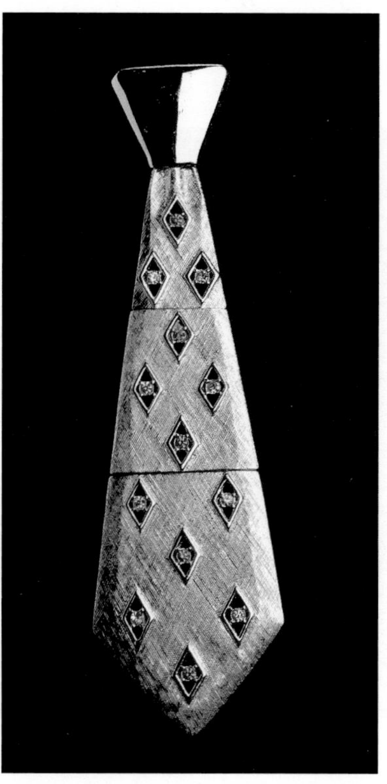

Three-part necktie pin. Chromium plated and set with simulated sapphires and peridots, 6" long. Marked J.J. (Jonette Jewelry). 1980s.

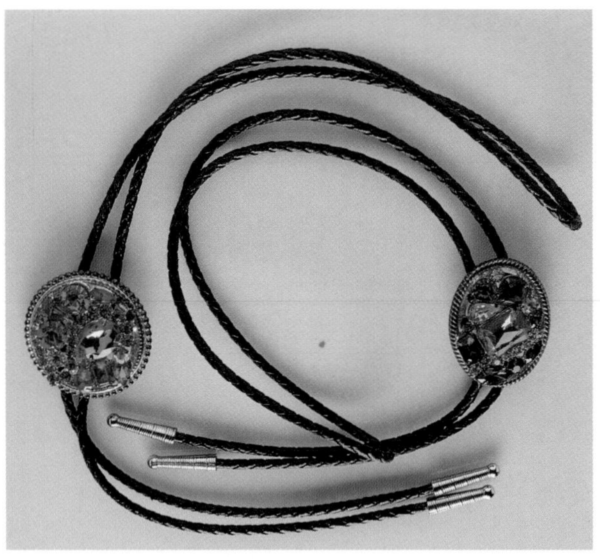

Western-style bolos on braided black leather slides. Sterling silver plated with prong-set rhinestones. The oval bolo is set with amethyst, peridot, and emerald rhinestones marquise, pear, chaton, and emerald cuts. The round bolo is set with fuchsia, orange, and golden yellow rhinestones in emerald, chaton, oval, marquise, and pear cuts. The round bolo is 2" in diameter and the oval is 1½" x 2". Unmarked. 1980s.

Italian-style antiqued gold-tone collar set with simulated pearls. The pearl disks are 1¼" x 1¼". Marked Dauplaise (Carol Dauplaise).

Heavy brush gold-tone pin and earrings set. Simulated cream and Tahitian pearls. Pin is 2" x 3¼" and the earrings are 1¾" long. Earrings have comfort clips. Marked YSL (Monet for Yves St. Laurent). 1980s.

Brushed silver-tone rigid bangle bracelet in a geometric design. Square-cut domed crackle glass in shades of green and blue. 1¼" wide. Marked YSL (Yves St. Laurent).

Brush silver-tone collar and drop earrings set. Contemporary design in traditional navy blue enameling. The collar is 1¼" wide and the pierced earrings are 2" long. Marked Anne Klein on a soldered on tag. 1990s.

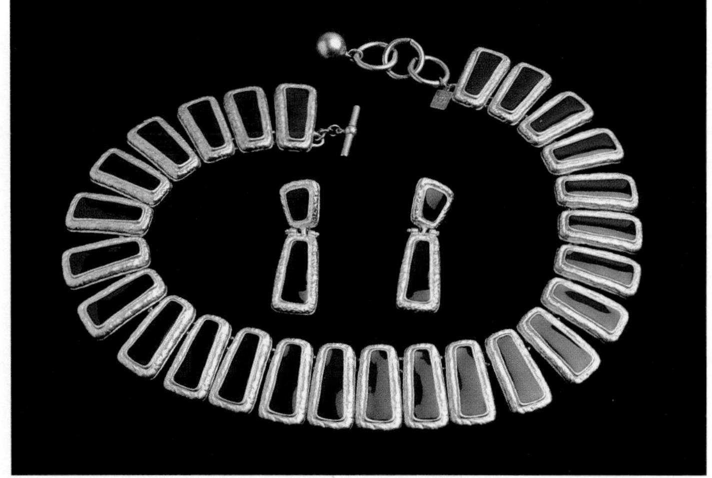

Abstract design collar and earrings set in brush gold tone with red, fuchsia, and orange enameling. The ¾" wide collar is marked Anne Klein on a soldered-on tag and the 2" long earrings are marked only with the copyright symbol (©). Brush silver-tone flower set with a central simulated pearl. Sapphire, turquoise, and aqua enameled petals. 2½" in diameter. Marked A.K. (Anne Klein). 1990s.

Carved ruby Lucite bangles with gold inset designs. Brush gold-tone earrings with coordinating ruby lucite stones and drops. The earrings are 1¾" long and one bangle is 1½" and the other is ½". The earrings are marked A.K. (Anne Klein) and the unsigned bracelets still have the original Anne Klein cardboard tags (not shown). 1990s.

Beautiful gold-plated crown pin set with simulated ruby, sapphire, diamond, and emerald rhinestones in chaton cuts with one inverted square cut sapphire rhinestone at the top. 1¾" x 2". Marked K.J.L. (Kenneth J. Lane). 1990s.

Heavy gold-plated necklace by Kenneth J. Lane for Avon. Glass cabochons in triangle, square, and oval cuts in shades of fuchsia, bright blue, emerald green, and ruby red. Has matching 1¾" x 1½" earrings in the diamond-shaped bright blue (not shown). Marked K.J.L. for Avon.

Kenneth J. Lane designs for Avon. Gold-plated sea shell charm necklace set with a single simulated pearl on the starfish. Gold-plated dragonfly pin with pearlized enamel wings. Tiny, clear chaton-cut rhinestone eyes. Body is set with a pink oval-cut rhinestone, and clear chaton and marquise-cut rhinestones. The pin is 1½" x 3¼". Both necklace and pin are marked K.J.L. for Avon.

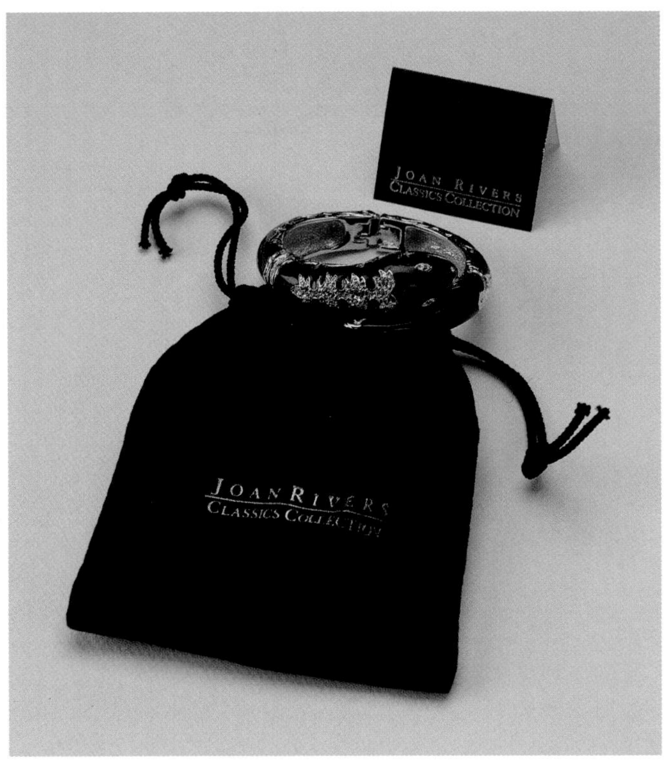

Victorian-inspired snake cuff. Gold plated with sapphire blue enameling and clear chaton-cut rhinestones. Excellent design and craftsmanship. This cuff is 1" wide at the widest point in front and ½" in the back. Original card and black velveteen pouch shown. Marked Joan Rivers. 1990s.

Two elegant watches by Kirk's Folly. Gold-plated pin/watch with prong-set clear rhinestones in pear and chaton cuts. The bow is set with glued-in clear rhinestone brilliants. Single simulated pearl drop accent at the bottom. 2" x 4½". Gold-plated wrist watch with marcasite accents. Twelve beaded chains are on each side. Push slot clasp with safety catch chain. Both are marked Kirk's. 1980s.

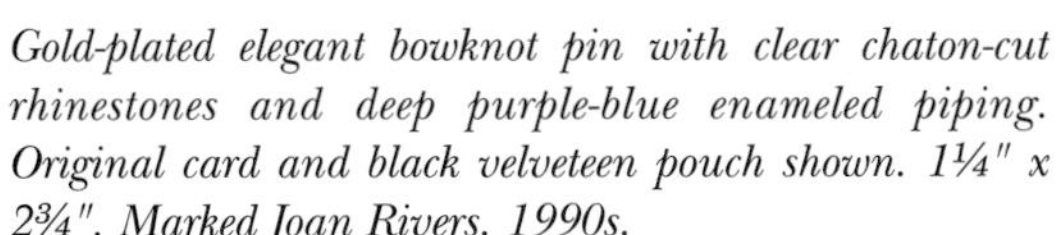

Gold-plated elegant bowknot pin with clear chaton-cut rhinestones and deep purple-blue enameled piping. Original card and black velveteen pouch shown. 1¼" x 2¾". Marked Joan Rivers. 1990s.

Dazzling retro-style pin from the Eisenberg Ice Classics collection made from an original Eisenberg mold. Rhodium plated with prong-set unfoiled sapphire Austrian crystal rhinestones (pear, emerald, star, and oval cuts). Clear chaton-cut brilliants. 2¼" x 2¾". Marked Eisenberg Ice. Still has original paper tag. Excellent Eisenberg quality that has been seen for over 60 years. Given to the author as a Christmas gift from her sister-in-law in 1996.

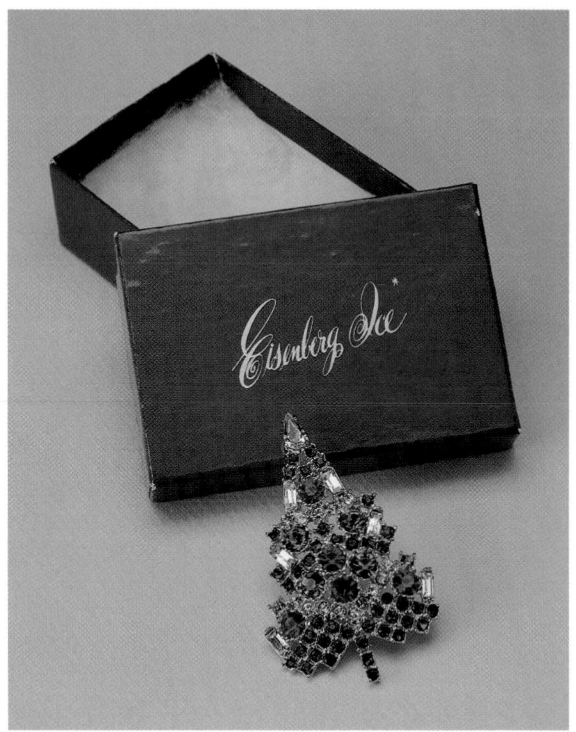

Classic Eisenberg Ice Christmas tree pin. Set with clear chaton, baguette, and pear-cut rhinestones. Chaton-cut rhinestones in ruby red, emerald green, sapphire blue, and citrine. Gold plated. 1½" x 2¼". Marked on back and shown with original box. Given to the author as a Christmas gift from her sister-in-law in 1995.

Contemporary and traditional designs by Eisenberg. Heart-shaped pin and dangle earrings set. Rhodium plated with prong-set clear Austrian crystal rhinestones and white simulated pearls. Prong-set clear rhinestone necklace and earrings set. Rhodium plated with chaton-cut rhinestones on the chain and marquise-cut rhinestones on the central pendant and earrings. Simulated white pearl drop. The pin is marked Eisenberg Ice, however the matching earrings are unmarked. The necklace and earrings set is only identified by the original Eisenberg Ice paper tag. The heart pin is 1½" x 1½" and the matching pierced earrings are 1¾" long. Both the necklace's central accent and earrings are 1¾" long. Given to the author as a Christmas gift from her sister-in-law in 1995.

Unusual papier maché earrings from the 1980s. These earrings have a dinosaur on one earring and a bone with a black wooden drop on the other. (Mismatched earrings were very popular during this time period.) Black papier maché with gold-painted spots. The earring tops are set with a large chaton-cut sapphire rhinestone and surrounded by prong set clear chaton-cut rhinestones. The dinosaur and bone are dotted with glued-on aurora borealis rose monteé-cut rhinestones. The dinosaur has a sapphire blue rose monteé rhinestone eye. The dinosaur earring is 2½" x 2½" and the bone earring is 2¾" x 1¼". Hand signed Gladstone and '87.

Pair of bronze mismatched dangle earrings from approximately 1987. Pear-cut ruby glass cabachons, red glass aurora borealis teardrops, and an aurora borealis rhinestone in the center of the star. Star earring is 3" long and the moon earring is 3¼" long. An early moon and stars design by Gladstone (unmarked).

Celtic pin from Ireland. Antiqued gold-tone with simulated lapis lazuli, malachite, black onyx, and purple venetian glass stones. Chaton-cut rhinestone brilliants in simulated sapphire, emerald and amethyst. 2¼" in diameter. Marked Sold'or. Shown on original cream velveteen card with burgundy velveteen pouch. 1990s. On the reverse side of the original card is printed: "It is in the Irish Isle and the Northern and Western rims of Britain that the heritage of the Celts has endured. These are the lands the Romans did not conquer or where they failed to implant their own culture. In the far West the Celtic culture continued to flourish. Their artistic ability and fine craftsmanship are shown in their ornamental and metal work. After the fall of Rome, Celtic culture flowed back into many regions of Western Britain, where their art and traditions have been faithfully maintained. Sold'or – Ireland."

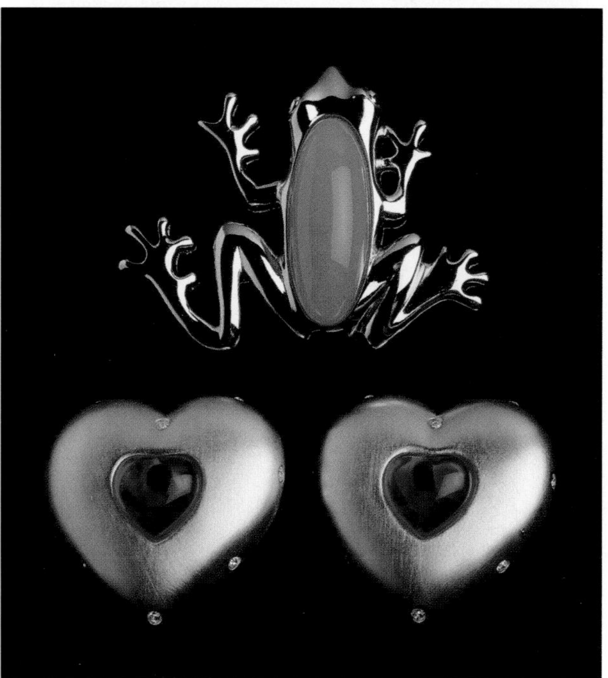

Jewelry designs by Givenchy. Gold-plated frog set with a turquoise-blue oval plastic back. Heart-shaped brush gold-tone earrings set with ruby glass heart-shaped cabochons and clear rhinestone accents. The frog is 2" x 2½" and the earrings are 1½" x 1¾". 1990s.

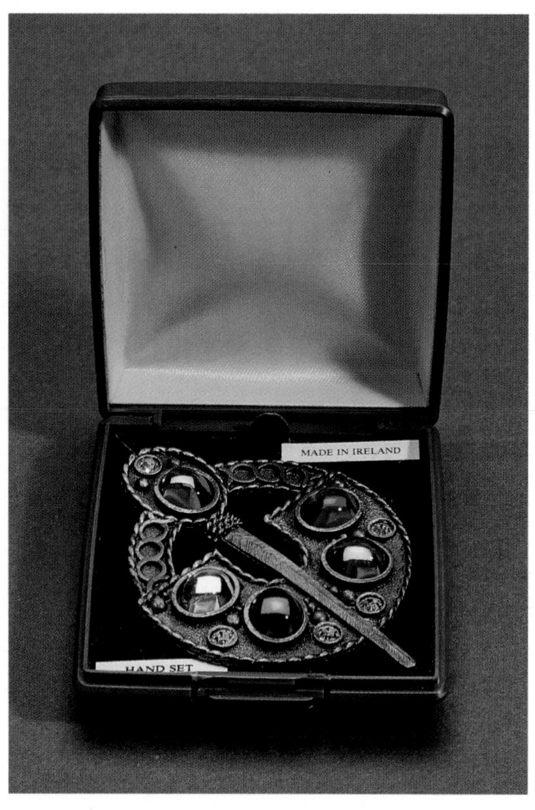

Pewter Kilt-style pin made in Ireland. Glass oval cabochons in clear, ruby, sapphire, and amethyst. Clear rhinestone accents. All cabochons and rhinestones are foil backed. 2¼" x 3¼". Unmarked. Shown in original plastic case marked "Hand set, made in Ireland." 1990s.

Antiqued bronze-tone drop earrings. Frogs with large prong-set topaz pear-cut rhinestones. French wire with topaz colored Austrian crystal beads. 2¼" long, including the wire. Marked Sadie Green.

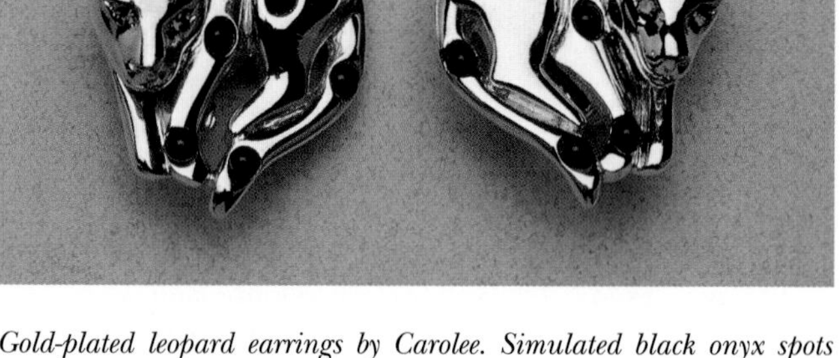

Gold-plated leopard earrings by Carolee. Simulated black onyx spots with emerald green rhinestone eyes. 1" x 1".

Swarovski enhancer. Rhodium plated with lozenge and pear-cut clear Austrian crystal rhinestones. Marked with the Swarovski Swan symbol. 2" long.

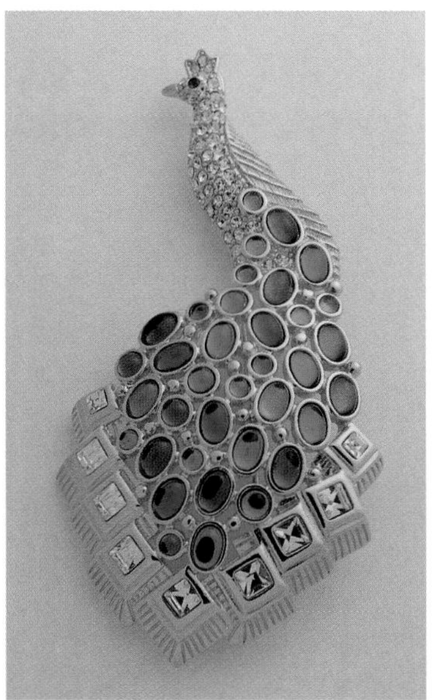

Elegant and appealing peacock pin. gold plated. Tiny green rhinestone eye and clear pavé rhinestone head and body. Oval and round glass cabochons in sapphire blue. Amethyst and emerald green accent the tail. the tail feathers end in clear square-cut Austrian crystal rhinestones. 3¾" long. Marked Nolan Miller. From the Nolan Miller Glamour Collection sold on QVC. 1990s.

Karl Lagerfeld cello pin. Brushed gold tone with black enameling and clear pavé rhinestones. 1¼" x 3¾". 1930s. Purchased in 1996 for $85.00.

Round button-style clip on earrings from the 1980s. Brushed silver tone with glass tortoise cabochons (glued in). 1¾" in diameter. Marked Kate Hines.

Highly detailed marine life rigid necklace, earring and gauntlet set. constructed of brass and copper with a baked lacquer coating. The pierced earrings are 2¼" long (including the wire), the gauntlet is 1¾" wide, and the rigid metal section of the necklace is 11" long. The necklace may be made as long as the wearer wishes by adjusting the satin cording. This set was designed by Pat Juneau of Scott, Louisiana and purchased by the author in the early 1990s.

Rigid cuff bracelet. Aqua Czech doublets mounted with clear Swarovski Austrian crystals. All rhinestones are prong-set. Sorrell Originals design (Robert Sorrell). Photo by Geoff Sokol.

Swarovski Austrian crystal fuchsia and rose brooch with detachable tassel and pendant chain. All rhinestones are prong-set. Sorrell Originals design (Robert Sorrell). Photo by Geoff Sokol.

Bangle bracelets: one with olivine, the other with ruby prong-set rhinestones. Sorrell Originals design (Robert Sorrell). Photo by Geoff Sokol.

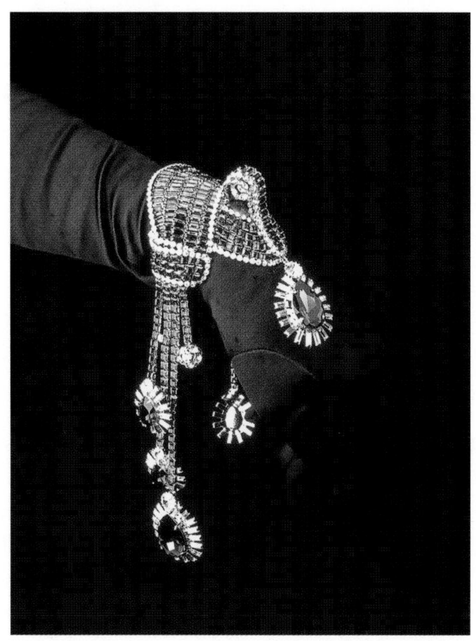

Haute couture runway jewelry. "Montana" blue necklace and bracelet created by Robert Sorrell for Thierry Mugler. Photo by Steve Skoll.

"Sea Monster" brooch next to the original Thierry Mugler design sketch. All the rhinestones are prong-set. Brooch executed by Robert Sorrell. Photo by Manfred Kolt.

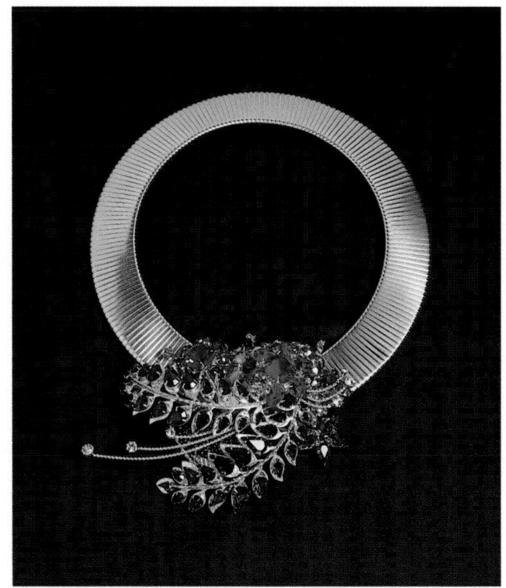

Cobra-style collar with detachable brooch comprised of prong-set multi-colored Swarovski Austrian crystal rhinestones. Sorrell Originals design (Robert Sorrell). Photo by Steve Skoll.

Glossary

alloy – a combination formed by the fusion of two or more metals. Also a combination of a base metal with a fine metal.

amber – a fossilized vegetable resin which is hard and brittle. Translucent colors range from yellow gold to brownish yellow.

aurora borealis – name derived from the colorful aurora seen in the high northern latitudes. Glass rhinestones that have been treated with metals to give it an iridescent quality. First introduced in the 1950s by Swarovski and used extensively by Christian Dior in his costume jewelry designs.

Bakelite – a phenol formaldehyde resin invented by Leo Hendrick Baekeland in 1909. Often a term inadvertently used to describe Catalin, Celluloid, and Galalith as well as other earlier plastics. Bakelite was available in a wide variety of colors and was used extensively in the production of costume jewelry as well as other accessories and household products. Bakelite was often carved and highly polished, whereas Catalin was a molded plastic and Celluloid an embossed plastic.

baroque pearl – an irregularly shaped pearl (simulated or genuine) often has a "lumpy" appearance.

base metal – a metal of low value (also called pot metal). A term often used interchangeably with brass, pinchbeck, and white metal.

Types of base metals:

brass: an alloy of copper, zinc, and sometimes tin.

pinchbeck: an alloy of copper, tin, and zinc in an imitation of gold. Named after its inventor Christopher Pinchbeck (1670 – 1732).

white metal: an alloy of pewter, lead, antimony, and copper — silver-tone in color. White metal is a term often used interchangeably with silver-tone metal and tin plate.

bezel setting – metal flanges holding a gemstone or rhinestone securely in its setting. The whole stone is enclosed by a strip of metal with its flanges folded over to secure it.

bracelet – a decorative band worn around the wrist or upper arm.

Types of bracelets:

bangle (gypsy bangle): a rigid bracelet without a clasp that slips over the hand.

charm: a link or chain bracelet with decorative ornaments (charms) suspended from it.

cuff: a rigid bracelet in the shape of a circle or oval with a clasp (usually a hinged clasp).

flexible or expandable: a flexible bracelet comprised of moveable metal links with metal joints attaching each link to the other. Also beads, pearls, or rhinestones strung on elastic cording. These bracelets do not have clasps — they expand to slip over the hand and then contract to fit snugly at the wrist. Flexible bracelets were popular during the 1950s. Also called expansion bracelets.

gauntlet: a rigid bracelet in the shape of a partial oval. The wrist fits through the opening at the underside of the wrist.

slave: a bracelet with a matching ring (or rings) connected by a chain.

spiral: an open-ended bracelet with rhinestones, pearls, or beads strung on flexible, expandable wire that wraps around the wrist or upper arm. Sometimes the open ends of the spiral bracelet have decorations or tassels. (Not to be confused with flexible, expansion, or expandible bracelets.)

tab: a bangle, cuff, or gauntlet with a suspended charm, drop, tassel, or decoration.

bib – a necklace of three or more concentric strands of beads or simulated pearls. Also a rigid, fringed, or decorative necklace that covers the area at the neck from no shorter than 14" to no longer than approximately 22".

bridge jewelry – a term given to jewelry that bridges the gap between fine jewelry and costume jewelry. Sterling silver jewelry and jewelry set with semi-precious stones often fall into this category.

brilliant – often refers to the tiny round rhinestones used for pavé.

brooch – derived from the French term broche. Often refers to pins of a large scale or pins made prior to the 1950s.

cabochon – an unfaceted stone, usually dome-shaped and round or oval-cut.

carnelian – also called cornelian. A waxy, translucent red to orange-red quartz in the chalcedony family. Often red to orange-red glass cabochons are mistakenly called carnelian.

casting – in costume jewelry this term is usually referred to as the lost wax casting method. The metal alloy is melted and poured into a pre-shaped mold then cooled. The hardened metal is then used in a three-dimensional shape. Not as cost-efficient as stamping. A method mainly used prior to the 1950s.

celluloid – an early plastic introduced in 1869 by J. W. Hyatt. A highly flammable plastic produced from a mixture of guncotton, camphor, and other substances. Could only be heated by hot water or hot air to be folded, rolled, or embossed. Could not be melted for molding purposes due to material decomposition. Was used in costume jewelry and hair accessories for a very short period of time.

chalcedony – also spelled calcedony. A porous stone of the quartz family. Sometimes this stone has dye added to it to enhance its natural color. Agate, onyx, carnelian, chrysophase, and jasper are all varieties of chalcedony.

channel setting – a groove or channel in the jewelry with the upper flange bent over to keep the stones from falling out. Also refers to a metal track with baguette stones set end-to-end with the upper flange folded over to support the stones.

charms – in olden times referred to an amulet worn to ward off evil or to bring good luck or fertility. Later the term was used to refer to a small decorative ornament suspended on a chain, bracelet, necklace, earring, etc. Especially popular in the 1950s.

chatelaine – the mistress of a household often wore a chain hanging from a belt to hold small household articles such as keys, a watch, a coin purse, and personal grooming items. Chatelaine later became a term used to describe a pair of pins connected by a chain (or several chains). Sometimes mistakenly called sweater guards.

choker – a necklace or ribbon with ornamentation worn high around the throat. 14" – 16" in length. Often a term mistakenly used to describe a dog collar.

chromium – a very hard grayish white metallic element that is resistant to corrosion. Often used for plating in costume jewelry and often mistaken for rhodium plating. Also called chrome.

citrine – also called citrin. A light yellow to golden yellow variety of quartz.

clasp – a releasable fastener for holding parts of jewelry together. Often prettily decorated as well as functional.

Common types of clasps:

fish hook: one end of the necklace or bracelet has a part of the clasp in the shape of a fishhook. The other end of the necklace or bracelet has a box which the hook slides in, catches, and locks.

jump-ring, spring-ring, or standard clasp: one end of the necklace or bracelet has a jump ring. The other end of the neck lace or bracelet has a ring with a slide that opens and closes to catch the jump ring. The most commonly used clasp style.

lobster-claw: one end of the necklace or bracelet has a jump ring. The other end of the neck lace or bracelet has a clasp that resembles a claw. When pushed, the claw opens and clos es to catch the jump ring.

mystery clasp: a screw clasp that is disguised as another bead or part of the necklace or bracelet.

push-slot clasp: one end of the necklace or bracelet has a piece that fits into a box at the other end of the necklace or bracelet. When the piece is pushed into the box it snaps closed. Often prettily decorated.

screw clasp – one end of the necklace or bracelet has screw threads and twists to screw into the other end.

claw setting – a setting with longer prongs used for cabochon stones.

clip – a spring clasp at the back of a pin or earrings. A clip can also refer to the spring clasp that has metal teeth or flanges or two long prongs. Dress clips in singles and pairs were popular during the 1930s through the 1940s.

cloisonné – metal wire or metal strips used to make a design, or cloison, and filled with colored enamel.

cluster setting – small rhinestones set clustered around a larger, central rhinestone.

coral – the skeletal remains of various small marine invertebrates. These remains range in color from a pinkish red to an orange-red.

cultured pearl – pearls cultivated in a controlled enviornment. Created in this fashion in order to ensure uniform size, dimension, and color.

die stamping – a method most often used for mass producing costume jewelry. This metal is mechanically shaped between a die and a counterdie. A cheaper and faster method of producing jewelry, replacing the lost wax casting method. Also called stamping.

dog collar – a broad necklace usually consisting of several strands of rhinestones, pearls, or beads worn tightly around the neck. A term often mistakenly used interchangeably with "choker".

drop – a small decorative object or ornament suspended from a brooch, necklace, earring, etc. Usually used to refer to a tear-drop shaped ornament. Also called dangle.

duette – a pin or brooch that can be taken apart to be worn as two separate clips or put back together and worn as one whole pin/brooch.

electroplate – usually used to describe a method of fusing a thin sheet of finer metal to a lesser base metal by means of electrolysis. Often electroplating is used to fuse several layers of different metals.

enamel – A process where opaque glass is fused to metal, porcelain, or other surfaces. A process which was popular in the 1940s. This old technique is costly and time-consuming. Today the term enameling is used to describe a process where a paint or lacquer is painted on the metal's surface and hardens after drying to resemble the old enameling techniques.

engraving – to etch a pattern or figure into a metal surface using a sharp graving tool (a burin).

faux – false, not genuine, simulated, counterfeit, or copied.

findings – catches, clasps, hooks, jump rings, springs, clips, pins, bezels, rivets, screws, wires, bolts, caps, loops, rings, and other functional parts of jewelry. Also called components.

filigree – lacy, intricate, and delicate ornamental work created by intertwisting gold, silver, brass, or other fine wire.

foil – a thin leaf of bright metal set behind a glass or crystal stone to add brilliance or color.

French jet – cut black glass used to imitate genuine jet. The supply of genuine jet was exhausted during the Victorian era and had to be simulated by this glass. First used in Victorian mourning jewelry and later in fashion jewelry. (Popular in the 1950s and 60s.)

freshwater pearl – a pearl produced by a mollusk in a non-brackish water environment. These pearls are usually elongated and lumpy or irregular in appearance and are not much larger than a grain of rice. Not considered a very desirable pearl and is thus usually priced inexpensively.

fur clip – a large, decorative brooch that has a metal spring clasp with metal teeth or flanges meant to hold a fur stole securely around the wearer's neck or shoulders. Larger in scale than the dress clip because it had to hold the thick fur together. Popular during the 1930s and 1940s.

gold filled – base or lesser metal sandwiched between two layers of gold. Usually hallmarked 18K g.f., 24K g.f., etc.

graduated strand – a strand of beads or simulated pearls of graduating sizes which start smaller in the back and get larger toward the center of the necklace.

hallmark – a mark or stamp on the back or inside of jewelry to guarantee purity. This term is often mistakenly interchanged with "signature" or "mark" which is used to identify the of manufacturer, designer, or patent information.

hammering – a technique of decorating jewelry using a hammer on the metal's surface.

intaglio – a design that is cut or carved into a gemstone, piece of glass, or plastic. Most often the design is of a woman (like in a cameo). Intaglio is the opposite of a cameo which is carved in relief.

ivory – tusks and/or teeth of the elephant, walrus, wild boar, and other select animals. Often found in the jewelry of the Art Deco period. Some early plastics were created as a cheap alternative to ivory, which was quite costly. Often bone jewelry is mistakenly identified as ivory. Today, ivory is illegal to trade and harvest.

japanned – a process which colors metal to a dull black. First used for mourning jewelry and often set with genuine or French jet.

jet – a coal fossil lignite of a glossy black color. Jet was used in Victorian jewelry — especially in mourning jewelry. Made acceptable by Queen Victoria who wore it during mourning. Usually was cut en cabochon. Often the term "jet" is mistakenly used when describing black glass used in jewelry.

lapis lazuli – a stone of the feldspar species that is a deep purple-blue. Sometimes has flecks of iron pyrite which give it a glittering quality.

lariat – a long necklace with open ends (without a clasp) that is knotted, looped, or held together by a ring. Popular in the 1920s and 1950s.

lavalliere – a thin chain with a single suspended drop or stone. A popular style during the Edwardian and Deco eras. Also spelled lavaliere.

man-made gold – a yellow metal alloy of zinc, tin, and copper. Also called imitation gold.

marcasite – white iron pyrite. Often mistaken for polished steel which can be cut in the same manner. Usually set in silver-tone or sterling jewelry.

marked – when the manufacturer's or designer's identifying mark or signature is etched, carved or stamped into the jewelry (usually located on the back of the jewelry). Sometimes this identifying mark or signature is accompanied by a date of manufacture, however this practice is rare. However, Hollycraft is known for dating a large portion of their jewelry. Mark is a term not to be confused with hallmark.

moonstone – adularia. A pearly, opalescent, bluish stone of the feldspar species. Popular use in jewelry during the 1930s and 40s. In costume jewelry usually used to describe glass with similar characteristics. Usually cut en cabochon. Often confused with "milkstone" which is a pearlized, opalescent white stone used in costume jewelry. Usually cut en cabochon.

mother-of-pearl – the pearly, iridescent internal layer of the abalone, mollusk, oyster, and sea snail.

nacre – a term often used interchangeably with mother-of-pearl. The outer pearlized shell of an imitation or simulated pearl.

obsidian – a black, glassy volcanic rock. Often used in Mexican sterling jewelry. Often mistakenly identified as onyx.

parure – a matching suite of jewelry often consisting of necklace, bracelet, earrings, pin (sometimes two pins), and sometimes a ring. A demi-parure is a partial matching set consisting of a pin and earrings, necklace and earrings, or necklace and bracelet, etc.

patina – a green rust that occurs on jewelry and other metal objects which have a high bronze or copper content.

Pat. Pend. – patent pending.

pavé – tiny rhinestones that are placed close to each other giving the jewelry the effect of being paved with rhinestones. Most of the time in costume jewelry these pavé rhinestones are glued in. However, some of the finer fashion jewelry has these stones prong set.

prong set – metal flanges (or prongs) are used to hold a stone securely in place. Later replaced in mass production of costume jewelry by cheaper, faster gluing in of stones. Also called claw-set when longer metal flanges are used.

prystal – a plastic substitute created to imitate glass. Often used in beads.

repoussé – a metal design formed in relief. These patterns and designs are produced by punches or chasing hammers.

retro – backward, behind, and prior. In costume jewelry refers to designs that have been done in the past and used again later.

rhinestone – a cut stone of glass with high light refraction and iridescence. Often backed with foil. Comes in clear to an endless color variety. The term "rhinestone" comes from the area near the Rhine river in Austria where these glass stones were originally produced. Also called diamante, strass, and paste.

rhodium – a whitish-gray silvery metal in the platinum family. Used for electroplating in costume jewelry due to its hardness and resistance to corrosion. Often mistaken for sterling silver and chromium.

rolled gold – a plating of gold which is laminated or rolled onto a base metal surface.

rondelle – small, round metal spacers used mostly in necklaces — strung between beads or faux pearls. When these spacers are made of glass they are often referred to as rondellas.

rose monteé – a flat back rhinestone that is usually foil backed.

sautoir – an open-ended long necklace of chains, pearls, beads, or cording ending in tassels, drops, or other decoration. A popular necklace style during the Deco era.

scatter pins – small conversation pins worn in groups. Scatter pins were popular in the 1950s.

signed – when the manufacturer's or designer's identifying mark or signature is etched, carved, or stamped into the jewelry (usually located on the back of the jewelry). Sometimes this identifying mark or signature is accompanied by a date of manufacture, however this practice is rare. However, Hollycraft is known for dating a large portion of their jewelry. Signed is a term not to be confused with hallmark.

simulated – to imitate or counterfeit something genuine. See faux.

soldering – the fusing of metals by solder. Solder is a fusible alloy with a lower melting point than most metals. Applied in the melted state — securely joins other metals together when cooled.

sweater guards – two decorative devices which resemble pins, but are held securely to the garment via alligator clips. Chains, pearls, or beads are suspended between the clasps. Used to secure a sweater about the neck when the sweater is not being worn. Popular in the 1950s. Often mistakenly called chatelaines or sweater pins.

Tahitian pearls – in costume jewelry, this term is used to describe simulated pearls in a dark gray to almost black or light gray color. Also called Polynesian pearls.

tremblant – a pin, brooch, clip, and sometimes necklaces which have a moveable part set on a tiny spring causing it to tremble when the wearer moves. Also called a nodder.

torsade – a necklace with several strands of different beads, pearls, and/or chains twisted together. (Example: remember the "twist-a-beads" from the 1980s?)

tortoise shell – a mottled brown to brownish gold horn-like substance derived from the marine turtle. Now illegal to harvest and sell the genuine tortoise shell. Often the term "tortoise shell" is used to describe the translucent mottled brownish-gold plastic used in combs, hair accessories, and jewelry.

trifanium – a special metal alloy patented by Trifari.

unsigned or unmarked – Manufacturer's or designer's identifying mark or signature is not etched, carved, or stamped into the item.

wax pearls – an imitation pearl created by filling clear, hollow glass beads with wax.

Standard Simulated Pearl and Beaded Necklace Lengths

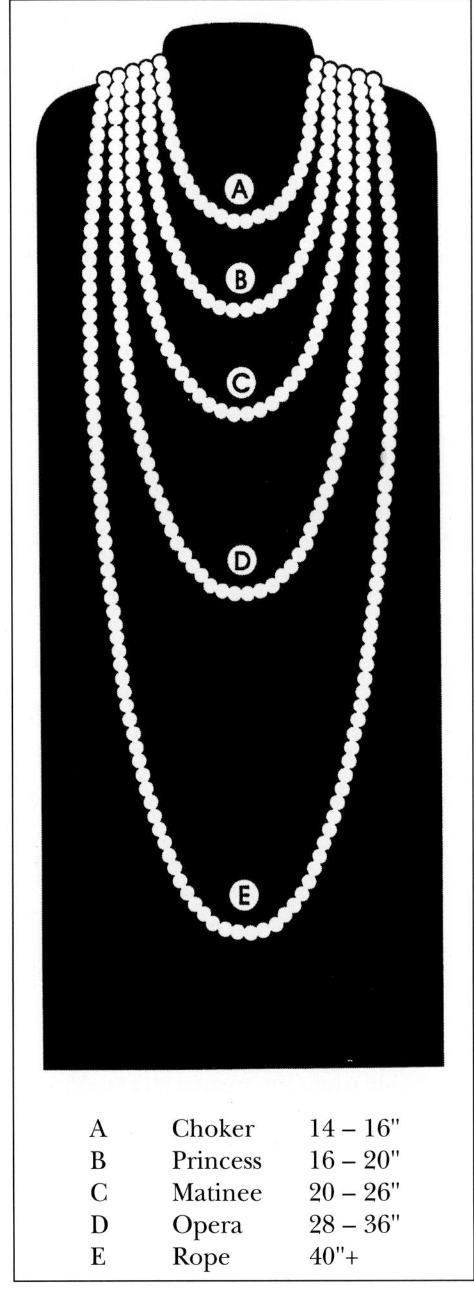

Popular Rhinestone Cuts

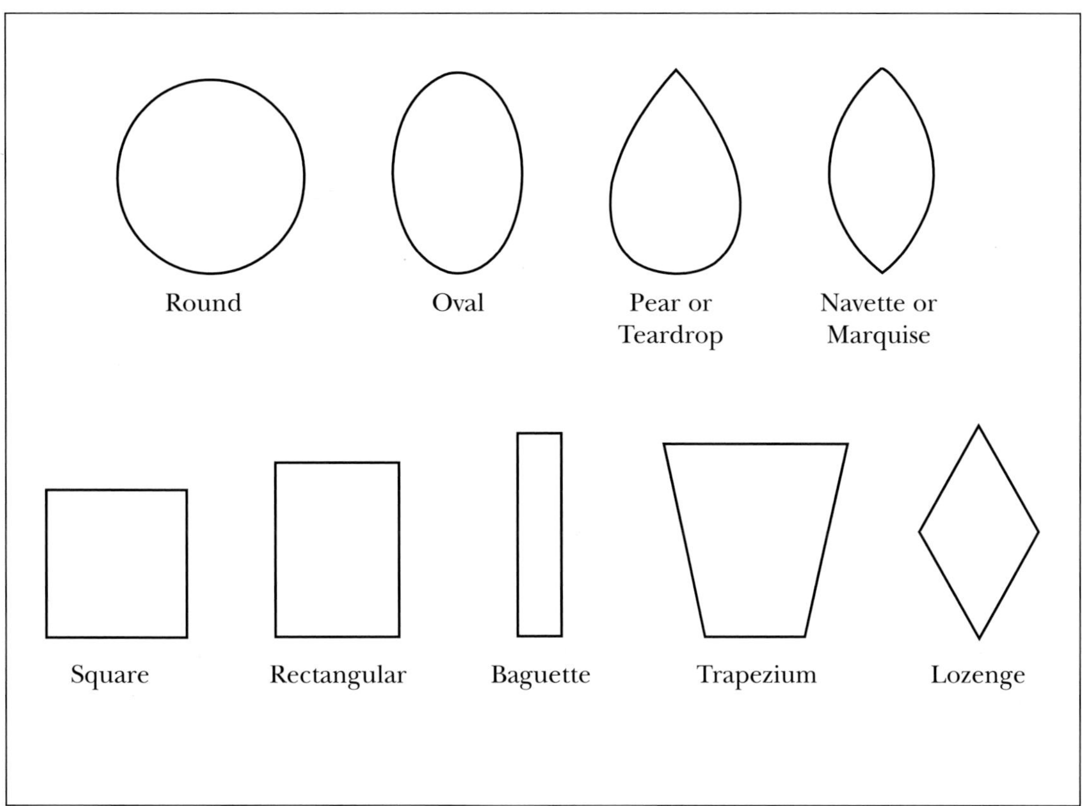

Types of Round Cuts
Typically Found in Costume Jewelry

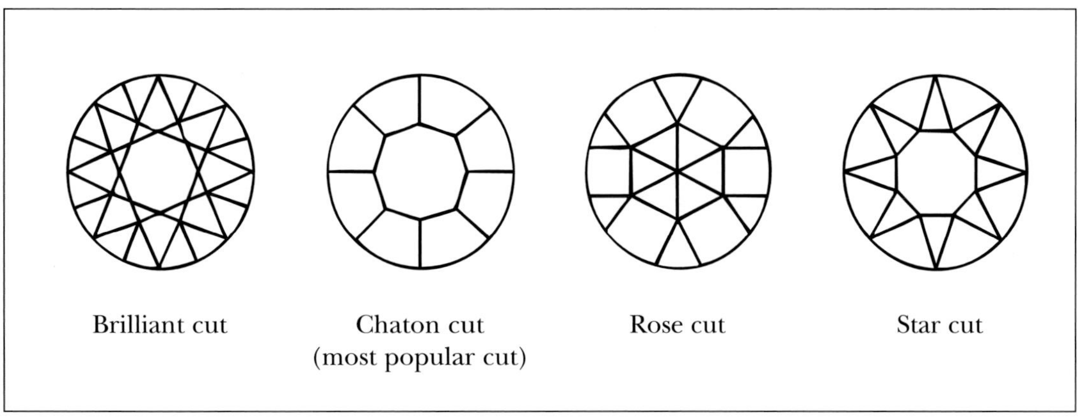

Bibliography

Baker, Lillian. *50 Years of Collectible Fashion Jewelry: 1925 - 1975.* Paducah, KY: Collector Books, 1992.

_____. *100 Years of Collectible Costume Jewelry.* Paducah, KY: Collector Books, 1993.

_____. *Twentieth Century Fashionable Plastic Jewelry.* Paducah, KY: Collector Books, 1992.

Ball, Joanne Dubbs. *Costume Jewelry Designers.* West Chester, PA: Schiffer Publishing.

_____. *Jewelry of the Stars: Creations from Joseff of Hollywood.* West Chester, PA: Schiffer Publishing, 1991.

Ball, Joanne Dubbs and Dorothy Hehl Torem. *Masterpieces of Costume Jewelry.* Atglen, PA: Schiffer Publishing, 1996.

Battle, Dee and Alayne Lesser. *The Best of Bakelite and Other Plastic Jewelry.* Atglen, PA: Schiffer Publishing, 1996.

Becker, Vivienne. *Fabulous Costume Jewelry.* Atglen, PA: Schiffer Publishing, 1993.

Cera, Deanna Farneti. *Jewels of Fantasy.* New York, New York: Abrams, 1992.

Davidov, Corrine and, Genny Redington Dawes. *The Bakelite Jewelry Book.* New York, NY: Abbeville Press, 1988.

Dolan, Maryanne. *Collecting Rhinestone Colored Jewelry.* Florence, AL: Books Americana.

Duncan, Alastair. *Art Deco.* London: Thames and Hudson, 1988.

Ettinger, Roseann. *Forties and Fifties Popular Jewelry.* Atglen, PA: Schiffer Publishing, 1994.

_____. *Popular Jewelry: 1840 - 1940.* West Chester, PA: Schiffer Publishing, 1990.

Field, Leslie. *The Queens Jewels.* New York, NY: Harry N. Abrams, Inc., Publishers, 1987.

Greindl, Gabriele. *Gems of Costume Jewelry.* New York, NY: Abbeville Press, 1990.

Heide, Robert. *Popular Art Deco: Depression Era Style and Design.* New York, NY: Abbeville Press, 1991.

Iovine, Julie. *Mirabella;* 'Gilty Pleasures.' October 1992.

_____. *Mirabella* 'Rhinestone Cowgirls.' October 1992.

Lynnlee, J. L. *All That Glitters.* Atglen, PA; Schiffer Publishing, 1986.

Kelly, Lyngerda and Nancy Schiffer. *Costume Jewelry: The Great Pretenders.* West Chester, PA: Schiffer Publishing, 1987.

_____. *Plastic Jewelry.* West Chester, PA: Schiffer Publishing, 1987.

Murray, Maggie Pexton. *Changing Styles of Fashion: Who, What, Why.* Fairchild Publications, 1989.

Menkes, Suzy. *The Windsor Style.* Salem House Publishers, 1988.

Miller, Harrice Simons. *The Confident Collector: Costume Jewelry,* 2nd Edition. New York: Avon Books, 1994.

Mitchell, Kimber. *Traditional Home;* "Spirited Scottish Agate." Des Moines, Iowa: Meredith Corporation, November 1994.

Morrill, Penny Chittim and Carole A. Berk. *Mexican Silver.* Atglen, PA: Schiffer Publishing, 1994.

Mulvagh, Jane. *Costume Jewelry in Vogue.* London: Thames and Hudson, 1988.

_____. *Vogue History of 20th Century Fashion.* Viking, 1988.

Rivers, Joan. *Jewelry By Joan Rivers.* New York, NY: Abbeville Press, 1995.

Ross, Heather Colyer. *The Art of Bedouin Jewellery.* Fribourg, Switzerland: Arabesque Commercial, 1981.

Schiffer, Nancy. *Costume Jewelry: The Fun of Collecting.* West Chester, PA: Schiffer Publishing, 1992.

_____. *Fun Jewelry.* West Chester, PA: Schiffer Publishing, 1991.

_____. *Rhinestones!* Atglen, PA: Schiffer Publishing, 1993.

_____. *Silver Jewelry Treasures.* Atglen, PA: Schiffer Publishing, 1993.

_____. *The Best of Costume Jewelry.* Atglen, PA: Schiffer Publishing, 1990.

Slowey, Anne. W. *Tales of Cartier.* March 1997.

Vintage Fashion & Costume Jewelry Newsletter. Glen Oaks, NY.

BY Adrian
©AK
ALEXIS © KIRK
©ALFRED
Hattie Carnegie
ALICE CAVINESS
ALICE CAVINESS
ANNE KLEIN
AVON
B. DAVID
B.K.
B.S.K.©
ANN-VIEN
ART©
BALLOU STERLING
BEAUJEWELS
©BOUCHER
AND CR
CHANEL
Carnegie
CAROLEE ©
Christian Dior
CARNEGIE
Celebrity Gems
CINER
Christian Dior
STERLING CRAFT BY CORO
Corocraft
Coro
Coro CRAFT
Coro
Coro
Coro Craft
©COVENTRY
CRAFT©
Corocraft
©CORO
DAUPLAISE
DE NICOLA ©
DE NICOLA
DeRosa
E
E
EISENBERG ICE
DE MARIO N.Y.
DUETTE
E.B.

Eisenberg Ice *

EISENBERG

EISENBERG ICE©

ELIZABETH TAYLOR E AVON

E

Eisenberg ORIGINAL

©EMMONS

FREIRICH

PARIS NEW YORK GIVENCHY

FLORENZA©

G.C.H

Goldette N.Y.

GERRY'S©

© GIVENCHY PARIS NEW YORK 1977

Hattie © Carnegie

Hattie Carnegie

Hattie Carnegie

Hobé

Hilco

Hobé

Hobé ©

Hobé

Hobé ©

Hobé

Hobé

Hobé

Hobé DESIGN PAT

Hobé DESIGN PAT

HOLLYCRAFT COPR. 1953

HOLLYCRAFT COPR. 1955

JEANNE©

JOAN RIVERS©

Joseff

Joseff

JOMAZ

©JJ

JUDY LEE

JUDY-LEE

Kirks

Karu

JOSEFF HOLLYWOOD

KATE HINES

KiM

KL

K.J.L. for AVON

©KJL

KRAMER

KRAMER	KRAMER OF NEW YORK	KTF INDUSTRIAL PRODUCTS	KTF.	Krementz
Krementz	KREMENTZ			Kunio Matsumot
BY Lampl STERLING	KREMENTZ			
	WL	Laurel Burch©®		©Laurel Burch
LA TAUSCA	Lavernia STERLING		Ledo	LES BERNARD
				©LISNER
LES BERNARD INC.	LEWIS SEGAL CALIFORNIA		MARCEL BOUCHER	
	MAJORICA		MARCEL BOUCHER	
	MARBOUX		MARVELLA	
MATISSE	Matisse		MBB ©DISNEY	MBB ©PELL
MBB	M W MATISSE	MAZER BROS.		
McClelland Barclay	MIMI diN		MIRACLE BRITAIN	MIRACLE A.S.
MIRIAM HASKELL	MIRIAM HASKELL		Miriam Haskell	
MIRIAM HASKELL	MIRIAM HASKELL		MONET©	Monet
			MONOCRAFT	

MOSELL
by Napier
NAPIER
N
Napier
NAPIER
Nellie Rosenstein
NOLAN MILLER ©
©PANETTA
PARKLANE
Park Lane
Park Lane
PAULINE RADER
PENNINO
Polcini ©
PERUZZI SILVER 800 FLORENCE
FROM POLLY BERGEN
R
RALPH LAUREN
©RAZZA
REBAJES
Rebajes
REED & BARTON STERLING ©
REGENCY
Réja
REINAD
REINAD
RÉJA
REJA
Réja
Renoir
ROBERT deMARIO N.Y.C.
original by Robért
Sadie Green
©SANDOR CO.
SARAH COV.
SANDOR
©SARAH COV.
©SARAH
SARAH COVENTRY
Schiaparelli
© SARAH COV
SCAASI
SCHIAPARELLI ©
SCHREINER NEW YORK
Sherman
STERLING Lang
STERLING by NORDIC
SILVER CHINA Bee
sol d'or
TANCER - II©
STERLING by Cini
43 THIEF OF BAGDAD KORDA © 61

THOMAS FATTORINI LTD REGENT STREET BIRMINGHAML TRIFARI	© Tortolani	TRIFARI	T	CLIP-MATES TRIFARI
TRIFARI TM	TRIFARI™	TRIFARI©	©VENDOME	
Vendôme	VOGUE	W.D.P.	MESH WHITING & DAVIS BAGS	
VOLUPTÉ	WARNER	WEISS	WIESNER	
WIESNER	YSL	MADE IN MEXICO ZZ 627	*Raised design that appears on the back of 1928 jewelry.*	

General Index

Schroeder's ANTIQUES Price Guide

. . . is the #1 best-selling antiques & collectibles value guide on the market today, and here's why . . .

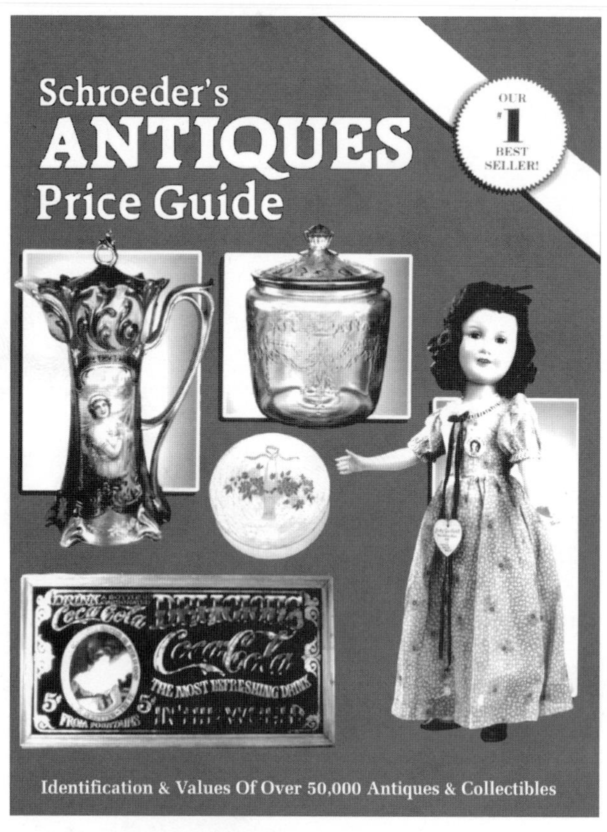

8½ x 11, 608 Pages, $12.95

• *More than 300 advisors, well-known dealers, and top-notch collectors work together with our editors to bring you accurate information regarding pricing and identification.*

• *More than 45,000 items in almost 500 categories are listed along with hundreds of sharp original photos that illustrate not only the rare and unusual, but the common, popular collectibles as well.*

• *Each large close-up shot shows important details clearly. Every subject is represented with histories and background information, a feature not found in any of our competitors' publications.*

• *Our editors keep abreast of newly developing trends, often adding several new categories a year as the need arises.*

If it merits the interest of today's collector, you'll find it in *Schroeder's*. And you can feel confident that the information we publish is up to date and accurate. Our advisors thoroughly check each category to spot inconsistencies, listings that may not be entirely reflective of market dealings, and lines too vague to be of merit. Only the best of the lot remains for publication.

Without doubt, you'll find
SCHROEDER'S ANTIQUES PRICE GUIDE
the only one to buy for
reliable information and values.

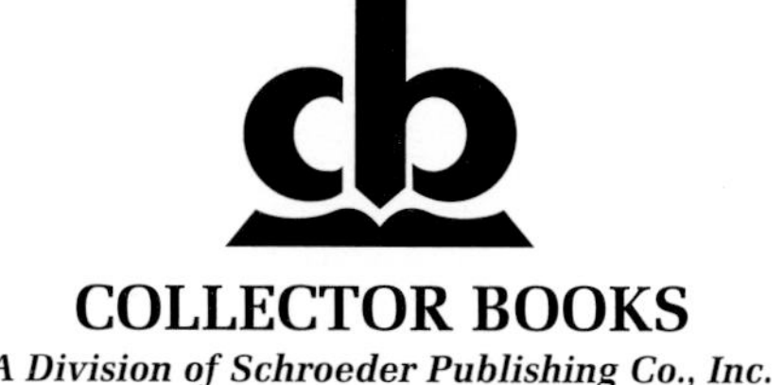

COLLECTOR BOOKS
A Division of Schroeder Publishing Co., Inc.